LITTLE SISTER

Advance Praise for
LITTLE SISTER

"Patricia Chadwick presents a riveting story of love and perseverance surviving religious beliefs and spirituality gone astray. A fascinating story presented by the person who was the child and daughter that lived through this harrowing experience. A must read for all!"

—KEN LANGONE

"Patricia Chadwick's *Little Sister* sheds light on a part of the history of American Catholicism that has been kept in the shadows. This fascinating, often horrifying story lets us in on the secrets of a cult that separated parents from children, fostered psychological abuse, and isolated its members from the modern world…all in the name of the One True Church."

—MARY GORDON

LITTLE SISTER

A MEMOIR

PATRICIA WALSH CHADWICK

A POST HILL PRESS BOOK

Little Sister:
A Memoir
© 2020 by Patricia Walsh Chadwick
All Rights Reserved
First Post Hill Hardcover Edition: April 2019

ISBN: 978-1-64293-355-0

Cover art by Cody Corcoran
Interior design and composition by Greg Johnson, Textbook Perfect
Digital images by Art Collector's Athenaeum
Image retouch by Nancy Gilbert

Post Hill Press
New York • Nashville
posthillpress.com

Published in the United States of America

To Mother and Daddy
For always letting me know they loved me.

Contents

PART 4: UNCLOISTERED

Prologue

Until the age of eighteen, I had never read a newspaper nor perused the pages of a magazine. I had never eaten in a restaurant nor shopped in a grocery store. I had never bought any clothes or cosmetics or a single item that could be called my own. I had never heard of Elvis Presley or Frank Sinatra, Marlon Brando, or Elizabeth Taylor. I had never watched television, nor made a phone call. I did not know how to dance.

I grew up in St. Benedict Center, a sequestered Catholic community headed by Leonard Feeney, an excommunicated priest, and his spiritual cohort, Catherine Clarke, a staunchly Catholic married woman with a strident disposition toward puritanism. "The Center," first located a short walk from Harvard Square in Cambridge, Massachusetts, and subsequently transported to the bucolic hamlet of Still River, Massachusetts, evolved into a social experiment of sorts, whose purpose was to create a pure-hearted community in which no material thing, no cultural influence, not even the bonds between family members, could impede the path to God.

Dedicated to a rigid adherence to Catholic orthodoxy, this community of nearly one hundred people, including my parents and thirty-nine children who were born into it, lived a life completely shielded from an outside world that was considered to be fraught with evil. I was educated within the confines of my community from nursery school through my senior year of high school.

For much of my childhood, I grew up without the daily love and attention of my parents. I was just six years old when Leonard Feeney and Catherine Clarke made the decision that my siblings and I were to live apart from our parents. Later, Leonard Feeney pressured my parents to forsake their marital vows, no longer living as husband and wife. A celibate existence, they were told, was more conducive to a life dedicated to God. And so my parents complied.

On only one occasion during my life at the Center was I allowed to listen to the radio. That was when the community assembled to hear the inaugural address of John Fitzgerald Kennedy, the country's first Catholic president. I felt transported at that moment into the vast unreachable outside world—a place I longed to experience. I was eleven years old at the time.

I had heard of the Beatles only because Leonard Feeney had once played a fifteen-second snippet of their hit song "I Want to Hold Your Hand" as a demonstration of "music of the devil." The eruption of rock and roll onto the world stage was lost on me, as was the sexual revolution that came in its wake.

Within my community, any personal attachment, any demonstration of familial affection, any expression of romantic love was prohibited. As for sex, the word itself was verboten. There was no explanation of the facts of life, as though by revealing nothing, the course of nature could be manipulated, and the lack of knowledge would lead to lack of interest.

But the absence of understanding such things did nothing to inhibit my natural desires. As I matured into my teenage years, I fell into a series of crushes on the grown men within the community, with not a glimmer of understanding about why it happened, what it meant, or what to do about it.

Though I'd never had a date, much less kissed a boy, my innocent interest was viewed as subverting God's will, which was deemed to be that each of the thirty-nine children should embrace religious life and celibacy. And so, just two months before my eighteenth birthday, I faced expulsion from the community, banished from my home, my parents, my siblings, and the only people I knew and loved.

An infant in the ways of modern life, I was being compelled to leave my family behind and make my way alone in a world I'd been taught to believe was full of sin and danger.

PART 1

WHERE IS GOD?

Grace

A Brief Meditation

The definition of Grace is *that free and unearned favor endowed by God.*

I believe in grace, although I have to admit I hadn't given it much thought until an event some years ago brought it into perspective for me.

The occasion was a visit in 2000 to Mother Mary Clare Vincent OSB, the seventy-five-year-old prioress of St. Scholastica Priory in Petersham, Massachusetts. She had known me all my life.

We were having a quiet tea together, when she suddenly took my hand and, looking into my eyes with her intense and bright black eyes, she said, "Darling, there's a special place in heaven for you on account of all your generosity."

I was taken aback. I had been visiting the priory since 1985 when Mother Mary Clare, with a small group of nuns, had set up the community under the auspices of the Benedictine order. While I was most assuredly not called to be a nun, much less lead a contemplative life, I adored Mother Mary Clare and came to love her band of Sisters.

We had a symbiotic relationship—I gave them advice on matters of finance and business and provided modest financial support. They, in turn, prayed for me, my intentions, and anyone for whom I asked them to pray. We were indeed family.

Listening to Mother's words about my place in heaven, I answered with a chuckle, "Mother Mary Clare, what I do is nothing special. It just comes naturally to me because I love you."

"Aha," she responded before I could speak another word. "Your generosity is a direct response to grace. Believe you me—that's what is so marvelous about you. You accept grace; you never reject it. For that you will be greatly rewarded, my darling."

She had silenced me and I contemplated her words, encouraging words for someone who was far from a model Catholic, much less saintly. A place in heaven, I thought. I hoped it would be close to her.

I took her reassuring words to heart and have been a believer in grace ever since. Grace received and embraced inspires the heart and soul to respond. How we respond to grace determines how we live our lives.

The millions of acts of daily human kindness throughout the world are evidence of man's innate goodness in response to God's grace and favor.

I like to think of grace as being granted in a variety of flavors— kindness, joy, patience (sadly that grace totally skipped me by), fortitude, faith, hope, humor, and so many more.

I feel blessed that the grace of generosity of spirit has imbued much of my life. And I believe that the grace of gratitude is what inspired me to write this memoir.

1

Sentencing

1965

I prayed. It was what I did when I faced trouble.

"*Jesus, Mary, and Joseph, please help me*," I whispered in my head as I made my way across the pebbled driveway to Sister Catherine's office.

It would be hard to count the number of times I'd been summoned to her office in the past few years. Even now at seventeen, I had difficulty keeping out of trouble.

What have I done wrong this time? I wondered as the familiar knot of anxiety twisted in my stomach.

Moments later I stood in the library and gave a timid knock on the wood-paneled door of her office.

"Come in," came the reply from inside.

Sister Catherine, seated tall in the straight-backed chair at her desk, swiveled to face me, her strong rectangular body softened by fine wisps of reddish blonde hair that danced like flickering candles around her flawless white complexion. Those wayward strands were the only bits of her not militantly managed. From her neck down, she was heavily garbed. A long black pleated skirt allowed only a sliver of ankle to appear above her black-laced shoes. A black jacket hung loosely over her collared white blouse, the ensemble intended, no doubt, to mask the shape that lay beneath.

As I took several steps toward Sister Catherine's desk, I attempted to surmise her mood, noting the tautness of her jaw, the line of her thin lips, the glint in her green eyes through her clear-rimmed eyeglasses. Long ago, I had mastered the art of reading her disposition, which had the capacity to run the gamut from maternal to malevolent.

But she preempted my analysis by greeting me with a pleasant, "Hello, dear, how are you?" The tension in my shoulders eased, and the nervousness in my stomach subsided.

To my astonishment, there in the office with Sister Catherine stood my mother, tall and silent, dressed identically to Sister Catherine but still, somehow slim and feminine in the same clothes. Never had my mother and I been in Sister Catherine's office together—for years, my siblings and I had been required to live separately from our parents, and our daily interactions had been carefully restricted. The novelty of the situation I now found myself in caused me to panic. I feared the worst, dreading that Sister Catherine might be about to give me bad news regarding my father. But my mother's smile reassured me. For sure, she would be crying if my father were sick, or worse.

Sister Catherine, her voice uncharacteristically warm, began to speak. "Dear, we want to have a little conversation with you about something."

The use of the pronoun "we" didn't fool me. I knew full well that it was Sister Catherine alone who had determined whatever was about to ensue. The momentary pause before she continued heightened my tension. I held my breath, not knowing what to expect in this "little conversation."

"You know, dear, religious life is not for everyone," she began, "and we have concluded that you do not have a vocation to be a nun. There's nothing to be ashamed of, because not everyone receives a higher calling from God. We will always love you and support you, and you will forever be my dearest godchild, whom I remember each day in my prayers."

I was stunned, trying to absorb Sister Catherine's words, which came to me almost like a foreign language because of their stark contrast to what she and Father (that was how everyone at the Center addressed Leonard Feeney) had repeated verbatim for as long as I could remember: "You thirty-nine children are among the chosen few who have been dedicated to God from your infancy. Each of you has received a special blessing and calling to follow His will in religious life."

All my life, I'd been raised to believe that my destiny was not mine to determine. Despite my intense curiosity about all things worldly, I was well aware that I would have to forgo a life in the real world. I was preordained to live within the confines of this community.

Having taken the first step toward the life of a nun—postulancy—at age sixteen, now a year later, I was nearing the day when I would enter the novitiate, one rung closer to taking final vows, which would signify my lifelong marriage to Christ and no other.

Suddenly, in a flash, Sister Catherine was reversing the course of my young life. She continued to speak as I tried to grapple with the full meaning of her enigmatic message.

"Many girls out in the world get married," she went on, her tone of voice uncharacteristically dulcet, her manner as though she were educating me on a subject I knew nothing about, which was mainly true. I had not borne witness to marriages, because marriages had been banished in the community, including that of my parents.

"But," she said, and there was a long pause before the sweet tone of her voice took on a more somber timbre, "you should know, dear, that life as a wife isn't as wonderful as it might seem in books. Each day before your husband comes home from work at five o'clock, you will have to stop whatever you're doing and make yourself look pretty for him by putting on lipstick and curling your hair."

I shifted my glance from Sister Catherine to my mother in a futile attempt to glean what this monologue meant, but she stood silent, a passive participant in this meeting. I could only listen in disbelief as Sister Catherine described as mine the very life she had been decrying for years.

Is she really telling me I can have a husband? And lipstick? And curl my hair?

For years, I had kept to myself my dreams of being married, having children, and living in an elegant house surrounded by rose-filled gardens. I dared not share those dreams with anyone, not even my parents, because I knew such longings were delusional. The course of my life had been laid out by Father and Sister Catherine, and it was out of my hands.

My mind went into overdrive as Sister Catherine spoke and then in an instant, the meaning of her words hit me with full force, and I grasped with horror what was unfolding. Gentle as her delivery sounded, Sister Catherine was issuing an eviction order, expelling me from my home. It felt like a death sentence.

The fantasies I had harbored of living a life in the world were suddenly replaced with the reality of being "kicked out"—the term that was used when someone was no longer part of our community. Sister Catherine was forcing me to leave the only people in the world I could call family. A feeling of nausea enveloped me. My throat went dry, and, behind my back, I gripped my long blue skirt with clammy hands.

For a moment my mind went blank, as though I had just hit a wall at full speed. Then questions toppled over one another inside my addled brain. *What does this mean? Where will I go? Where will I live? Why is this happening?*

Sister Catherine shifted in her seat and rearranged her skirt, taking a deep breath before she spoke again, and now she altered the tenor of her voice from gentle to serious.

"And, dear, I must warn you about two words you will hear when you go out into the world."

She stopped, and in the ensuing silence, I wondered whether she was having second thoughts about sharing them.

"They are diet and rape." She said them in an almost haphazard way, as though once delivered, she was rid of the burden of disclosing them.

Diet and rape? I repeated them in my head.

I knew the word "diet." Father had described many times the Diet of Worms, that monumental event in church history convened by the Emperor Charles V to condemn Martin Luther and his writings.

But I was lost when Sister Catherine added in an all-knowing way, "Diet is something that lots of girls in their teens do because they think it will make them more attractive."

She offered not a shred of light on that enigmatic sentence. The very words "make them more attractive" denoted a concept verboten in the community. Our homemade clothing had been crafted to hide any semblance of femininity. I had never worn lipstick, much less put on makeup. I had no idea if I was attractive or not.

As for the word "rape," it was devoid of any meaning for me. Rigorously schooled in Latin and Greek, I wracked my brain for a root word I could associate it with in order to give it some semblance of a definition.

Sister Catherine elaborated no more. For my part, I buried those two words in my memory, with the intention of heading for a dictionary when I left her office.

Her monologue was over. Silence fell in the room and it was now my turn to speak. All I had were questions, plaintive questions.

Did my father know?

Yes, he did.

Did the whole community know, I asked, certain that if Sister Catherine had already told the adults, I would be marked as an outcast. There was an ignominy associated with leaving the community. When people left or were sent away, they were reviled and then never spoken of again. It was as though they were dead.

"Oh, no, dear, this is our secret, and you must keep it to yourself. We don't want to upset the rest of the community."

Upset, she said. The community would be upset to know that I was leaving.

"Will I be allowed to finish school here?" I asked, terrified the answer might be "No," and I'd be whisked away overnight.

"Of course, dear. You may stay and graduate with your class next June."

That was a relief. The questions spilled out like a litany of earnest supplications, each begging for an answer, as I did my best to conceal the panic that gripped me inside.

Where would I go? What would I do? Could I come back and visit?

Sister Catherine alone provided answers, and they were vague—platitudes that did nothing to allay my fears.

My mother was merely a witness to the scene. I knew her role was to listen, but not to speak. Within our community, all the power lay with Sister Catherine, and she wielded it with immense supremacy. It had been that way almost as far back as I could remember, when she had snatched parental roles from mothers and fathers.

Now, as my mother was hearing that I would be banished, I wondered what she was thinking. *If she could intercede for me, what would she say?* I knew her heart. I had never doubted her love, silent though it had been for most of my life.

How I wished she could say something encouraging, just a word that might calm the panic inside me and reassure me that I would still be able to see her and my father and my four younger siblings.

I was mentally depleted and needed to be alone to digest the enormity of what had befallen me. In the silence, Sister Catherine spoke.

"We all love you, dear."

"Thank you, Sister Catherine," I replied. As I turned to leave, my mother gave me a reassuring smile, one that seemed to say, "I'm with you, darling. Don't worry." I returned her smile with a fainthearted one of my own. I could muster nothing more.

Closing the door behind me, I felt an unbearable sadness. This was worse than getting into trouble—this was forever. As I made my way slowly to the refectory, I felt forsaken, abandoned by the whole court of heaven. For years I had prayed to them to sustain me in times of trouble, and now they had deserted me. I was a failure.

And worse, I now faced a time bomb, a countdown to my graduation, just seven months away. On that day in June, I would lose the only thing in the world that was dear to me—my home and my huge extended family.

What had I done to deserve this punishment? What could I do to change Sister Catherine's mind?

That became my mission, and instinctively I prayed once again for help from heaven.

2

A Moment of Grace

1935

Six-year-old Betsy Ann McKinley stood on the sidewalk outside the Willard Elementary School in Cambridge, Massachusetts, next to her best friend, Peter Bailey, as they waited for their mothers to pick them up at the end of the school day.

The sound of singing distracted them, and they turned to witness a procession coming in their direction through the park. Betsy stared at the sight of a white and gold canopy held aloft by four men who walked slowly, providing cover for a priest who wore an enormous, radiantly embroidered cape and held high a gold monstrance, as though inviting the entire world to view it.

Behind the priest came the congregation, solemn and reverent, singing hymns in unison. Nuns, wearing long black habits and wimpled veils, escorted their charges—schoolchildren in blue-and-white uniforms. Following them were the parishioners, men wearing suits and hats, and women in modest dress with kerchief veils on their heads.

As the procession drew nearer, an elderly lady next to Betsy got down on her knees, bowed her head, and made the sign of the cross.

Betsy was mesmerized by the giant gold monstrance and the circular glass window in its center, displaying a white object. She nudged Peter and whispered, "What's happening?"

Peter turned to look at her. "It's the feast of Corpus Christi. Aren't you a Catholic?"

"No," said Betsy, "I'm Episcopalian. What's the priest carrying?"

Peter replied, "That's God."

Betsy's eyes opened wide. "God? I'm looking at God?"

"Yup," said Peter.

She grew silent and watched as the procession passed in front of them and the old lady on her knees, and then disappeared around the corner at the end of the block.

On that day, Betsy Ann McKinley vowed to herself, "I'm going to become a Catholic so that I can see God."

3

Quest for Knowledge

1946

A young man wearing the uniform of the United States Navy walked to the back of a Boston College classroom and sat down to await the arrival of the professor. Tall and handsome, with curly black hair and pale blue eyes, Lt. James Richard Walsh was soon to be discharged after a four-year tour of duty aboard the aircraft carrier *USS Enterprise*. Having received an undergraduate degree from Bates College prior to his enlistment, he was now enrolled as a graduate student in philosophy, thanks to the G.I. Bill, at this Jesuit college on the outskirts of Boston. To supplement his government support, he would be teaching mathematics as an assistant professor at the college.

Born in Quincy, Massachusetts, Jim Walsh had been raised in a strongly Catholic family. He and his younger sister Eleanor attended parochial grammar school, and after his father's untimely demise, Jim attended Boston College High School and then Bates College, where he earned a degree in mathematics. He was teaching high school mathematics, but after the Japanese attacked Pearl Harbor, he enlisted in the Navy.

Catholicism had been the foundation of Jim Walsh's life. His father had died when Jim was only eleven years old, and it was his mother and two maiden aunts who inspired his Catholicism. At Bates he had founded the Newman Society, an organization that promoted Catholic faith and morals among students and faculty. For him, faith was an intellectual endeavor rather than an emotional exercise. Observing the atrocities of war firsthand only strengthened his determination to explore the realm of God through the study of Catholic philosophy.

Jim Walsh's presence in the Boston College classroom did not escape the notice of the professor, the renowned Dr. Fakhri Maluf. Originally from Lebanon and with a Ph.D. in philosophy from the University of Michigan, Maluf had done postdoctoral work at Harvard, and now, at age thirty-three, he held a prestigious position on the faculty of Boston College. The two men introduced themselves at the end of class.

A few weeks later, Dr. Maluf invited Jim to join him on a visit to St. Benedict Center, a Catholic meeting place for Harvard and Radcliffe students, a stone's throw from Harvard Square, where he offered free lectures in philosophy every Tuesday evening. Jim accepted the invitation and, before long, found himself engrossed in the energetic life of "the Center," as it was called.

To have walked into the Center on that day would have been to encounter a buzz. It came from the mingling of intellectual energy and youthful gaiety as scores of students congregated, many far from their families, who found it also to be a gracious home-away-from-home, a welcoming environment for socializing.

The chaplain at the Center was Father Leonard Feeney, a fifty-year-old world-renowned Jesuit priest, poet, author, lecturer, and teacher. In addition to his role as spiritual leader, Leonard Feeney enjoyed acting as social intermediary among the vibrant young men and women who frequented the Center. He took an immediate liking to Jim, going so far as to introduce the twenty-eight-year-old bachelor to a number of young Radcliffe graduates who were attending classes

Lt. James R. Walsh–1946.   Betsy Ann McKinley–1947.

at the Center. But Jim did not find his soul mate among the young women there.

Then on March 7, 1947, Betsy Ann McKinley, a tall, slender young woman with lively blue eyes and shoulder-length brown hair, walked into the Center for the first time. Just eighteen years old, she had grown up on Ellery Street in the shadow of Harvard Yard and was now a freshman at Boston University.

Betsy was accompanied by Father Collins, a priest who had been instructing her in the teachings of the Roman Catholic Church. He introduced her to Leonard Feeney. Three weeks later Leonard Feeney baptized her, allowing her to fulfill the vow she had made at age six. Her staunch Episcopalian parents were not pleased, but they knew better than to try to dissuade their strong-willed daughter.

Jim Walsh met Betsy within an hour of her arrival at the Center. He was instantly smitten by her beauty and impressed by her commitment to Catholicism. The two were soon inseparable, and within three months they were engaged to be married. Six months after they met,

Leonard Feeney married the couple at St. Paul's Catholic Church, not more than twenty yards from the front door of St. Benedict Center, which would come to be the center of their social, spiritual, and intellectual lives for the next twenty-five years.

Eleven months later, they had a daughter, whom they named Mary Patricia. I am that child.

Clockwise from top left: Leonard Feeney with my parents. My parents' wedding. The day of my baptism, September 12, 1948, with my mother, Grandma Walsh, and father. Jim and Betsy Walsh shortly after I was born.

My father and my mother, each with me at the age of two months, in the Halloween costume my mother made–1948.

4

In the Beginning, It Was Good

1940

Catherine Clarke was a woman of strong faith, and possessed with a mission to foster the spirit of Catholicism, in particular among the students attending Harvard and Radcliffe.

In 1940, she took the first step toward achieving that goal. Together with Avery Dulles (who would one day be named a cardinal by Pope John Paul II) and Chris Huntington, both recent graduates of Harvard College and converts to the Catholic faith, she established Saint Benedict Center, a place for young Catholic students to meet, study, and engage intellectually on matters of religion, ethics, philosophy, and theology. In addition to spearheading religious classes at the Center, Catherine brought her own natural charm, hosting daily afternoon teas, which became immensely popular with the students.

Within a few years, the visitors to the Center had become so numerous that Catherine Clarke petitioned Archbishop Richard Cushing, the popular Irish American bishop of the diocese of Boston, to appoint the renowned Jesuit writer Leonard Feeney, then forty-seven, as the spiritual director of the Center. She had been impressed

Leonard Feeney as a young priest.

Leonard Feeney, as I remember him
as a young child.

with the brilliance of his intellect and his immense appeal to young
people on the occasions he had been a visiting speaker there.

Catherine's decision was instrumental to the burgeoning success
of the Center. Leonard Feeney's popularity was enormous—his
Thursday-evening lectures on theology were standing-room-only
events, where hundreds of young people, Catholic and non-Catholic,
crowded in to hear him, often spilling onto the sidewalk outside. Over
the course of the next several years, Feeney was credited with bringing hundreds of young men and women into the Catholic Church.

In 1946, Catherine Clarke and Leonard Feeney encouraged
students at the Center to start a quarterly publication, *From the House-
tops*, which in short order attracted high profile contributors such as
bishops, theologians and professors from area colleges. It enjoyed
worldwide subscribership and was noticed and praised by no less an
authority than Pope Pius XII, who sent his handwritten blessing as
the footer to a life-sized photograph, which hung prominently on the
long gray wall on the ground floor of the Center. John F. Kennedy

St. Benedict Center in the 1940s, at the intersection of Bow and Arrow Streets.

visited the Center more than once, most memorably in 1946, shortly after having been elected U.S. congressman from Massachusetts. On that occasion, Leonard Feeney retrieved one of his treasured possessions, *the* brown derby, which had been made famous by New York Governor Al Smith, the first Catholic candidate for president of the United States. Smith had given the hat to Feeney following his crushing defeat by Herbert Hoover, in appreciation of an open letter entitled "The Brown Derby," which Feeney had written and which was published in *America,* the Jesuit weekly magazine. In essence, the letter credited Smith with remaining staunchly Catholic, even though it cost him the election. Some eighteen years later, Leonard Feeney placed the famous derby on Kennedy's head and pronounced, "One day, you will be President."

The Center had quickly become a seat of intellectual discourse, and at the end of World War II, it also served as a welcome home-away-from-home for many war-weary veterans (both men and women) attending college on the G.I. Bill. The Center itself was accredited

(Left) Catherine Clark in the mid-1940s.

(Right) Leonard Feeney, Catherine Clark, and Avery Dulles (later made Cardinal by Pope John Paul II) in the mid-1940s on the steps of the Center.

through the G.I. Bill to offer college courses, including Greek, Latin, logic, and philosophy. Numerous students participated in the program. For nearly seven years, from its inception in 1940, the story of Saint Benedict Center was one of resounding success.

5

Then Came the Decline, and a Fall

1946 and 1949

The first sign of a change in the air came after the United States bombed Hiroshima and Nagasaki in August 1945. Leonard Feeney decried the bombings. They were a moral outrage, he said, a callous disregard for human life and an un-Christian act. He blamed a godless society for such atrocities and channeled his indignation at the faculties of colleges and universities, arguing that liberalism was corrupting the morals of students.

Within a couple of years, a number of his adherents—intellectuals like himself—had become convinced by the passion of his arguments. One of those was Dr. Fakhri Maluf, the man who had invited my father to the Center. In September 1947, Fakhri published an article in the Center's quarterly entitled "Sentimental Theology" that boldly proclaimed, "There is no salvation outside the Catholic Church." In other words, the only way for a person to be saved and reach heaven after this life was to be Roman Catholic.

Over the centuries, no less than half a dozen popes had championed that dogma and it was so stated in the Baltimore catechism that was part of every parochial school child's religious education. But in the aftermath of World War II, the Catholic Church turned its focus to fostering ecumenism between Catholics and non-Catholics. The previous hard-line position was deemed too doctrinaire.

Feeney railed against ecumenism, against the professors at Harvard for their liberalism, and against Catholic colleges and universities for compromising their faith by suggesting that non-Catholics might find a way to heaven. But the fire of his rhetoric was aimed mostly at the Jews, whose crime was killing Jesus.

As Feeney's vitriol increased, many of his adherents grew wary and stopped attending his lectures at the Center. But a small cadre of followers found inspiration in his oratory and became ardent adherents. Before long, the message of the Center had morphed into a one-issue mantra: "No Salvation Outside the Catholic Church."

My father, as an intellectual and a student of theology, wholeheartedly subscribed to the dogma of "no salvation." His graduate studies at Boston College only strengthened his orthodoxy in this regard.

My mother's long road to Catholicism had imbued her with a zealous ardor for her faith. There was nothing capricious about her spirituality. She was convinced that she had received a grace from God as a small child that led her to renounce her Episcopalian heritage and convert to Catholicism. Father Feeney had guided her through those final steps and had baptized her into the Catholic Church. She would remain loyal to her priest and her faith. Catholicism was her salvation.

In a defiant, and seemingly rash, show of allegiance to Feeney, more than a dozen young, brilliant students at Harvard and Radcliffe resigned from their colleges during the scholastic year of 1947 and 1948, most of them just months away from graduation. Anguished parents, whose families had, in many cases, sent their sons to Harvard for generations and provided generous support for the institution, turned to the archbishop, beseeching him to intervene.

At the same time, in May 1948, the dean of the College of Arts and Sciences of Boston College met with my father to offer him the position of instructor in philosophy for the upcoming scholastic year. But that offer came with a condition that he not teach Feeney's doctrine (as he put it) that espoused "No Salvation Outside the Catholic Church." My father refused to agree to that stipulation. He was, nonetheless, allowed to teach philosophy, but was aware that he was under scrutiny.

This confluence of events led Feeney's Jesuit superior to address the situation by ordering him to leave his post as chaplain at the Center and to report to Holy Cross College (forty-five miles away in the diocese of Worcester, Massachusetts) as an English teacher for the fall semester in 1948. Feeney refused.

In December of that year, the Jesuit provincial (Feeney's superior) informed him in a letter that as of the year-end, he would no longer be allowed to exercise his priestly duties in the Boston diocese. The Center was now under siege.

Three weeks later, on January 19, 1949, Feeney, Catherine Clarke, and fifty-one followers—students and married couples, including my parents, Jim and Betsy Walsh—signed a document establishing themselves as a religious order, with Father Leonard Feeney, S.J., as their spiritual director. They signed under a statement that read: "We, the undersigned, having banded together as a religious order, dedicated to the glory of God and the protection of the doctrines of the Holy Catholic Apostolic Roman Church, have made our vows under the title of The Slaves of the Immaculate Heart of Mary."

Each one of them took simple vows as religious members, promising "to make the first interest of my life the doctrinal crusade of Saint Benedict Center...." In other words, they were dedicating their lives to the doctrine of "No Salvation Outside the Catholic Church." There was an irony in that declaration, because they were heading down a path that would end in Feeney's excommunication. In addition, each of the signors pledged blind allegiance to Feeney, promising "obedience to Father [Leonard Feeney] and to whomever he may delegate."

The members of the newly formed religious community continued to work in their professions and support their families. My father, together with Fakhri Maluf and Charlie Ewaskio, carried on as teachers at Boston College, but less than three months later, each of them received a letter from the president of the college requesting their presence in his office. In the verbal confrontation that ensued, the "three professors" (as they were referred to by the members of the Center) maintained their commitment to teaching strict orthodox Catholic doctrine. The meeting ended in their dismissal. The date was April 13, 1949, the Wednesday before Easter Sunday.

The headlines in all the Boston newspapers the following morning screamed "B.C. Teachers Fired after Probe," and the story covered the front pages of the papers.

The community, consisting of nearly sixty members, was in shock. As they gathered together in the cavernous main room of the Center on that day in 1949, I was among them, just eight months old.

The two photos on the opposite page display the joviality of the Center shortly before the troubles unfolded.

Four days later, on Easter Sunday, the professors appealed by cablegram to the Vatican, and the following day they met in person with Archbishop Cushing.

But the most shocking news was yet to come. On Easter Monday, the afternoon editions of the Boston newspapers ran the story that the archbishop had officially silenced Father. The decree, which came without any warning, read:

> The Rev. Leonard Feeney, S.J., because of grave offense against the laws of the Catholic Church, has lost the right to perform any priestly function, including preaching and teaching of religion.
>
> Any Catholics who frequent Saint Benedict's Center, or who in any way take part in or assist its activities forfeit the right to receive the Sacrament of Penance and Holy Eucharist.
>
> Given at Boston on the 18th day of April 1949.
>
> —Richard J. Cushing, Archbishop of Boston

Center members at the beach in the summer of 1948. The child in the fore-
ground is Mariam Maluf, and her father, Fakhri, is on the right.

A picnic of Center members at the estate of a wealthy friend of the Center.
My mother, standing in the middle, is eight months pregnant with me, and my
father is slightly above and to the left of her. Leonard Feeney is in the front
row. July 1948.

(Left) Leonard
Feeney and the three
professors: (L to R)
Charlie Ewaskio, my
father, and Fakhri
Maluf, with David
Supple in the front
(he taught at BC High
School and was fired
along with my father
and the others).

(Bottom) On the day
Father Feeney was
censured–1949.

Leonard Feeney
with Fakhri Maluf
when the Center
closed its doors to
Harvard and Radcliffe
students–1949.

Those "grave offense[s]" were embodied in Feeney's refusal to obey his Jesuit superior's order to leave the Center and report to Holy Cross College. Truth be told, the edict was a political gesture designed to silence a man who was embarrassing the Catholic hierarchy with his refusal to soft-pedal the doctrine of the Church that stated in no uncertain terms that salvation was granted only to those who were Catholics.

This monumental announcement by the archbishop of the diocese of Boston acted as a catalyst in forging a spiritual and emotional bond among the members of Saint Benedict Center. Three months earlier, they had constituted their own religious community, some of them single and some married, but all of them more Catholic than the Church itself. A number of couples had become engaged and, when the Church authorities refused to grant them a Catholic wedding,

Fakhri Maluf giving a class to members of the Center after the silencing of
Leonard Feeney.

they faced a quandary. Some parted ways with the Center, but four
couples remained, and Father performed the marriage ceremony in
secret. Each couple then went to Cambridge city hall and was married
in a civil ceremony, as a security measure lest the Catholic authorities
decree the Catholic nuptials invalid.

Young and idealistic, the members of the Center found ways to
support each other financially, some doing menial jobs and bringing
home money for the rest. Before long, the men and women, married
and single, were pooling their resources—incomes, automobiles, and
soon even homes and furniture. My parents sold the three-family
house in North Cambridge that they had bought on the G.I. Bill and
gave the proceeds to the Center.

The community expanded to nearly one hundred members over
the next five years, in large part because the twelve married couples

brought the number of children from five in January 1949 to thirty-nine. With money donated from the sale of personal property and family homes, Catherine Clarke bought a cluster of seven houses off Putnam Avenue, a few blocks from Harvard Square, into which the families moved. Twelve couples, each looking forward to the joys and challenges of child-rearing and, at the same time, dedicated to ensuring that, however many children God chose to bless them with, each child would be raised with a rigid adherence to traditional Roman Catholic doctrine. That was their life's work.

My home was the top-floor apartment of a three-family house, which Father named Saint Francis Xavier's House. The Malufs and the Ewaskios—the families of the two married professors who, with my father, had been fired from Boston College—moved into the second and first floors. Ours was a spacious apartment, with large bay windows that overlooked the street below. It suited us well, and before long my parents had five children.

PART 2

LEAVING THE WORLD BEHIND

6

A Family of the Heart

1951–1952

My earliest memories are filled with the sounds of laughter. Though I was only three years old, I knew each of the more than sixty adults at the Center by name. We were family. Three times a day we gathered for meals. We prayed together in the morning at Mass and in the evening at Benediction. The men and women of the Center became an array of "uncles and aunts," with someone ready at any time of the day to play games with me, read to me, or take me for a walk.

My favorite "aunt" was Betty Sullivan, a soft-spoken woman with gentle brown eyes and shoulder-length dark hair much like my mother's. When my parents attended the frequent evening lectures at the Center, she would come to our apartment and babysit. Sunday mornings were made extra special when she'd take me to the banks of the Charles River where I'd pick daffodils or buttercups. Most mornings after breakfast, I'd put my hand in hers, and we'd make the ten-minute trip along the streets of Cambridge to the Center. I knew the route by heart.

As we walked, I'd skip around Betty, grabbing first her right hand and then her left as I circled her, while she seemed to glide along the sidewalk like a guardian angel before delivering me safely into the hubbub at the Center.

The Center was a four-story gray building at the junction of Bow and Arrow Streets, fronted with floor-to-ceiling plate glass windows that faced both St. Paul's Church and Harvard's renowned Adams House. The ground floor consisted of one long rectangular room, its stucco walls painted a dull white and its concrete floor covered in an array of Persian rugs. Half of the cavernous space was like a living room, with sofas and comfortable chairs. The rest was organized with tables and folding chairs, where the adults met for their classes.

While they studied, I'd play on the floor with the Maluf children. Mariam Maluf was the first child born to the Center parents. At nearly six years old, she was a full two-and-a-half years older than I was. She had large brown eyes like her father's and long, straight, almost black hair. Her skin color was darker than mine. Mariam said with pride that it was "olive colored," and she explained why to me.

"I'm a Semite," she said in her all-knowing way, "and you're a Japhethite."

Then she went into detail about how her father, Fakhri, who was from Syria, was descended from Sem, the oldest son of Noah from the Old Testament. I, on the other hand, was descended from Japheth, Noah's youngest son, whose offspring settled in Europe. She made it sound as though that was inferior to coming from the Middle East.

"That's why you have blue eyes, and I have brown eyes," Mariam said with authority. Fakhri had told her these things, she said, and, at three years old, I believed whatever she told me. But I was happy to have blue eyes.

Sometimes Mariam seemed like an older sister because she knew so much more than I did. She had an answer for everything, and I didn't dare question her authority. Her two younger brothers were Peter, who was nine months older than I was, and Leonard, who was nine months younger. Leonard was my best friend and we were never far apart—playing together, sharing everything, and racing each other, whether it be up and down the stairs between our apartments or along the banks of the river.

When the adults' morning classes were over, Father would sit in the middle of the Center on what seemed like his throne, a vast, low-slung armchair of crinkly, cracked red leather. Slouched in his seat, he'd stretch his legs out and rest his feet on a matching footstool. He was old (just like the chair, I thought), the oldest person at the Center, and unlike the rest of the adults, who wore colorful clothes or suits with ties, he was always dressed in black, except for the white Roman collar that signified he was a priest.

As Father reclined, the women would gather around him, some sitting at his feet and others kneeling at his side. They all seemed to wait for him to say something, and while he spoke, the room was silent. If he said something funny, everyone laughed; if he was serious, so were they.

When he finished talking, and it was time to leave the Center for lunch or dinner, there was always a hand for me to grab as we headed back through the streets of Cambridge to the house on Putnam Avenue where everyone at the Center gathered for meals. We called that house Sacred Heart Hall.

While dinner was being prepared, some of the adults would gather in the parlor room upstairs, where sofas and comfortable chairs were scattered around a coffee table. The women wore lipstick and pretty dresses, and the men smoked cigarettes as they sipped iced drinks and talked about what they did during "the war." Their peals of laughter floated toward me as I'd sit at the top of the stairs with my elbows on my knees and my chin in my hands. I didn't understand much of what they said, but I was mesmerized.

Sometimes Leonard joined me. Together we'd sit in silence, absorbed in the adults' revelry and awaiting the clang of the bell that signaled dinner was ready. Then, holding hands, we'd sprint down the

Father and Catherine with me (lower left), Mariam, and another Center child, on the lawn of Sacred Heart Hall, November 1950.

stairs and into the refectory. That's what everyone called the makeshift dining room, where three long picnic tables were set up with folding chairs. We sat anywhere we wanted, adults and children side by side. I needed a stack of books underneath me, and still my chin barely came over the top of the table. But there was always a friendly "aunt" or "uncle" ready to help cut my food.

If the weather was hot, we'd have our dessert sitting on the miniature rectangle of lawn between Sacred Heart Hall and the white picket fence that bordered the sidewalk. Father himself would often bring it to me. "What kind of ice cream would you like, dear?" he'd ask.

"Strawberry, please, Father," I'd say.

Always strawberry, and always "please" and "thank you," as I took the bowl with both hands. I'd let the ice cream melt in the summer's

The grownup women as I remembered them before they discarded their "worldly" clothes.

heat, then slurp down the liquid—careful not to spill any on my white summer dress.

It was around this time that the women at the Center stopped wearing their colorful clothes. Floral patterned dresses, royal-blue jackets, and cinched waist suits were replaced by long black skirts and white blouses covered by a black jacket. Instead of a pocketbook, my mother now carried a small black fabric satchel. Her shoes were lace-up—no longer the heels and open-toed shoes she used to wear. The men wore identical black suits and white shirts, except when they were working and had to wear overalls. Even my own clothes changed. Now I wore the same kind of blouse and jumper as the other little girls. But I was unfazed by the new wardrobe. My life centered around the array of loving people that poured attention on my daily activities.

It wasn't until I was four that I started to become aware that we at the Center were different from the people who lived "out in the world"— that's how we referred to everything that existed beyond our realm.

That world presented danger and Mariam tried to explain it to me.

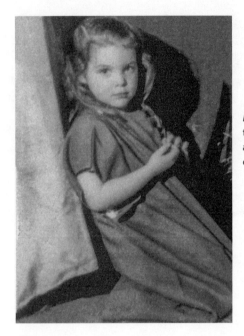

Me as a shepherd in
the Christmas pageant,
around the age of three
or four.

"The bad people hate us," she said. "So, you can't tell anyone that Father says Mass. If you do," she warned, sounding every bit like a seven-year-old grown-up, "the police will come and put us in jail."

"Put us in jail?" The specter was terrifying.

Father had been deprived of his priestly faculties, but that did not deter him from continuing to celebrate Mass for the community. His defiance, however, was a matter of secrecy and to ensure that no slip of the tongue inadvertently alerted the local church authorities of his continued insubordination, we devised code words to describe our religious activities. Mass was called "First Breakfast," and the real breakfast that followed, we referred to as "second breakfast." Benediction, which Father said each afternoon, was "tea," and if we were to say the Rosary at Benediction, we were having "tea and biscuits." Father heard confessions each Saturday, but we called it "*cubiculo*,"

Around Christmas, 1951. My parents were now wearing the "religious" garb. I am in the snow suit, my sister Cathy is holding Dad's hand, and Mother is holding David, who is about five months old.

the Latin word for "bedroom." These terms and others became part of our vernacular and I knew them all by heart.

When the weather was sunny and warm, Father would celebrate First Breakfast on the rooftop of Sacred Heart Hall. I knelt in fear, convinced that the people on the street below would hear us singing our hymns and would call the police, who would come crashing through the doors with guns drawn and haul us off to jail, just as Mariam told me.

Jail was never far from my mind, and with good reason. To raise money for their daily sustenance, the men and women of the Center peddled books that Father and Catherine Clarke were writing, books that stressed the doctrine of "No Salvation Outside the Catholic Church."

Each week, in groups of six men in one car and six women in another, they set out to places as far away as New Orleans, Chicago, and St. Louis. Bookselling was what we called it, and it was the primary source of income for the community. Even the parents went on those trips, except for the women who were expecting a baby, a common occurrence during those early years.

The ecclesiastical authorities in Boston got wind of the bookselling and alerted Catholic parishes across the country to be on the lookout for us and to call the police if we were in town. Our books were not sanctioned by the Church, they said, and we should be arrested for trespassing.

The members of the Center community, dressed identically in black, were easy to spot. Hardly a week went by without one or more of the men and women, including my father on one occasion, being arrested on their bookselling journeys. Often they were confined in jail until Bill Shea, the Harvard-educated lawyer and Center member, would pay a visit to "friends in high places," as he described his lawyer friends in Boston. Within a few hours, he had managed to free the booksellers.

Bookselling wasn't the only cause for anxiety in our secluded life. Each Sunday afternoon, regardless of the season or the weather, the adult members of the community drove from Cambridge to the Boston Common, a sprawling public park in downtown Boston. With Father in the lead, and surrounded by his "bodyguards"—half a dozen of the burliest of the Center men—they processed, fifty strong, men and women, and took up their station on the western corner of the Common, where for an hour or more, Father would address the throngs that gathered, haranguing the audience, blaring epithets against the Jews "who killed Jesus," and the Freemasons, the

Leonard Feeney leading the men (followed by the women) on the Boston Common on a Sunday afternoon in the 1950s.

Protestants, and anyone who didn't believe in the doctrine of "No Salvation Outside the Catholic Church."

The listening public, in particular those who felt under attack, including Jewish students from nearby Brandeis University, would shout back and, on occasion, the confrontation erupted into violence and the police would appear. But rain or shine, winter and summer, Sunday afternoons were dedicated to a confrontational exchange between the Center and the people of Boston.

Though none of us children were ever brought to "the Common," as we referred to those Sunday afternoon sessions, I developed a clear, if perhaps exaggerated, depiction of what had transpired because at dinner that evening the adults would regale themselves with rehashing the most lurid incidents of the afternoon. On more than one occasion, one of the men came home with a gash in his head or a black eye.

Despite the lightheartedness with which the Center members treated these Sunday incidents, I was beginning to wish it all would end. Why was it, I wondered, that we were hated by everyone "out in the world"?

The stimulating interaction with the many adult members of our community served to offset the lack of communication with the outside world. I devoured every snippet of information I could glean from them. While the Center's mission was a somber one, the highly intellectual, spirited men and women didn't shy away from having a good time. Much of their free time was spent in writing and performing skits that covered a broad array of topics, all done with a level of humor and sophistication far beyond my ken. But that did nothing to diminish my enjoyment on skit nights, when the community, adults and children, gathered at the Center several evenings a week after dinner to be entertained as the adults performed, donning as costumes the worldly clothes they had forsaken. Oblivious to the black wit of their parodies of well-known lyrics, I memorized the words in their many spoofs, including two from Gilbert and Sullivan's *H.M.S. Pinafore.*

"The Captain's Song"
I am the Captain of the Queen's Navee,
And a right good captain too.
I'm very, very good, but be it understood
That at heart I'm a great big Jew.

Chorus: *He's very, very good but be it understood that at heart he's a great big Jew.*

"The First Lord's Song"
I polished brass for her Majesty to win the title of nobility.
But England isn't what she used to be; she sold out to the Jews financially.
If Buttercup would marry me, we could both live on her pocketbook quite happily.

It would be a couple of decades before I came to learn the true words.

7

The Noose Tightens

1953

I had an enormous appetite for asking questions. "What does that word mean?" was my constant refrain as I'd hover around the adults who chatted among themselves on matters far beyond my comprehension.

When one of them would offer to take me for a walk, the questions bursting inside my head would spill out in a torrent.

"Why are buttercups yellow?" "Why does the moon change its shape?" "What city were you born in?" "What do the cedars of Lebanon look like?" "Can you speak Italian?" "French?" "Russian?"

Not a day passed that I didn't glean a smidgeon of knowledge from the ever-ready "uncles" and "aunts" in my life. But those resources started to become restricted, as Father and Catherine Clarke imposed regulations on the Slaves of the Immaculate Heart of Mary that increasingly bordered on monastic and religious discipline.

One of the first was an edict by Father prohibiting members of the community from discussing their past lives—what they did in the world before joining the Center. He referred to this rule in code, calling it PL (past life) and I felt it in a personal way. No longer could

I listen with rapture to the adults' stories that brought the outside world into my imagination—about their time in the war in Germany, Japan, the South Pacific, and Africa; how Fakhri had crossed the Atlantic Ocean on a boat and saw the Statue of Liberty when he reached America; how others came to America from Lebanon and Spain and Italy.

"What did you do in the war?" had been my favorite question to ask. I thought that everyone in the Center had been "in the war."

"How did you get out of the Navy?" I'd asked my father over and over, knowing the silly answer he'd give me.

"I snuck out the back door," he'd reply, and I'd try to imagine what the back door of the Navy looked like.

Now those questions were forbidden.

More crushing was the follow-on restriction that forbade anyone at the Center to contact their family members who lived "out in the world."

Until then, my favorite Saturday pastime had been visiting my Grandma Walsh.

"Let's go for a ride," my father would say, and I knew what that meant—we were heading to Quincy for the afternoon to see my relatives. Entering the house where my father had grown up, I'd run to my grandmother as she sat in her usual spot on the couch in the living room. Though her hair was white and she wore eyeglasses, I didn't think of her as old, as I'd sit in her lap and hold her hand and rest my head on her bosom while my father and she chatted. I adored her.

Then without explanation, the trips stopped. "When are we going to see Grandma?" I'd ask my father.

"Soon, my little princess," he'd say. (That was his pet name for me.) But it didn't happen, and after a while, I stopped asking.

It wasn't long before I was aware that the PL rule didn't apply to Father. The much anticipated trips to my grandmother's were soon supplanted by visits to the Feeney house and *his* parents, who lived in the Boston suburb of Lynn. The dark mahogany-paneled rooms of the

Holding my Grandma Walsh's hand with my father, sister Cathy, and brother David–1952.

Feeney home were in sharp contrast to the light-filled and cheerful home of my grandmother. A large vase of faded hydrangeas that sat on a round marble-topped table in the front hall set the stage for the gloom that permeated the house.

"They're dried flowers," Mariam told me on one occasion when I wrinkled my nose at them.

Dead was a better description, I thought.

Mr. Feeney sat like a crumpled rag doll on a sofa in front of two tall windows covered with red velvet drapes that obliterated daylight. His wife brought us cookies and milk and in between nibbles and sips, we had to recite poems Father had written once upon a time when he was the famous and beloved American Catholic poet, long before his fall from grace. For my part, I couldn't wait to get back home.

* * *

With a shovel in his hand, my dad started digging.

"Daddy, what are you doing?" I asked, ever curious and fascinated by the multiple deep holes that lined up like sentinels along the sidewalk.

"Building a fence, my little princess," he replied. "Now stay away, so you don't get hurt."

Mariam filled me in on the rest. "The fence is going to go all around our houses."

She was right. It took weeks, but little by little, the fence was erected and the outside world disappeared—the people who lived in the multifamily houses across the street, the open field where children played, the rag man and his horse and buggy, the banana man who pulled his cart and shouted, "Whoop! Ripe bananas, ten cents a pound apiece."

The fence was painted red, and it formed the circumference of the walled city that encompassed the seven houses in which the married couples and their children lived and where we now had our communal meals and the chapel. The nearly forty single adults continued to live in two separate houses, one each for the men and the women, outside of the red fence. The phrase "out in the world" came to represent the world beyond our compound.

"That's where the bad people live," Mariam told me in her know-it-all way, as we sat eating our bread, butter, and oregano sandwiches on the picnic bench in our enclosure.

I knew the litany of who the bad people were—the Jews, the pagans, the heretics, the infidels, the Protestants, the Freemasons, and the pious frauds, or as Father called them, "PFs." They were the Irish Catholics of Boston who had turned against him and sided with Archbishop Cushing.

The more the world was shut out, the more I longed to see it. One evening, while playing in the newly enclosed yard, I made a discovery. By putting my right eye up to the small sliver of space between the gate and the post to which it was hinged, I was able to spy the top

The entire adult community in the summer of 1953. My mother is fourth from the right in the front row; my father is on the far right in the back row.

of Boston's tallest building, the John Hancock in Copley Square. In the fading daylight I could see the steady blue light shining from the weather beacon.

"It's going to be sunny tomorrow," I announced with confidence to my father. He had taught me the verse that interpreted the color of the light, which was a weather beacon.

Steady blue, clear view.
Flashing blue, clouds due.
Steady red, rain ahead.
Flashing red, snow instead.

The only other glimpse I now had into the world beyond the red fence was on Thursday evenings when Father continued to give his once-famous lectures. The throngs of listeners in his heyday were now replaced by a small coterie of ladies, loyalists to Father. Their arrival in an array of "worldly" attire—hats and high-heeled shoes, pocketbooks, and all manner of coats, furs, dresses, and suits—was a feast for my eyes.

When a couple of them would head off to "powder their noses," an expression I found baffling, I followed them to the ladies' room.

Once inside, I stood silently, my back against the wall, observing their rituals. The click of the clasp on the pocketbook opened up a profusion of items both novel and exotic. *Was the gold-colored powder compact made of real gold?* I committed to memory their beauty routine—the multiple dabs of the powder puff on each check (but seldom on their nose) followed by several deft sweeps of the lipstick tube across the top and then the bottom lip, then a smacking of two lips together over a tissue and running the tongue across the front teeth.

This was an education I could never get at the Center. All those "worldly" lipstick tubes and powder puffs had been banned.

St. John's House, with the red fence in the far background.

8

Identity Crisis

1953–1954

I was not quite five years old when Father Feeney decreed that the adults, including my parents, would change their names, in some cases getting rid of nicknames and in others replacing their "worldly" names with saints' names, as is the practice when Catholics enter religious life. My mother, whom everyone had called Betsy, became Sister Elizabeth Ann, and my father Jim was now Brother James Aloysius. Within the community, the adults were referred to as the Big Brothers and Big Sisters, and the children as the Little Brothers and Little Sisters. As members of the religious order—the Slaves of the Immaculate Heart of Mary—each of the adults now used the abbreviation, MICM, following their signature on correspondence among themselves. (MICM stood for the first initial of the Latin translation of the order: Mancipia Immaculati Cordis Mariae.)

Sixty plus people, each with a new name, was a memory challenge I took as a game. But more difficult was being expected to address my parents by their new religious names. Only in the privacy of our apartment, could I still call them Mama and Daddy.

Then Father decided to change some of the children's names. Grace, a little girl about two years younger than I was, became Claudette, a name I'd never heard of before. My sister, Cathy (whose full name was Catherine Mary Joan Leonard), became Mary Catherine, as Father chose to switch her first two names as if to say that Mary was more important than Catherine. He made a number of other reorganizations of the names parents had given to their children.

Each day, it appeared as though another child succumbed to Father's name-changing spell, and I grew wary, desperate that my name not be altered in any way. I was Mary Patricia, proud to be named for St. Patrick, the patron saint of Ireland, who was Irish like my father. I did my best to avoid Father and was successful until one morning after second breakfast as I was walking through the basement refectory hand in hand with my mother. Suddenly Father appeared at the far end of the room. His stride was strong as he closed the distance between us. I gripped my mother's hand, dreading what might be coming.

Bending down and touching my head, he said, "Mary Patricia, dear, how would you like to change your name?"

What could I say? He was Father. Nobody said no to him. I remained silent, looking down at my shoes and still holding on tightly to my mother. I wished I could whisper to her, "Please tell him I don't want to change my name." But that wasn't how things were done at the Center. Father was in charge, and he always had his way. He took it personally if anyone disagreed with him. He may have fallen off his pedestal in the eyes of the rest of the world, but within the confines of the Center, he was lord of the manor. He never let any member forget the vow they took when they joined—"obedience to Father and to whomever he may delegate."

"How would you like to be called Anastasia?" he asked.

Anastasia? What kind of a name was that? I'd never heard of any St. Anastasia. I wanted no part of it. But I was trapped—the nightmare I had dreaded was unfolding, and I couldn't run away from it.

Father stood before me waiting for an answer. "She was a virgin and a martyr," he added, as though that information would encourage me.

I wanted nothing to do with martyrs. If I had to change my name, I wanted it to be for a beautiful queen, like St. Helena, the mother of Constantine the Great, or St. Margaret of Scotland or St. Elizabeth of Hungary, my mother's patron saint. Now as I stood before Father, still clutching my mother's hand, I nodded, as I knew I had to, and the deed was done. In a flash, I was no longer Mary Patricia. I was now Anastasia.

That evening at dinner, Father took me by the hand and led me to the head of the refectory. He announced to the whole community that I had a new name—Anastasia—and everyone clapped. I wanted to cry.

During recreation in the yard after dinner, I pretended to be excited about the change in my name, but my outward smile belied my inner feelings. What I really wanted to do was stamp my foot and scream at the top of my lungs, "I hate being called Anastasia—I hate my new name!"

But that wasn't done at the Center. And besides, if my parents saw me upset, they'd want to fix it for me. This couldn't be fixed.

Despite the wave of name changes, family life within our apartment remained much the same. My father participated fully in the evening rituals of giving the oldest of us baths while my mother nursed the newest baby, my sister Veronica, the number five child in our family, born just two months before my sixth birthday.

"Daddy, will you sing me a song?" was my nightly request.

"Of course, my little princess," he'd say, and then he'd settle into the heavy oak chair in the middle of the family room. I'd scramble onto one of his black-trousered legs and dangle my own legs between his, kicking back and forth. Often, my sister Mary Catherine joined me, sitting on his other leg.

"And what song would you like tonight?"

My answer never varied.

"You know—'La Très Sainte Vierge'!"

It was one of several French-Canadian songs in his vast repertoire, a song about Our Lady when she was a little girl, walking to school. My dad would stroke my own long brown hair as he sang "avec les beaux cheveux pendant," which he explained meant "with her beautiful long hair hanging down."

And later when he tucked me into bed, I held my breath, waiting for the words I knew he would whisper in my ear: "Good night, my little princess."

On nights when my parents attended classes at the Center, one of the Big Brothers or Big Sisters would be our "Angel," the Center's word for babysitter.

I had a few favorite Angels: Brother Sebastian was one of them. His role as my brother's godfather gave him a special place within our family and his bedtime stories were legion—St. Patrick came to Ireland and kicked out all the snakes; St. Francis tamed the wolf in Gubbio; St. George killed the dragon; St. Frances Cabrini sailed on a ship to America from Italy and traveled throughout South America riding on a donkey. Those tales of the saints became my internal encyclopedia, and I relished memorizing facts about countries and cities, history and nature, all intertwined in a riveting story about life long ago and out in the now-verboten world.

I imagined visiting each city where a saint grew up—Rome, Constantinople, Besançon, the Isle of Lindisfarne, Lisieux, Padua, and on and on. I tried to picture the hills of Tuscany and the Arno River, the Sea of Galilee with fishermen throwing out their fishing nets. Then, as I fell off to sleep, I vowed to myself that someday I would visit those places.

But my favorite Angel was Sister Mary Elizabeth, whom I still thought of as Betty Sullivan. The red fence had put an end to our time together picking flowers by the river or walking to the Center, but the bond we had forged since my infancy only grew. When I was too young to understand such things, she had been engaged to marry one of the men at the Center—but that was before they all took vows. Perhaps I represented the child she knew she would never have.

Then one day, she was gone. I didn't see her at First Breakfast or second breakfast. She didn't come out to the yard and play with me after dinner. A sense of dread mounted inside me: *Had she been kicked out?*

Kicked out was the term we used when someone was no longer with us. It meant they were no good. It meant they would never go to heaven, because in my world, there was no salvation outside of the Center, or as I thought about it, outside the red fence.

That evening as my mother was combing the snarls out of my long, wet hair, I asked her, "Where is Sister Mary Elizabeth?"

She responded softly, as though knowing how much her answer would hurt me. "She's gone, darling."

"Gone? Why?" I was horrified at the thought that I might never see her again.

My mother paused and the words came out as though it was the only explanation she could give, "Because she wasn't a good girl."

Tears streamed down my face, a silent requiem for the woman I loved who was so suddenly gone forever. I knew then, though, that there was no point in making a scene. I knew my mother could do nothing to bring her back. Father and Sister Catherine kicked people out of the Center.

But why? What could she have done that was so awful?

9

Separation

1954

"This is a glorious day."

That was how Father began his sermon on a crisp Sunday morning in November.

"Today is the Feast of the Presentation of Our Lady in the Temple. On this very day, nearly two thousand years ago, Our Blessed Mother's parents, St. Ann and St. Joachim, brought their precious little girl to the temple and consecrated her to God. She was exactly three years, two months and thirteen days old. As she stood on the first step, she let go of her parents' hands."

Then Father lifted his right hand and demonstrated with two fingers as though they were walking, while he went on. "Her little feet went pitter-patter as she ran up the twenty-one steps that led into the temple. Never once did she look back. At the top step, she was met by the high priest, who took her into the temple where she was raised until she was ready to become the Mother of God."

Father told endless stories in vivid detail about the Holy Family. It was as though he knew them personally. I reveled in the myriad tales that included how St. Joseph, who was a carpenter, taught the child Jesus to use a hammer and nails; how the Holy Family had to flee into Egypt on the back of a donkey in the middle of a cold night so that Herod wouldn't kill Baby Jesus. My six-year-old imagination was stimulated by the images Father created—Our Lady holding Baby Jesus snuggly against her so that the desert wind wouldn't make Him cold. I believed every word of those stories.

As Father spoke that morning, I envisioned Our Lady as a little three-year-old, with long brown hair like mine, dressed in a pale blue dress that came to her ankles—the way she was depicted in holy cards. I imagined her as a person out in the world, beyond the red fence.

But there was a more sinister meaning to Father's story that morning, and it would have an imminent significance on the trajectory of my life.

The weather that day was sunny, and the air was brisk. After second breakfast, we bundled up in our homemade sweaters and mittens and headed out to play in the yard. As I climbed the willow tree with Leonard and Mariam, we were oblivious to the several Big Brothers who had entered our apartment house. When sometime later they emerged carrying my parents' bed and my favorite upholstered chair—the one my mother sat in as she nursed my baby sister—I was aghast.

In stunned silence, we watched as the furniture from our homes was carried off, piece by piece. What did it mean? Confused, we whispered among ourselves. At lunchtime, I looked for my parents to ask them what was happening, but they had left with Father and most of the other adults to go to Boston Common. Even Mariam, who was quick to share her superior knowledge on nearly every matter, seemed stumped.

It wasn't until after dinner when we were playing in the yard that my mother explained in cryptic fashion what was happening.

"You and Mary Catherine and David are big girls and boys now, and you're going to live with the other children who are your age" was how she put it in a gentle and encouraging tone of voice. "Don't worry, darling, we'll still be nearby," she said as she gave me a kiss, "just across the yard in St. John's House."

The reality of her words sank in slowly. *We aren't going to live together as a family anymore?* I bit my lip to keep from crying.

My mother was right that St. John's House was nearby. But as far as I was concerned, it might as well have been outside the red fence. I did my best to put on a brave face. As the oldest, at six, I felt a sudden sense of responsibility for my little sister, Mary Catherine. Only four years old, she seemed bewildered, while David, my three-year-old brother, was oblivious to the change he was about to face.

When the bell rang indicating the end of evening recreation, my parents kissed me goodnight.

"Little Sisters and Brothers, please stand in line along the side of the house, in order of age and in silence."

The order came from Sister Matilda, herself the mother of five of the children. She directed the Little Sisters to face the front door and the Little Brothers the side door. Her broad shoulders displayed an air of authority. The tone of her voice was anything but motherly.

I took my place, third in line among the twelve Little Sisters. In drill sergeant fashion, Sister Matilda walked from the head of the line to the end. "Hands by your side," she said sternly and I stiffened to attention.

As she patrolled the long line of children standing in military formation, I turned to watch my parents walking out of the far side of the yard carrying my two youngest sisters, Margaret Mary (who was just two) and five-month-old Veronica, and heading to their new home in St. John's House.

"Eyes straight ahead," Sister Matilda barked at me.

Then she led us up the stairs to the third floor—to the apartment that had, until a few hours earlier, been my family home.

I stared in astonishment at the change that had taken place since I left that morning. There were now two twin beds in each of the four rooms. With no explanation, Sister Matilda assigned us to our bedrooms and I was distraught to discover that I would no longer share a room with Mary Catherine.

Following orders, we prepared for bed in silence, taking turns washing at the sink, brushing our teeth, and donning the white cotton nightgowns assigned to each of us.

"Everyone, line up with your hands folded."

It was time for night prayers. In single file, our hands folded as instructed, we descended to the second floor, where the front room had been converted into a chapel. Kneeling on the wooden floor in assigned places, we said, in unison, the Our Father, the Hail Mary, the Act of Contrition, and the prayer to our Guardian Angel. Then Sister Matilda rose, and we followed her in silence, returning to the third floor and our assigned beds. There was no bedtime story.

Surrounded by darkness in my new bedroom, I tried to absorb the crushing realization that in a flash, my family had been split up. As I lay alone in my bed without a goodnight kiss from my parents, without the bedtime story of one of my favorite saints, without tucking my baby sister Veronica into her crib, without the whispered, "Good night, my little princess," from my father, I let the tears flow down my cheeks. It was safe to cry silently—no one could hear me. I couldn't fathom why my family had been taken away.

I fell into an unsettled sleep. When I woke the next morning to the harsh clang of a bell that was our wakeup call, I realized I wasn't in a dream. This was my new life.

10

From Carefree to Caged

1954

Father and Sister Catherine had assigned Sister Matilda as the Angel in charge of the children.

"Dear Sister in the Immaculate Heart of Mary, sometimes you have a bad temper."

Those words were addressed to me as I knelt on the linoleum floor of the kitchen in what used to by my family's apartment. With my eyes focused on the floor and my hands folded as if in prayer, I gritted my teeth and swallowed hard, forcing back the words I wanted to yell—"I do *not* have a bad temper."

But such remonstration was not allowed. This was a Chapter Meeting, a throwback ritual to the ancient Benedictine custom known as "Chapter of Faults," at which adult monks and nuns corrected each other for infractions of the monastic rule.

I was hardly six years old, and I detested this humiliating Saturday morning ritual that Sister Matilda initiated almost as soon as she was put in charge of the children. Kneeling in silence, I listened as each of the seven other Little Sisters with whom I now lived on the third floor of St. Francis Xavier's House took a turn pointing out my faults to me.

"You broke silence last night after the lights were out," said another Little Sister.

"You are proud."

"You cry too easily."

It will be over soon, I repeated to myself, as I bit the inside of my cheek and felt my face becoming increasingly flush with rage.

Much as I dreaded Saturday morning Chapter Meetings, I knew I could look forward to Saturday afternoon when I had my hour-long sewing and knitting lesson. What made it special was that my mother, Sister Elizabeth Ann, was our teacher.

This weekly session was the only opportunity, outside of Sunday mornings and our thirty-minute recreation in the evening, that I had to spend time with her. Each of the Big Brothers and Sisters had assigned chores, and my mother spent her days making clothes and knitting sweaters for the children.

Lunch had no appeal for me on Saturdays—I gobbled it down and raced through the two tiny yards to Blessed Sacrament House, deliberately arriving well before the other Little Sisters, so as to have a few extra minutes alone with Sister Elizabeth Ann. She kissed me, and I watched in fascination as she set up our lesson, laying out the fabrics, threading the needles, and arranging the chairs.

Our sewing projects were simple—making rolled hems on the handkerchiefs for the Big Brothers and Big Sisters or working on the altar linens.

As the six of us children, ranging in age from five to nine, sat in a circle on folding chairs, Sister Elizabeth Ann went from one to the other of us, always with a kind word or small piece of advice. When the frustration of a lost stitch or a bungled row of knitting brought me close to tears, she'd whisper in my ear, "Don't get upset, darling. Let me help you."

She'd take my project in her hands, and adjusting her eyeglasses on her nose, she'd undo my mistake and give it back to me as good as new. "You're doing beautifully, darling. There's no need to rush. Just take your time."

"Thank you, Sister," I replied, inwardly reveling at the attention she was paying to me. I kept an eye on the clock on the wall, and as the sewing lesson was coming to an end, sadness crept up inside me. I blinked my eyes hard to push back the tears. It would be a whole week before we had this special time together again.

Militaristic was the best way to describe our daily routine. At seven o'clock each morning, one of the four assistant Angels, each of whom reported to Sister Matilda, arrived on the third floor and rang a bell to wake us. They rotated a week at a time in the role of Angel for the eight of us Little Sisters who lived on the top floor. My mother was not one of them.

The ringing of the bell signaled that I had ten minutes to rise, put on my clothes, wash my face, and brush my teeth, all the while observing the rule of silence. When the bell was rung again at precisely 7:10, it was time to make my bed, with perfect hospital corners and the spread tucked under the pillow so that there wasn't a wrinkle to be seen. The third clang of the bell five minutes later told me to brush my hair, braid it, and tie ribbons on the ends of the braids.

When Sister Mary Laurence was the assistant Angel, she marched through the four bedrooms checking on the eight of us Little Sisters as we rushed through our tasks. In her hand she carried a hairbrush, not as an aid for a Little Sister with snarls in her hair, but as a weapon to punish a straggler. I knew I could finish in time, but I worried about Mary Catherine, whom I couldn't observe because her bedroom was around the corner.

By 7:25 each morning, the eight of us were standing in line, facing the stairwell door. In silence we descended to the second floor, where the younger Little Sisters lived. Together, hands folded as if in prayer, and with the Little Brothers following, we filed across the yard to St. Gabriel's House, walked up the stairs to the third floor, and took our assigned places on benches in the chapel, awaiting the start of First Breakfast at 7:30.

The bedtime ritual was much the same. After preparing for bed, which included polishing our own shoes, spot-cleaning our jumpers, and washing out our white blouses in the deep sink, we headed downstairs to the chapel for night prayers, which were led by Sister Matilda.

Our new regime was a tortuous adjustment. When my baby sister Veronica was born only five months before the separation, I had felt like a mother myself, carrying my sister Margaret Mary (just eighteen months old) on my hip around the apartment and helping my mother by changing her diaper and dressing her. Now, the only time I could spend with my baby sisters were those few minutes of recreation each night after dinner in the yard. And that pleasure, too, was stultified when Sister Matilda announced a new rule one Saturday morning after Chapter Meeting.

"From now on, you may no longer hold the hands of the younger children."

I was stunned. *Why*, I thought, but no answer came to mind. I felt as though that new, hideous rule was somehow directed at me. Veronica was almost a year old and nearly ready to take her first steps. Each evening during our thirty-minute recreation, I'd let her toddle toward me with her tiny hands grasping my fingers, as I walked backward with arms outstretched.

I couldn't concoct the right words to tell my parents about this new restriction, so I tried my best to act as though nothing had changed. But one evening, when Sister Matilda wasn't in the yard during recreation, I couldn't resist taking Veronica's hand. As I led her across the yard, her tiny feet making progress with my guidance, I glanced up and caught sight of Sister Matilda watching me from the second-floor window of St. Francis Xavier's House. I gulped, knowing I would soon be in trouble. Within a minute she was standing in the doorway, beckoning to me. Without as much as a kiss good night to my parents, I headed into the house, fully aware of what lay ahead—a paddling with whatever instrument Sister Matilda deemed appropriate. Would it be her latest instrument of torture, the two-foot-long board that only she, with her Paul Bunyan–size hands, could handle? She chose instead a shoe brush, and in the soundproof stairwell, she laid into me as I was bent over her lap.

"This will teach you not to break the rules," she thundered as the powerful force of her blows hit my bare bottom.

On another morning, Sister Matilda called the eight oldest of us Little Sisters in from our recreation in the yard. Leading us up to the third floor, she waited as we assembled in order of age. Then, striding back and forth in front of us, she fired a question: "Which of you didn't wash your face this morning before First Breakfast?"

I hadn't the slightest recollection of whether I'd remembered to wash my face in my rush to be ready on time, but Sister Matilda had apparently discovered the infraction by inspecting the towel racks after second breakfast to make sure all the facecloths were wet.

When no one responded, she said, "Well, maybe this will help you to remember."

She approached Mariam, saying, "This will hurt me as much as you," but she didn't seem to mean it as she brought the full force of her open hand across Mariam's face. She did the same to Rene, and then came to me. After slapping me, she said, "And a second one for you," as her left hand came crashing into the other side of my face. I nearly fell over. The rest of the Little Sisters each received a single resounding slap. We then had to sit in silence for an hour as further punishment.

Was I the culprit? I wondered. We were sent back out to play, but I lingered and when the others headed down the stairs, I took the opportunity to check the facecloths—mine was damp. The only dry one belonged to Sister Matilda's daughter.

It's not fair—why does she dislike me?

A powerful slap in the face became one of her favorite modes of discipline. I could feel the marks left by the impact of her hand on my cheek. But I soon observed that she was careful not to use that form of punishment if I was heading out to recreation in the evening with my parents, so they never saw the redness on my face.

At another of our Saturday morning Chapter Meetings, as Sister Matilda entered the kitchen where the eight of us sat on the bench awaiting the start of the meeting, the force of her step told me there was trouble. She took her seat at the table and wasted no time.

"It has come to my attention," she announced, and the tone in her voice made my stomach churn, "that all of you were rude to Father last week when he took you for a ride in the car. Who wants to tell me about it?"

I was stunned and, along with the Little Sisters, sat in silence, wracking my brain to recollect what had happened a few days back, when Father had taken us to the Italian market in Boston's North End, where the merchants sold meat, fruits, and vegetables. Those occasional forays into the outside world were a treat. As he always did on such occasions, Father had asked us to sing some hymns for the vendors, whom he described as "good Italian Catholics." When we were through, one of the men offered Father peaches and plums for us.

Holding the fruit in his hands, Father turned to us and asked, "What would you like, dear, a peach or a plum?"

I loved both and thought about it before saying, "A plum, please, Father." The other Little Sisters made their choices. I could remember nothing else about the excursion.

"Well, let me remind you." There was an edge of sarcasm in the tone of her voice. "When Father asked you if you wanted a peach or a plum, you had the nerve to make the choice yourself instead of letting him decide."

She slammed her hand down on the table next to her chair with such impact that all eight of us jumped and her voice became thunderous. "From now on, if Father asks you what you would like, you are to reply, 'Whatever you would like me to have, Father.' Do you understand?"

"Yes, Sister Matilda."

"Good. Now you're going to practice it." She turned to Mariam and asked, "What would you like to have—a peach or a plum?"

Mariam replied, "Whatever you would like me to have, Father."

Then she turned to Rene and asked the same question, and then to me. And when she had finished with Claudette, the youngest, she started again with Mariam. There was no way I'd ever forget the obligatory response.

Once the hour of terror was over each Saturday, I threw myself with abandon into the games we created among ourselves—marbles and jacks, games of hide-and-seek and tag. Dolls, coloring books, and toy cars or plastic animals were not in our collection of playthings, but we used our imaginations to make up our own games. One of my favorites was our version of Twenty Questions that we called "I'm Thinking of a Saint." The stories of the lives of the saints were woven into the fabric of our daily life, whether through listening each evening at dinnertime as one of the Big Brothers read from *The Roman Martyrology*, that ancient compendium of facts about Catholic saints, or from being regaled at recreation by my "aunts and uncles" who had an endless array of stories about the saints—virgins (whatever that meant) who had their eyes plucked out or their breasts cut off because they refused to give up their Catholic faith, or (more to my liking) queens and kings who spread the Catholic faith throughout Europe. I excelled at our game, and there was almost no saint I couldn't eventually guess.

11

Troubles

1955

Mary Catherine stopped eating—she was not quite five years old. One morning, at second breakfast, she refused to eat her cereal, staring at her bowl without lifting her spoon.

Sister Matilda's voice was harsh. "Mary Catherine, eat your cereal right now."

But she didn't respond. She simply looked at the food with her hands in her lap. I wanted to catch her eye and give her a nod or a hint of a smile as encouragement, but she seemed to be in another world, almost oblivious to my existence.

It was only a few months since the day we were separated from our parents. I had settled in to the new way of life, at least outwardly. But Mary Catherine had lost much of her vivacity. Now, as we sat at the refectory table, I felt my stomach wrench, knowing she was in for a spanking with the dreaded plank if she didn't eat.

Maybe she's sick, I thought. *Why doesn't Sister Matilda ask her if she has a tummy ache?*

At the end of the meal, I headed upstairs to tutoring. That's what we called our school, where I was now in the second grade. My growing anxiety dulled my usual exuberance in the classroom. I hoped that by lunchtime, Mary Catherine would be hungry enough to eat a big meal.

But when we sat down to our soup and sandwiches, Sister Matilda put the bowl of uneaten, now-cold oatmeal in front of Mary Catherine as her lunch.

Again she refused to eat. During afternoon recreation, I cornered Mary Catherine.

"Did you get a spanking?" I whispered to her. She nodded her head, and I wracked my brain for a solution. Nothing came to mind. "Why can't you eat?" I asked in desperation.

"I don't know" was her response. That only increased my anxiety. I wanted a solution, whatever it was, so that Mary Catherine would be happy again.

The bowl of cereal was brought back for dinner.

"*Now* eat it," said Sister Matilda.

Mary Catherine couldn't. Nobody could eat that hideous lump of cold, dried-out oatmeal.

I fell into a troubled sleep, and when I woke the next morning, the knot in my stomach told me something was wrong. *What could it be?* And then I recalled the events of the previous day.

Since the day my parents were taken away, it had become my daily habit to pray during First Breakfast to a litany of saints, as well as to my guardian angel, beseeching heavenly help as I braced for the daunting task of getting through the day without incurring the wrath of Sister Matilda. On this morning, as I knelt on the hardwood floor of the chapel during First Breakfast, I ignored the prayers on my own behalf, concentrating instead on Mary Catherine's patron saint. With all the fervor I could muster, I prayed to St. Catherine of Siena. *Please help Mary Catherine eat all her breakfast so that she won't get punished.*

I was starting to realize that it was always a gamble with my prayers—sometimes they were answered, but just as often, they seemed to miss being heard.

On this morning, however, I was rewarded. As we sat down for second breakfast, Mary Catherine picked up her spoon and ate as though yesterday had never existed. I silently thanked the whole court of heaven. My faith in prayer was restored—for the moment.

Mary Catherine's "recovery," however, didn't last for long. Her "non-eating" episodes, as I called them to myself, seemed to come out of the blue. For a few weeks she'd be vivacious and energetic, and then one morning, she'd have a certain look in her eye—doleful and haunting—and I knew we were in trouble. I thought of her problem as my problem. Only I couldn't solve it for her. All I could do was worry.

As her bouts of inability to eat increased, I schemed to devise creative ways to help her, but they came with danger—the risk of getting caught. On one occasion when the meal was beef stew, a dinner I detested because of the small white boiled onions that made me gag, I managed to swallow my meal with the help of giant gulps of milk, but Mary Catherine, who was sitting beside me, wouldn't touch hers. From the look on her face, I could tell she wasn't going to eat at all.

I sprang into action. Scanning the table to make sure nobody else was watching me, I swapped my bowl for hers. Gagging and shaking, I shoveled a second helping of stew—onions and all—into my mouth, down my gullet, and in the pockets of my cheeks. It was done. Mary Catherine's stew was gone.

As I finished the last bite, I sped to the bathroom. Locking the door behind me, I heaved up the still unchewed onions, the thick gravy, the potatoes and carrots, flushing them down the toilet. From the faucet I filled my cupped hands with water to rinse out my mouth. I patted my face dry and returned to my place at the table next to Mary Catherine. She gave me a silent look of gratitude with a feeble smile. I felt victorious. We had won the battle that day. But what would tomorrow bring?

I was sure my parents knew nothing about Mary Catherine's eating problem. The Big Sisters and Brothers sat at the far end of the refectory, out of earshot and view of the children's tables. What I wasn't sure about was what would happen if I told them. *Could they help her?* They were no longer in charge of her, my brother, or me. *Would I get into trouble if I spoke to them about it?* I didn't have the courage to dare.

* * *

I was about seven years old, just a year after the separation, when "pilgrimages" became part of our religious life. On the first Saturday of each month, the thirteen oldest children—we ranged in age from Mariam, who was now ten, to the youngest, who had recently turned five—made an all-morning trip outside our enclosure to visit one of the many parish churches in Boston.

Initially, the idea seemed exciting—an opportunity to see the real world. But the reality was a far cry from the vision that danced in my head. These excursions were designed as a religious mission—to defy the Catholic authorities in the diocese of Boston who had brought about Father's excommunication. By marching into parish churches and singing hymns, we were showing the world that we *were* indeed still Catholics, excommunicated or not.

When word spread of our monthly escapade, Archbishop Cushing's office notified the local parishes to be on the lookout for us.

One sunny Saturday, the thirteen of us, chaperoned by Sister Maria Crucis and chauffeured by two of the Big Brothers, arrived midmorning at a nearly empty church. As we gathered in the vestibule, I was fascinated by the sunlight reflected in myriad colors through the stained glass windows and I breathed in the smell of the incense that hung in the air.

We marched two by two in silence up the aisle, and when we reached the sanctuary, Sister Maria Crucis lined us up in front of the

Communion rail, instructing us to kneel down. Dressed identically in our blue and white uniforms and with our hair in two long braids, there was no mistaking who we were—"Feeneyites," the disparaging term the press used to describe us.

Then in her bold soprano voice, Sister Maria Crucis led us in singing one of Father's songs, the one we sang whenever we were feeling defiant. We all knew it by heart.

Holy Michael, great archangel, with a bright sword at his side.
Satan routed, while he shouted, "Who is like to God," he cried!
Light eternal, dark infernal—let the hosts of hell decide.

Suddenly a priest burst through the sacristy doors, waving his hands at us as though to shoo us away like a flock of errant chickens.

But Sister Maria Crucis raised her voice. "Children, hold on to the railing! Don't let go! Keep singing!"

Kneeling at the Communion rail, I grasped the wooden spindles with all the strength my tiny fingers could muster while doing my best to squeeze a note out of my vocal chords, which suddenly were paralyzed.

Some of the younger children started to cry. *Be brave,* I told myself.

"Get out!" yelled the priest. He was now breathing down on me as I knelt in frozen rigor.

"No, we won't," Sister Maria Crucis shouted back. "Children, stay right where you are."

Just then, through a side window of the church, I saw the reflection of flashing lights and turned around to see a policeman coming up the aisle of the church. All the while, the priest and Sister Maria Crucis continued yelling.

We're going to be arrested, I thought in panic, *and they're going to throw us in jail.*

The policeman took the lead, and with his hand respectfully guiding the shoulder of the priest, they and the two Big Brothers, who were the chauffeurs on this ill-fated mission, left through the side door of the sanctuary into the sacristy and out of sight. In the meantime, Sister Maria Crucis, undaunted in her zealotry, led us in another hymn, her strong vibrato drowning out my own thin, shaking voice. I prayed frantically to my guardian angel, expecting to be handcuffed at any moment.

After what seemed like an eternity, the Big Brothers returned without the priest or the policeman, and Sister Maria Crucis instructed us to rise. Together the thirteen of us stood up, genuflected, and in silence filed two by two down the aisle and out onto the sidewalk. We entered our cars, and we were taken home. My hands were still shaking when we drove through the massive gates to safety behind the red fence.

12

Sister Catherine

1956

Father and Sister Catherine seemed like deities to me. I saw them only at First Breakfast and at meals, where they sat prominently at their own special table, which was covered in a white linen tablecloth. They dined on delicate china and drank from crystal goblets, while the rest of the community sat at long wooden tables and ate from sturdy melamine dishes. Their utensils were real silver, while ours were stainless steel.

Sister Catherine was my godmother, and at the Center each godparent played a special role in the life of his or her godchild. But because Sister Catherine seldom came to visit us behind the red fence, I missed out on much of that bonding. I accepted the fact that she must be too busy running the Center with Father to spend time with me, but I longed for that personal attention.

So I was thrilled when one Saturday morning, Sister Catherine invited me, along with Mariam and Rene, the two oldest Little Sisters, to spend the day at her office. This meant a trip beyond the red fence, a rare treat.

We played quietly while she worked, and as morning became early afternoon, I found myself getting hungry. Sister Catherine had not offered us lunch, and there was no food in sight.

Maybe if I tell Sister Catherine I'm hungry, she'll take us out to eat, I thought to myself. Excitement over the idea of an excursion into Harvard Square grew faster than my hunger. At the age of eight, I'd never been to a restaurant. The picture in my mind's eye took shape— Sister Catherine would take me by the hand and off we'd go, down the stairs and out into the bright sunlight, up the street and into a restaurant, where we'd sit down and have a sandwich and a glass of milk.

Gathering up my nerve, because I was not used to asking for a special favor like this one, I walked to the entrance to her office and said, "Sister Catherine, I'm hungry. Could I please have something to eat?"

Her response came as a shock. Rising from her desk chair, she strode past me and into the living room where we'd been playing.

"Very well, then," she said in a stern, cold voice, her nearly six-foot frame towering over me. "If you're hungry, you can head right back to St. Francis Xavier's House. Come, the car is here."

We followed her down the stairs, where she instructed Brother David to take us back home. With neither a kiss, nor even a wave goodbye, we were ushered out.

I sat in numb silence during the short car ride back to life behind the red fence, stunned by Sister Catherine's reaction and devastated by the failure of my ploy.

What did I do wrong? I wondered. Did she think I was complaining? Or did she see through me and could tell I was angling for an excursion into the "real world"?

I beheld my godmother in a new light—no longer the charming, smiling, grandmotherly figure, but an enigma.

It was a few months later when Sister Catherine made another appearance in St. Francis Xavier's yard, this time with Father. I was wary.

Father spoke. "Come," he said, motioning to me, and to Mariam, Rene, Peter, and Leonard. Then, turning on his heel, he headed through the maze of houses to our enclosed parking lot. We followed as though behind the Pied Piper and scrambled into the back seat of the black Oldsmobile—all five of us. Sister Catherine drove, explaining little other than that we were going to see a surprise.

Nearly an hour later, we arrived at our destination—a mansion (or so it appeared to me) with large picture windows and a huge wraparound porch dotted with wicker rocking chairs and cushioned sofas. The sprawling house sat on a promontory, overlooking the ocean. A broad stretch of green lawn sloped down from the house. Countless bushes of beach roses in full bloom surrounded the house, and the breeze in the air was filled with their exquisite scent.

I held my breath as Sister Catherine unlocked the front door and led us into an expansive hallway that opened up to a wide, carpeted staircase. A pink glow poured down from the paned windows on the second floor, lending an almost magical aura to the house.

"This is where you're going to come all summer," Sister Catherine said as she invited us to explore. "The Little Sisters on one day and the Little Brothers the next. We're naming it St. Pius X House."

The five of us ran from room to room on our own. I marveled at the mystery of the sliding doors that disappeared into the walls, turning two rooms into one. I peered into the seemingly endless array of bedrooms and bathrooms.

This must be what it's like to live in a palace, I thought.

And when I tumbled head over heels down the long stairway, unused to carpeting under foot, I dusted myself off and pretended nothing had happened. Better to not let Sister Catherine know, lest my calamity change her mind about our summer here.

And for the whole summer, three times a week, twenty of us Little Sisters crowded into two black cars and a station wagon and were driven from the heart of Cambridge to the seaside town of Nahant. On the first day of our vacation, Sister Matilda gave each of us a pair of brand-new white sneakers. Then, in single file, we followed her down the steep road to the stony beach at the bottom of the hill, next to a Coast Guard station.

I took off my sneakers and wobbled barefoot to the edge of the water, my feet not yet hardened to the sharp edges and the heat of the stones underfoot. Holding up my long navy-blue jumper just high enough to keep it from getting wet, but not so high as to show my knees, I put one foot and then the other into the sea. The shock of the cold water was exhilarating. I wiggled my toes into the pebbly sand under the shallow water. Sister Matilda had laid down the rule—we were not to go in any deeper than our ankles.

As the gentle waves rippled over my toes, then my feet and ankles, I bent down and swirled my fingers in the sea and then put them into my mouth, hoping it would be salty the way I had heard the ocean was supposed to be. It was. I felt carried away by the novelty of the experience.

Staring at the vast ocean in front of me, I wondered, *Is this the very same water that Christopher Columbus sailed on?*

Squinting at the wavy line of a horizon where ocean met sky, I was sure I was looking at Spain, which I knew was three thousand miles across the Atlantic from Boston. Suddenly I felt part of the world that was beyond the red fence, a world that I was aching to discover.

Even the ride itself to Nahant provided an intriguing education about the world outside my sphere. Along Route 1, which took us through less-than-fashionable towns before we reached the needle causeway that brought us to our beach house, there were endless billboards. I read and memorized the slogans on the larger-than-life pictures that peppered the route.

"Wonder Bread—Helps build strong bodies twelve ways." (What they were remained a mystery to me.) The little red-haired boy with the black eye and the slogan, "He tried to take my Drakes cookies." Ads for cigarettes and Coca-Cola—items that were foreign to me.

"Mansion" in Nahant where we spent days during the summer I turned eight years old.

Whether the days were hot and sunny or rainy, each visit provided a new opportunity for exploration—gathering periwinkles at low tide or discovering miniscule fish in the shallow pools of tepid water that formed in rock crevices, remnants of high tide.

Exploring was my passion. Grabbing onto seaweed embedded in the steep wall of rock that rose like a monolith from the ocean, I could hoist myself to the top of boulders where the surface was flat. I'd find a solitary spot, sit down, and let the warmth of the stone heat my legs through my long jumper, which I fanned out around me. And as I ate a banana or a candy bar, I'd gaze out to the open sea, drinking in the warm, salty sea air. For once, silence did not feel like an obligation but part of the beauty that spread out before me, broken only by the lapping of the waves on the shore.

We were still several weeks away from the end of summer, when our trips to the beach house ended abruptly—the owner had discovered that we were Feeneyites and ordered us to leave. In a flash, my sole means of exploring the world beyond the red fence vanished. But with the start of tutoring in September, when I entered the third grade, I found another way to explore life outside the Center.

I was an avid reader, devouring any book I could get my hands on. My favorites were the twin stories by Lucy Fitch Perkins—Dutch, Italian, Norwegian, Filipino, Spartan, and more. Each volume was like a trip to a family home in a foreign country. There, a pair of twins, always a boy and a girl, lived with their parents. And somewhere in the middle of the book, the children would head out on their own for an adventure that invariably went terribly wrong. Gypsies kidnapped the Italian twins, and the Filipino twins were marooned in a typhoon, while the Norwegian twins had to kill a wolf. I was spellbound. Reading the stories again and again, I imagined myself as one of the twins, always relieved when they made it safely back to their home and their parents. It wasn't lost on me that children in the storybooks were able to live with their parents.

13

A New Home

1957

While the red fence was meant to shield us from the evils of the world beyond, it was failing to protect us. One afternoon, during our music lesson, a pellet from a BB gun flew through the open window, hitting our tutor's eyeglasses and knocking them off her face and onto the floor. From the street, hidden from view by the red fence, came the sound of boys' laughter. We sat in fright as Big Sister picked up her shattered glasses and hurried us out of the room.

A few weeks later, while I was getting ready for bed in my third-floor room that overlooked the street, a crashing thud startled me. I looked toward the window, expecting to see the venetian blind had fallen, but it was still in its place. As I glanced at the floor, I became paralyzed with fear. There, not two feet from where I stood, was a rock so large I couldn't pick it up in one hand.

For a few seconds I stood frozen in place, unable to speak or even move. Then I let out a bloodcurdling shriek as I flew from my bedroom around the corner and into the kitchen where the other Little Sisters were drying their hair or polishing their shoes. Sister Colette, the

Angel in charge that week, leapt up and held my shoulders in an effort to calm me.

"What *is* it?" she asked.

The only word I could manage to gasp was "rock." Taking me by the hand, she brought me back to my room. I pulled back as she entered, fearful of what might happen, but she strode past the rock and the shattered glass to the window, peering through the wide-slatted venetian blind to look down on the street below.

Then turning to me, she muttered, "Those dogs!" and shook her head. As she swept up the hundreds of shards of glass strewn across the floor, I asked her, "Did they hurt the dogs, too?"

She laughed softly. "No, honey," she said. "That's what those scoundrels are. No better than dogs."

Sleep eluded me for what seemed hours, as I saw visions of "punks," as Father called them, and the "dogs," Sister Colette's word, hurling stones at my window.

The attacks against us were gaining momentum. In the darkness of night, vandals smashed the plate glass windows of the Center and damaged the life-size marble statue of the Virgin Mary that stood in the garden next to the house.

It was starting to dawn on me, that our "cause" (as Father described the dogma of "No Salvation Outside the Catholic Church") was the source of the vitriol that was launched against us. That cause represented everything I wished I could change—the separation from my parents, the endless arrests on the bookselling trips, the Sunday afternoons when Father and the Big Brothers and Sisters went to Boston Common, the rules and punishments, the ban on seeing my grandmother and even our name, Slaves of the Immaculate Heart of Mary. I had no wish to be a slave and I didn't want my parents to be slaves either—not even to Our Lady.

And why did we have to have a cause that made everyone hate us? The very logic of the "No Salvation" dogma confounded me, and

I posed the innocent question, at the age of eight, to one of the Big Brothers during recreation one night, "How can people who live on a faraway island be sent to hell for all eternity when they never had a chance to be converted to the Catholic faith?" The response, "If they were of good faith, God would have sent them a missionary." I was skeptical because it seemed so unfair. How could God be so cruel? But I knew better than to give voice to my incredulity.

By now, the rigidity of our daily regime seemed normal. Even calling my parents Brother James Aloysius and Sister Elizabeth Ann felt more natural than saying Daddy or Mama. And when, a few weeks after my eighth birthday, we had a surprise visit from my father's family, I adored the reunion with my grandmother after a four-year hiatus. Nothing had changed about her—I saw the same twinkle in her eye, the same white hair and eyeglasses. But with my cousins, I found myself more embarrassed than excited. I stared at their worldly clothes and wondered what they thought of me in my long blue jumper, dressed exactly like my sisters. I felt out of place, particularly when my mother asked us to sing some of the religious songs we'd been taught. I'd have preferred to show them how my father had taught me to play chess on my birthday.

* * *

As the next summer rolled around, Sister Catherine came back into our lives, taking the oldest of us on a trip to a property she had bought in Still River, a hamlet about thirty miles west of Cambridge.

"This is where we'll soon be living," she told us as she led us through the stately white clapboard colonial-style house on eighteen acres of land. Then bringing us to the vast green field, she beckoned us to run around. Putting my arms out like wings, I sped through grass as tall as my shoulders. The smell of hay and the tickling sensation of the dried grass on my legs and arms were novel and exhilarating—different from the ocean, but full of newness and freedom.

"And when we move here next year," Sister Catherine said, as though letting us in on a secret, "we'll have cows and chickens, and you can each have a pet of your own."

A pet of my own! It was almost too good to be true. This was Sister Catherine the way I wished she would be all the time—jovial and full of promises of good things to happen.

Toward the end of September, the flu pandemic that had started in Asia reached the United States with full force and the red fence was unable to keep it at bay. Tutoring was cancelled, as all thirty-nine of us children fell victim. After a week of being confined to bed in a state of forced silence, it was Sister Catherine who came to the rescue, bringing us coloring books and crayons, jigsaw puzzles and Little Golden Books of nursery rhymes and fairy tales. Best of all, she dispensed with the rule of silence.

Where was Sister Matilda? I wondered. She, who for the last three years had been solely in command of every facet of our lives, was suddenly no longer the head Angel. It was now Sister Catherine herself who assumed that role, becoming an omnipresent force in our daily life.

Why? I pondered this unannounced but significant shift in power but knew to keep my questions to myself. At the Center, one didn't ask aloud why things changed.

Sister Catherine's motherly demeanor that afternoon turned to rage a few days later when Mary Catherine, who was now just seven years old, refused to eat her breakfast. She and I were having our meal together at a small table set up in the kitchen on our floor.

As Mary Catherine, still ridden with the flu, sat stone-faced looking at her scrambled eggs, her hands in her lap, the Angel in charge tried to cajole her.

"Be a good girl now and eat your eggs. Do it for the souls in purgatory so that they can go to heaven."

Offering things up for the souls in purgatory was a common exhortation at the Center. I was convinced that a battalion of souls had been released from their purgatorial sojourn and had floated on their way to the beatific vision because of my sufferings—each soul the beneficiary of a scraped knee or elbow, the toothaches, earaches and headaches that often ravaged me.

But on this morning, Mary Catherine, in her yellow and white flowered pajamas, did nothing but stare at her plate. I wanted to grab her fork and shovel the eggs into my *own* mouth, but I didn't dare under the hovering presence of the Angel.

I was sent back to my bed when I had finished eating, and a moment later I heard the Angel say, "What a good girl—you ate up all your eggs. I'm so proud of you."

I peered around the corner, hoping to give Mary Catherine a reassuring smile as she headed toward her bedroom. But she had gone only a few steps before a napkin stuffed full of scrambled eggs came tumbling out of the bottom of her pajamas. I watched in horror as she tried unsuccessfully to pick up the mess without being discovered. Her deception was out in the open, and it wasn't long before Sister Catherine was summoned to the scene.

"You're a willful, horrid girl," she yelled, her fury evident in the redness of her face. Then she took her powerful hand and whacked Mary Catherine on the arm before sending her, tearful and humiliated, back to her bed.

I was stunned—Sister Catherine hitting one of the children? How could she be so kind one day, showering us with toys and books, and then turn so fearful the next? I started to dread her.

As one of the first children to recuperate, I was moved from St. Francis Xavier's House to one of the other houses at the far end of the property, together with other Little Sisters and Brothers who were no longer ill. For the first time in our lives, Mary Catherine and I were now living in separate houses, and it worried me that I couldn't keep a constant eye on her.

A week or so later when she was well enough to play outside, she confided in me.

"They locked me in the cellar," she said.

I swallowed hard.

"Was it because you didn't eat?" I asked, but I was sure I knew the answer.

She nodded her head, her lower lip quivering as it did when she was frightened.

"Which cellar?" I asked

"St. Ann's House."

I shuddered. Of all the basements in the seven houses behind the red fence, St. Ann's was the worst. It had a dirt floor and no lights. I imagined that rats lived there.

Little by little, I elicited the full story from her. One of the Angels had forced her to sit on a stool in the pitch-black basement when she hadn't eaten her dinner.

That night I lay sleepless.

Where's Mary Catherine now? Is she possibly back in that basement?

I thought of sneaking out of the house in the dark, tiptoeing down the narrow walkway along the red fence, past Blessed Sacrament House to St. Ann's House. Then I could peer into the basement window, and if she was there, I could keep her company from outside. My fear of the dark was not the impediment. What stopped me was that I was sure I'd be caught as I tried to unbolt the front door of the house. I felt powerless.

Maybe when we move to Still River, Mary Catherine will eat again. Maybe if she has a pony and a kitty cat, the way Sister Catherine said, she'll become happy again and start to eat.

Then I prayed. *Dear Jesus, Mary, and Joseph, please let us move to Still River soon. And please make Mary Catherine all better again. I promise I will be good for the rest of my life.*

14

Countdown

1957–1958

January 31, 1958, couldn't come fast enough. Sister Catherine had announced that was when we'd be moving to Still River.

Tutoring filled much of the day, but I found it hard to concentrate. My mind drifted away from my books as I daydreamed about our move and the new life that lay ahead. I felt as though I was embarking on an adventure—it was like a new start to my life.

Especially thrilling was the idea that, come summer, I would celebrate my tenth birthday in our new home. I had it planned out in my mind. We'd play all day. I'd run through the fields with grass as high as my waist and let the wind blow through my hair. And after dinner, there would be a big chocolate cake with chocolate frosting and ten candles just for me, and the whole community would sing "Happy Birthday" in rapturous harmony as I blew out all ten candles in one breath.

After the New Year arrived, the days seemed to grind too slowly, so I occupied myself by helping the Big Sisters pack up the pots and pans, carving knives, and cooking utensils. Even as I taped and marked the boxes, a small worry lurked in the back of my head—that something might happen that would prevent us from moving. But as the boxes piled high, that gnawing anxiety gradually faded away like an evaporating fog. *It really is going to happen,* I told myself.

By mid-January, it was time to pack my own possessions. Everything I owned fit into one small, rectangular cardboard box. First my clothes: two pairs of navy-blue socks, two white long-sleeve blouses, a petticoat, bloomers, two pairs of flowered pajamas, and my extra blue jumper. As I packed, I imagined my new room in Still River. Sister Catherine had described it to us—a "cubicle" she called it, where I'd have my own dresser instead of having to share drawers and shelves with other Little Sisters.

My half-filled box sat at the end of my bed awaiting the final possessions that would go in on the last morning: a coloring book and crayons, my hairbrush and comb, my toothbrush, my crucifix, and my own small copy of the New Testament with my name embossed on the front.

In the hectic final days of packing, the rule of silence seemed to slip away as Big Brothers and Big Sisters alike packed and stacked boxes, loaded up vehicles, and made round trips to Still River. Meals were served on paper plates, and recreation was barely supervised. I reveled in what felt like a newfound freedom.

Will it be this way in Still River? I wondered. *Will we be able to run around and laugh all day with no rule of silence?*

Seven days, six days, five days. January 31 was almost here. It was hard to fall asleep at night.

Then one evening, with only a few days to go, an announcement was made at dinner—the Big Sisters would be going on the last book-selling trip before moving day. *Please don't let it be Sister Elizabeth Ann,* I prayed in my head, invoking every saint I could imagine.

The following morning, I stood at my bedroom window craning my neck as the Big Sisters who were heading out on that final bookselling trip put their suitcases into the trunk of the car. Hard as I tried, I couldn't make out who they were. I waited, knowing that the car would have to pass by my window on its way through the big red gate. As it slowly came into view, all polished and washed to a sleek black gleam, my heart sank. There in the driver's seat was my mother.

The car glided through the open red gate and turned right onto Hayes Street, as one of the Big Brothers closed and bolted the gate. Tears rolled down my cheeks.

Throwing myself on my bed, I buried my head in the pillow. With the relaxation of rules, I'd been hoping that Sister Elizabeth Ann might be allowed to help me do the last bit of packing. I even imagined being lucky enough to ride in her car for the final exciting trip from Cambridge to Still River. And now she was gone. *What if she couldn't find her way?* Despondent, I turned to prayer.

Jesus, Mary, and Joseph, please bring Sister Elizabeth Ann safely to Still River.

15

Still River

1958

I t was late in the afternoon when we assembled in the main house in Still River—a large, rambling, white clapboard structure that Sister Catherine named St. Therese's House in honor of one of her favorite saints. The original part of the house had been built in 1683 and was rumored to have served as Major Simon Willard's headquarters during the French and Indian War. On its front door was a carved wooden pineapple, the emblem of New England hospitality. Three of the four front rooms had a giant working fireplace, including an oven for baking bread. Those rooms in the original part of the house would serve as refectories where we would gather to eat our meals. A more recent addition included a small guest dining room, an elegant wood-paneled library, off which there was a sunny sitting room that was to be Father's and Sister Catherine's office, and a huge living room that overlooked the sprawling fields and woods. Upstairs was where the Big Brothers would live. Attached to the main structure was a carriage shed as old as the original building itself. It had been outfitted as our new chapel.

St. Therese's House in Still River. The tall wing on the right was added later.

A stone's throw from St. Therese's House was a brand new house that had been built over the prior summer and fall. Sister Catherine named it St. Ann's House, in honor of the mother of Our Lady. This was where the children and Big Sisters would live. It also had a number of small rooms for tutoring.

From these two houses, the nearly eighteen acres of our property gently sloped down to the Nashua River, the boundary between us and Fort Devens, an active Army base. On the distant horizon was the rounded dome of Mount Wachusett.

It was dusk. As we headed toward St. Ann's House to see our new living quarters, an anxious thought went through my mind. *Where is Sister Elizabeth Ann? How come she hasn't arrived yet? Could she have lost her way?*

But on entering St. Ann's House with the other Little Sisters, my concern evaporated as I was overcome with the breathtaking newness of everything around me. It was better than I had dreamed it might be—spotless white walls in the front hall and gleaming wood floors that exuded the pungent odor of shellac, as though they had been finished only minutes before we arrived.

Off the front hall ran a long corridor, on both sides of which were the Little Sisters' cubicles—ten on the right and ten on the left, one for each of us. As I made my way down the corridor, peeking into each one, identical in shape and size, the pink-and-yellow-flowered bedspreads looked like miniature gardens.

Big Sisters floated in and out of cubicles that had already been assigned to each of us. Entering mine, I unpacked my clothes and a few possessions from the box that lay at the foot of my bed, reveling in the freedom to set up my small space as I wished, and all the while gabbing and laughing with the other Little Sisters, uninhibited by the rule of silence that had ordered our lives for the past few years.

Is this the way it's going to be from now on? I wondered, hoping I might be lucky.

Already feeling a sense of giddiness over the newness of life in the country, I was even more elated when Sister Elizabeth Ann walked through the front door of St. Ann's House. She was safely home. I couldn't ask for more.

Snuggling under the crisp white sheets of my newly made bed and pulling up the heavy woolen blanket around my neck, I imagined all the things Sister Catherine had promised us—pets and farm animals and swimming lessons and walks in the woods. This was surely the beginning of a new and wonderful life.

Reality hit home when, early the following morning, while still in my bathrobe, I came face to face with a sign in the Little Sisters' bathroom in large, bold, black letters, posted prominently on the pink tiled wall above the four pretty pink porcelain sinks. It was a single word: SILENCE.

PART 3

PREPARING FOR THE CLOISTER

16

New Life, New Rules

1958

Sister Catherine stood tall and powerful in the doorway that separated the Little Brothers' and Sisters' refectories. We had been in our new home for less than a week.

"Little Sisters and Brothers," she said, her green eyes scanning the two rooms as we sat at tables of five, each with an Angel at the head. "I want to talk to you about your wonderful Big Brothers and Sisters."

From the endearing tone of her voice, I perked up, expecting a surprise. She paused, heightening the tension, and then went on. "As Slaves of the Immaculate Heart of Mary, they want to spend more time praying and meditating. I'm sure you would like to help them to do that. Wouldn't you, dears?"

From both refectories there was a combination of mumbled "Yes, Sister Catherine" and head-nodding.

"How wonderful, darlings. So this is our decision together."

She went on to instruct us that no longer were we to speak to any of the adults, not even our own parents, and they would no longer speak to us. Conversation would be allowed on Sundays only, when we would have what she described as a "community meeting," a specially designated time with our parents.

It didn't sink in immediately, the enormity of this "decision" that we (Sister Catherine and the thirty-nine of us children) jointly had just made. Much less did I grasp the duplicity embedded in her tactic, one she would use again and again.

Her chicanery only dawned on me over time when she'd excoriate us for violating an "agreed-upon" regulation.

"But it's *your* rule—*you* made it. Remember, dears?"

Family life had already been sundered in Cambridge. Now what remained of familial bonds was being strangled little by little, rule by rule, supplanted with Sister Catherine's vision of a monastic life for all one hundred of us—men, women, and children.

The exhilaration I had felt about our new life in Still River, with its promises of open fields and pets, began to dissipate, marred by what seemed like a daily onslaught of restrictions and new regulations. Silence was the constant, enforced at all times and in all places except during recreation.

As the cold winter weeks turned into spring, the novelty and excitement of the move from Cambridge to Still River began to wear off, and a new regimen, so different from life behind the red fence, revealed itself. Each day offered a few pieces of the jigsaw puzzle. Now, my first thought on waking was: *What new rules will there be today?*

Sister Catherine was fully entrenched as the rule-maker, the de facto leader, and the chief disciplinarian at the Center. By springtime, birthday celebrations had been outlawed, supplanted by feast days. Father seemed thrilled by the idea. Rubbing his hands together, the gesture he used when he was agitated, he spoke from the altar. "Birthdays are worldly and of the devil. Who needs birthdays anyway?" he declared. "From now on, we're going to celebrate only our feast days—no more birthdays."

For months I'd been dreaming about my tenth birthday, on August 16. The sun had a way of always shining on that day, and I'd been fantasizing about how magical it would be to spend the day playing in the fields. Now in a flash, my dream was dashed. Adding to the insult was the fact that the feast of my patron saint, Saint Anastasia, was celebrated on Christmas Day.

No one will even think of me on Christmas, I thought, feeling cheated out of both a birthday *and* a feast day.

* * *

A few weeks after our move, Sister Catherine introduced the tea party. Was it a nostalgic throwback to the early days of the Center? Or was it perhaps a way for her to teach us old-fashioned manners? It was held each Thursday afternoon in the library, a large book-lined, wood-paneled room adjacent to Sister Catherine's office. She herself played the role of hostess, sitting erect and cheerful at one end of the long library table, an elegant silver samovar set up in front of her. The Big Brothers and Sisters were invited, and the oldest of us children, wearing white gloves and having been instructed by Sister Catherine on the protocols, acted as servers.

We were to be "seen but not heard," she advised us as we took our seats silently on the brocade-covered, tall-backed, oak library chairs stationed along the side wall. That was until the adults entered, when we went into action.

I could count on my parents to arrive early (and separately) and to stay until the very end. The moment they set foot in the library, I made a beeline for one of them.

"Sister Elizabeth Ann, would you like some tea?"

She answered with a smile, "Yes, please, dear."

"With milk or lemon?"

Then I hurried over to Brother James Aloysius before anyone else could get to him. He would wink at me as I approached him, and he always said, "Thank you, my little princess," as he selected cookies from the china platter I held with both hands. I felt like a princess serving my king.

As much as I loved our tea parties, it was the Sunday morning community meeting that I lived for, counting down the days as the week wore on. Then for two blissful hours, it was family time, unrestricted by rules or oversight by the Angels.

"How is my little princess?" Brother James Aloysius would greet me and each of my three younger sisters.

Taking my father's hand one Sunday morning, I felt something was different. I looked at his fingers: His wedding ring was gone.

"Where's your ring?" I asked. He grew silent and paused as he did when he was thinking. Then pointing to his chest, he said softly, "It's right here, safe and sound in my scapular."

Everyone at the Center, adults and children, wore a scapular, a Catholic tradition. A simple square of sackcloth that had been blessed by a priest, the scapular was worn next to the skin. Father had told us again and again that if you died with your scapular on, you would never go to hell.

I saw that my mother's ring was gone as well.

"Is yours in your scapular, too?" I asked her.

"I gave my diamond ring to the Little Infant of Prague," she replied, referring to the statue of the Child Jesus that had been a gift to the Center in its heyday. What she didn't tell me was that she had turned over her simple gold wedding band to Sister Catherine as requested. Apparently, my father had chosen not to obey.

I found an excuse to go to the front room and stood in front of the statue of the Infant of Prague, looking up at the crown on His head. There were sparkles in the crown, but I couldn't tell what they were. All I knew was that somewhere in that elegant crown was my mother's ring.

One person at the Center continued to wear a wedding band—Sister Catherine. From my earliest memories, I knew she had a husband, Hank, and two children, Nancy and Joey. Hank had never come to visit the Center, neither in Cambridge nor in Still River, but Nancy, who was a few years younger than my mother, had joined the community briefly while we were still in Cambridge, taking the name of Sister Nancy Marie.

Before we moved to Still River, Sister Catherine, after spending the day at the Center, returned each evening to the house she and her husband owned in Waltham. After the married couples were coerced into taking vows of celibacy (shortly after the separation of children from their parents), some chose to live separately, with the single men and women, while a few, including my parents, continued to live together under the same roof. My father sought out Sister Catherine, telling her that he hoped that the families could be reunited when we moved to Still River, and she gave him assurances that it would happen.

Nothing could have been further from the truth. With the move came the enforced physical separation of all the married couples. Sister Catherine was the exception. Every Wednesday, Saturday, and Sunday, shortly after lunch, she left the property in her own car and drove home, where she spent the night with her husband and Nancy, their unmarried daughter.

It's not fair, I thought over and over as I watched her car head up the driveway and turn on to the highway, headed for Waltham. But at the Center, rank had its privilege.

I used Sister Catherine's absence to breathe easier, enjoying a brief respite from the perpetual tension that hung in the atmosphere, brought on by her overpowering presence. I sensed that even the Angels relaxed a bit when Sister Catherine was gone. But the anxiety resurfaced promptly at one o'clock the following day when she returned in time for the lunch that was waiting to be served to her on fine china in her office.

Sister Catherine
with her husband,
Hank, around 1960.

The idea of Sister Catherine at home in Waltham with her family sent questions cascading through my mind. Does she wear her nun's habit when she goes home? Does she cook, or does her daughter Nancy do the cooking for her? Does she share a bedroom with Hank? Does she listen to the radio and watch television?

We had no radio or television at the Center because Father and Sister Catherine said they were the "ruin of the country" and would cause us to "lose our souls."

Over and over again, I asked myself. *Why is she allowed to live with her family and I can't?* I had no answer and I dared not share my resentment with anyone.

When one of the youngest children, who had no idea that Sister Catherine had a husband and a home away from the Center, asked her why she had to leave, she replied wistfully, "Oh, darling, it's the cross I have to bear. How I wish I didn't have to go."

I was not yet ten years old, but I found her answer implausible. *A cross to bear? It wouldn't be a cross for me to live with my family.*

17

Sister Maria Crucis

1958

Sister Maria Crucis was my Angel—the person Sister Catherine selected to take the place of my mother. She was a petite woman with hair that was almost black. Her nose, although large and aquiline, somehow looked right on her face, and her huge, dark eyes were magnified behind the thick eyeglasses she wore at all times. Nearly everything else about her was tiny—her feet, her hands, her waist—all, that is, but the protrusion from beneath her white cotton blouse and modest, straight-hanging, short black jacket that was meant to hide her well-endowed bosom. When she smiled, which wasn't as often as I wished, her black eyes glowed, and she displayed two lines of straight white teeth.

Unlike most of the eight Angels, Sister Maria Crucis was unmarried. From back when we lived in Cambridge, before the PL rule was in place and when she was still Alberta Maria Rensaglia, I knew she had graduated from Radcliffe College and spoke both Italian and French fluently. She was also an artist, but most intriguing to me was that she had studied to be an opera singer.

Now garbed in her nun's attire, Sister Maria Crucis displayed none of that worldliness that fascinated me; on the contrary, she invoked an asceticism that I bridled against. She demanded an almost obsequious reverence from the five of us Little Sisters who were her charges. She was Queen Bee, and we the humble drones did her bidding, following her smothering set of rules.

A hypochondriac, perhaps from being a pampered only child, Sister Maria Crucis took to bed at the first sign of a sniffle. And she treated us similarly, as though we were delicate china, fragile and breakable.

It was late February, a month after we'd moved, and the flu epidemic returned. I prided myself on being one of the few children who hadn't succumbed. Then one night, I coughed as Sister Maria Crucis came into my cubicle to kiss me goodnight. Just a little nothing cough.

"I think you're coming down with the flu," she exclaimed.

"Oh, no, I'm fine," I responded, desperate to maintain my status as one of the "strong" and "healthy" children.

But to her my cough was an opportunity to envelop me in her protective cocoon. She swooped into action, armed with a jar of Vicks VapoRub that she proceeded to slather on my chest.

"I'll be back with some brandy," she said as she headed off down the corridor to return with the only enjoyable part of the treatment— warm brandy mixed with honey that, with the help of additional heavy woolen blankets that she piled on top of me, was meant to sweat the flu out of me.

Even story time (Sister Catherine reintroduced bedtime stories) was ritualized. Sister Maria Crucis would position herself in the middle of the bed in one of our cubicles, with her back against the wall. Once she had sorted her long black skirt so that it lay in a tidy fashion around her legs, she signaled the five of us to set ourselves up on either side of her, with our hands in our laps and our bathrobes neatly closed and tied.

As Sister Maria Crucis read to us, my mind would wander.... *What is Sister Elizabeth Ann doing? Why can't she be reading to me?*

18

Leonard

1958

As I reached the edge of the pine forest, I bounded ahead of the other children with my best friend, Leonard. Nine months younger than I was, Leonard was like a brother to me. We'd been almost inseparable since birth.

We both loved nature. Now hand in hand, we ran through the woods. With my free hand holding on to my long, pleated skirt so as not to let it catch on the thorns from the barberry bushes, Leonard and I stomped down the brambles to make a path for the other children to follow. We stopped at a narrow brook that flowed from the hill above down toward the fields below and then gingerly made our way across the gentle rippling stream, with arms outstretched to balance ourselves atop the larger stones that poked through the running water. Once across, we scrambled up the gentle embankment, dotted with miniature gray patches of half-melted snow, into the wooded pine forest beyond.

A broad, green bed of princess pine unfolded at our feet, under the shade provided by white pine trees that seemed to reach the sky.

Leonard and I dropped down on the plush carpet to wait for the others to catch up. As we lay on our backs looking up at the sky, we played guessing games—how tall were the trees—thirty feet, fifty feet, a hundred feet? What birds were singing—was that a robin? A Baltimore oriole returning from a winter in the south?

Then we were silent, and I inhaled the crisp spring air, with its mixture of the earthy scents from the forest floor and the tangy aroma of surrounding evergreens. In the bliss of that moment, I was content to lie in silence—a state of mind distinct from the coerced rule of silence that accompanied our daily lives.

This is how heaven must be, I thought.

Within a few moments, the rest of the children caught up with us, and Sister Maria Crucis led us on an expedition in search of pheasant and grouse nests. We tiptoed our way in silence through the woods, never so excited as when we startled a setting hen who squawked away, allowing us a peek at the many speckled eggs camouflaged among the sticks and down of the nest floor. At the end of the morning, Sister Maria Crucis promised to take us hunting for lady slippers, the rare wild orchid that grew in the dense New England forests, when the weather got warmer. In every way, it was a splendid day, and I could hardly wait for the next excursion.

"Anastasia, I would like to see you in my office after dinner."

I was startled. Sister Catherine was addressing me in front of all the Little Brothers and Sisters as she stood in the doorway between our refectories. Although her voice was pleasant, my stomach instantly twisted into a knot.

Had I done something wrong? I couldn't fathom what.

After dinner, I stood anxiously outside Sister Catherine's office as I put my ear to the door and heard voices, too muffled to make out the words. When Sister Catherine responded to my timid knock, I entered. She swiveled in her chair and faced me. I looked for a sign of her mood, but I couldn't judge. Was there the slight hint of a smile, or was that my imagination? I tried to appear relaxed, but inside I was shaking.

Father was slouched in his red leather chair, and sitting on the bench across from Sister Catherine was Sister Mary Laurence. I was puzzled. Why was she here? Sister Mary Laurence was one of the Little Brothers' Angels—the most detested, in fact, with a reputation for giving them endlessly long beatings. The only two Little Brothers who seemed to escape her wrath were her own sons, Adrian and Alexander.

"Anastasia, listen to me carefully." Sister Catherine's voice was serious. She paused and I thought she must have been able to hear my heart pounding.

"From now on you are to have nothing more to do with Leonard. You are not to speak to him or play with him. Do you understand me completely?"

I replied automatically, "Yes, Sister Catherine," but my mind was racing.

Leonard? My best friend and playmate? Why?

"Very well, then," she said, and she seemed to soften for a moment. "I know you will remember that rule, won't you, dear? You may leave now."

That was it. The meeting was over. It was now clear to me why Sister Mary Laurence was there. She was Leonard's Angel. I glanced over at her and caught the menacing combination of grin and grimace on her face that told me she would play the role of spy and report me to Sister Catherine should I ever break this rule, this secret rule, made only for me.

As I turned to leave, Father, still in his near supine position, reached out his hand toward me. I put my hand in his.

"Let me bless you, darling," he said in a gentle voice. I knelt down, and he made the sign of the cross on my forehead. *He's trying to make it seem not so bad.* I stood up and fled the room.

That night, as Sister Maria Crucis read us our bedtime story, she gave no indication that she knew about this new rule Sister Catherine had made for me. *Should I tell her? What should I say? What will* she *say?* Best to keep it to myself, this worrying, frightening dictate.

As I lay in bed, I pondered my fate. *Does Leonard know? If he doesn't know, and he tries to talk to me, what should I do? Why am I being singled out?*

My confusion was entangled with fear. There had to be some meaning behind Sister Catherine's decision, but I couldn't understand it.

It was a long time before I fell into a troubled sleep.

19

New Neighbors

1958

Without the stricture of the red fence, bits of the outside world managed to creep into life at the Center. Our new neighbors were mostly "Yankees," as Father referred to them. They were different from us. They had names like Bigelow, Haskell, Sprague, Dudley, Hazel. There were no other nationalities—like Italian or German or Irish or Lebanese—the way it was at the Center.

Our neighbors in Still River were mostly farmers like their ancestors. Father made friends with them almost as soon as we settled into our new home. On many a Saturday morning, he'd take a small group of us children next door to visit Mrs. Bigelow, a frail, wheelchair-bound elderly lady who told us stories about how she used to sled down the hills on which we now sledded. Other times, we'd walk with Father across the highway to visit the Haskells, an elderly brother and sister who doted on their pet parakeet. No sooner would we sit down in their cheery, sunlit living room than Miss Haskell would produce a box of chocolates, a rare treat for us. To be embraced by our neighbors was a novelty and a relief after the experiences with the stone-throwing hoodlums in Cambridge.

But something puzzled me. None of these Yankees were Catholics. Most of them were Unitarians, a religion Father liked to say "stands for nothing." Yet, for some unexplained reason, these Protestant Yankees were our friends.

How come the Protestants in Still River are our friends, but all the Catholics were our enemies in Cambridge? I mulled this over endlessly but realized there was no way to get an answer. Asking questions only got me into trouble.

Here in Still River, at least, I could observe the outside world a bit more successfully than when we lived behind the red fence. Every day, the local dairy farmer, Buzzy Watt, delivered fresh milk. He arrived at the same time each morning, just as we were finishing second breakfast. When I spotted his truck coming down the driveway, I'd put on my winter coat and head out the door so that our paths would cross.

Ever cheerful, Buzzy, a short, rectangular man with bright blue eyes and a Hollywood smile, walked up the pathway to the basement kitchen door carrying cartons of freshly bottled milk, his one-year-old son John in tow.

"Guh monning," he would say in his clipped Yankee accent and then follow up with a quip, "Nice one, isn't it?" or, when it was snowing, "Good for sleddin.'"

"Good morning, Mr. Watt," I replied.

I reveled in this brief exchange, in the ability to talk to someone who lived out in the world. As I then crossed the yard to St. Ann's House, I imagined what life was like in the Watt family house. What did Mrs. Watt look like? Was John their only child? Would they have more?

Every glimpse at outsiders, every stare at visitors, brought to mind the same questions over and over. What is their family life like? What would it be like to live out in the world the way they do, with my own family?

20

Relapse

1958

My curiosity about the world beyond the Center was matched by my concern for the members of my family inside our community. Mary Catherine, especially, was my constant worry. Moment by moment, I feared that she might relapse into her "non-eating."

This was a burden I carried alone. Brother James Aloysius and Sister Elizabeth Ann were unaware of Mary Catherine's problem. Their involvement in our daily lives had ended long ago. Their roles as parents had been subsumed by Sister Catherine and the Angels. If they were to discover my sister's plight, it would only make them unhappy, and there would be nothing they could do. I was sure of that.

My sole recourse was to heaven, and I prayed each night in bed: *Jesus, Mary, and Joseph, please watch out for Mary Catherine, and make her eat all her food. I promise to be good for the rest of my life.*

In the refectory, I did my best not to look as though I was keeping an eye on her. But it was difficult to hide my sideways glances over at her table as I checked to see whether she was eating her food.

For the first few weeks after our move, Mary Catherine was lively, and I started to hope that her problems were over. Then one early spring morning, as we sat down to second breakfast, she gave me her sad look from across the room, the all-too-familiar vacant stare that told me trouble was coming. I prayed frantically inside myself, but to no avail. Mary Catherine's French toast sat untouched on her plate.

I glanced at Sister Teresa, her Angel, hoping that she might find a way to encourage Mary Catherine to eat. But she remained silent. Instead, Sister Catherine herself swooped onto the scene with fierce energy, her green eyes cold and narrow, her mouth taut and hard. She was like a hawk fixed on its prey.

"We'll have none of this nonsense," she said in a voice like thunder, glaring down at Mary Catherine. "You will eat everything on your plate now, or you will be punished."

Sister Catherine's threat, however, did nothing to induce her to eat. At the end of second breakfast, Sister Teresa picked up her plate of uneaten food, brought it to the kitchen, and put it in the refrigerator. I shuddered. The cold French toast would be Mary Catherine's lunch, and possibly her dinner. This was just as it had been back in Cambridge.

For the next few days, Mary Catherine ate nothing at all. At recreation, she played half-heartedly, as though fearful of the next meal. I was tormented. What had I done that my prayers had gone unanswered? Why was no one in heaven listening to me?

Then on Sunday morning, Mary Catherine sat down at her table for second breakfast with a cheerfulness that had eluded her for a week. Gone was the hollow-eyed stare as she gobbled down fried eggs, bacon, coffee cake, and milk.

"What a good girl you are," said Sister Catherine in the well-practiced motherly voice she could use when she wanted to. The tension eased in my stomach, and I ate my own breakfast with a relief I hadn't felt in days. Mary Catherine smiled and seemed to be her old self once more.

Maybe this will be the last time, I thought, with a hopeful prayer. But it wasn't. Mary Catherine's episodes became more and more frequent. One Saturday morning, Sister Catherine tried a new tactic. After she'd spoken to us from the doorway between our refectories, she approached Mary Catherine's table.

In a quiet voice, she said, "Mary Catherine, I want to see you in my office after breakfast."

Maybe she's going to try kindness, I thought, hoping that would work. But it was hard to tell with Sister Catherine; she could play tricks on you.

Mary Catherine was gone for the entire morning and I spent the time in lackluster play but inwardly was racked with anxiety. When we gathered for lunch, I held my breath as the bowl of soup was set in front of Mary Catherine. She picked up her spoon, dipped it into the bowl, and brought it to her mouth, without hesitation.

Thank you, God, I prayed. *It's a miracle.*

Cornering my sister that afternoon, I questioned her. "What did Sister Catherine say to you this morning?" I said.

"I'm not supposed to tell you," she replied, turning away from me.

I was hurt. "Not supposed to tell me? Why?" I asked.

"Sister Catherine said it was a secret," was all she said.

A secret from me? That couldn't be. I was the one watching out for her. I was the only one she had.

21

Father

1958

With the move to Still River, power shifted from Father to Sister Catherine. He now seemed older and frailer. At sixty-one, his black hair had turned to gray and was thinning. His jacket sagged on his sloping shoulders, and his walk, once bold, had now slowed to a shuffle. His thin lips turned downward, making him look melancholy, and his once-piercing black eyes now often seemed dull and faded. Alongside Sister Catherine, who was nearly six feet tall and had a stately carriage, Father looked broken down, worn out.

Father was a social person. He enjoyed the bustle of life in an urban setting like Cambridge. Still River offered none of that stimulation, so he created his own social life by spending each afternoon off the property, making acquaintance with merchants in the surrounding towns.

To have company on his daily trips, he often invited a few of the children to go with him. Some afternoons were eye-opening adventures for me, and I soaked up every detail of what I could absorb about the outside world—the particulars of clothing and hairstyles and handbags I encountered as we made our way along the streets of nearby towns.

On one occasion, Father brought the six oldest of us Little Sisters to the home of an elderly Yankee woman he had befriended, a widow named Trudy Byrd. The startled look on her face as we barged into her small, wood-paneled living room made it clear that we'd arrived uninvited. Father never made an appointment to visit with anyone—he simply showed up. On this occasion, he promptly seated himself in one of her chairs.

"Trudy," he said, "I have a special treat for you."

Father motioned to the six of us to gather in a semicircle in front of Mrs. Byrd and said in a cheerful voice, "Little Sisters, recite the twenty-nine Doctors of the Church for Trudy."

In unison we began: "Athanasius, Basil, Cyril of Jerusalem…." and on through the list to Alphonsus Maria de Liguori, number twenty-nine.

No sooner had we finished than Father, without a moment's hesitation, said, "Now, dears, sing a song for Trudy. How about the 'Te Deum'?"

I cringed. The "Te Deum" was the longest piece of Gregorian chant, all in Latin. Poor Mrs. Byrd sat patiently as we sang away, falling farther and farther off-key without the benefit of an accompanying organ. When we reached the end of the hymn, Father stood up and with a quick goodbye, we left as abruptly as we had entered. Embarrassed by our rudeness, I turned to Mrs. Byrd and gave her a small wave and a tiny bow.

As we drove away, Father rubbed his hands together in excitement, saying, "Trudy Byrd will become a Catholic one day, I promise you. She received a grace today when you recited the Doctors of the Church and sang the 'Te Deum.' You just wait and see. God and Our Blessed Mother work in wonderful ways."

Father's mood was lifted when he was doing what he most loved to do—trying to convert non-Catholics. Barging in on unsuspecting Protestants was part of his sacred mission to save souls.

Sometime later when Mrs. Byrd died, Father announced her death from the altar.

"Trudy, our dear friend Trudy Byrd, has died. She is now enjoying the beatific vision." He paused and then went on. "I am sure that on her deathbed she made an act of contrition and that her soul has been saved."

I was stunned. How could this Protestant lady be seeing God for all eternity, while all the Catholics who lived out in the world, the pious frauds as Father referred to them, were going to land in hell? But Father was infallible within our midst, and if he said that Mrs. Byrd was in heaven, I had to believe it.

22

Bookselling

1958

For an hour every Saturday afternoon, I was assigned to make lunches for the upcoming bookselling trip. Three days' lunches for six Big Brothers and six Big Sisters meant thirty-six sandwiches. Everything was counted out in advance—exactly thirty-six apples and thirty-six candy bars, which made it impossible to sneak a snack on the side.

Working in silence, I laid out seventy-two pieces of homemade brown bread in rows across the sprawling kitchen table, spreading each with mayonnaise, mustard, and then whatever filling had been provided—ham, cheese, or tuna salad.

Bookselling continued to be the way the Center financed itself. The trips started each Sunday when the Big Brothers and Sisters, in separate cars, drove to their varied destinations. After five days of pounding the pavement on a dual mission to save souls and maximize sales, all the while keeping a wary eye out for the police, the team called home on Friday evening during the dinner hour to give Father a report on the week's financial success.

One such evening, Father burst into our refectory as Sister Catherine was holding court. His black eyes beaming with excitement, he rubbed his hands together and nearly shouted.

"Guess what? The Sisters did five times the conversion of Greenland, plus the death of St. Augustine. Isn't that great?"

Father was speaking in code, one I'd memorized years earlier while we were still living in Cambridge. It was embedded in the myriad dates we were obligated to memorize—dates entwined in the history of the Catholic Church.

I started to calculate. I knew that (according to Catholic lore) Leif Eriksson had sailed to Greenland in the year 1000 to bring the faith to its people. I knew, too, that St. Augustine died in the year 430. Five times the conversion of Greenland was therefore $5,000 plus $430 meant that the Big Sisters had made $5,430 that week.

Knowing how much money the Center made in a week was of little actual use to me, however. I had no concept of what $5,430 was, or how much it could buy. No one at the Center was allowed to keep any money; Sister Catherine alone held tight control of the purse strings.

Despite no visible trappings of wealth within our community, successful booksellers (Big Brothers or Big Sisters) seemed to find a special place in Father's heart.

We children, especially, had no need for money. The Big Sisters made our clothes. The only store we ever visited was a shoe store, where our feet were measured for an order of identical shoes. If we asked Sister Catherine for a pet—the only significant possession any of us thought of requesting—we usually got it. Ponies, donkeys, dogs, horses, cats, ducks, and rabbits made up our menagerie of pets. If we wanted a holy card, a book of prayers, or a story about the saints, Sister Catherine was happy to provide it.

My only experience with money came from tutoring. In the fourth grade, Sister Ann Mary brought in play money that looked like the real thing, and we learned to make change and recognize the bills and coins.

As I played with the fake currency, I pretended it was real and thought of the many things I could buy. Alone in my cubicle, where I did most of my thinking at night, I imagined buying jewels like the ones worn by some of the lady guests who came to visit or pretty dresses or shoes with open toes or hats that sat like small boxes on their heads. Oblivious to Father's warnings about the sin of vanity, I spent many an hour in carefree reverie before falling off to sleep, fantasizing about what I would look like in worldly clothes.

23

Treading Carefully

1958

When we moved to Still River, the daily classes in Latin and Greek, theology and church history, ethics and philosophy, so much a part of the life of the Center in Cambridge, became a thing of the past. With the migration of power from Father to Sister Catherine came a seismic shift in focus within the Center—from academic to anti-intellectual, from confrontational to contemplative. That about-face reverberated through the community and was reinforced in terms of the daily responsibilities delegated to a number of the Big Brothers. It didn't go unnoticed by me, even at the age of nine, that the "three professors"—my father and the two other Big Brothers who, ten years earlier, had been fired from Boston College for their support of Father—were now relegated to manual labor jobs in Still River.

My father was assigned to work on our fleet of cars, a far cry from his intended career as a teacher of philosophy. The best thing about his job, in my mind, was that I got to see him every day because the garage opened onto the driveway at the foot of the stepping-stones that led from St. Therese's House. In my mind, it was a far better chore than what the two other professors were assigned—doing the Big Brothers' laundry and sewing their black cassocks, the floor length habit they now wore.

The prohibition against speaking to the Big Brothers and Sisters only increased my longing for a glimpse of my father. Sometimes it was just his feet as they stuck out in front of a vehicle while he worked on its undercarriage.

One day I came up behind him while he was occupied under the hood of a vehicle. As I walked slowly past him, he turned his head, and with a wink and a broad smile, he lifted a grease-smeared little finger, wiggling it as if to say, "Hi, my little princess."

I smiled back at him, without saying a word, not daring to violate the rule of silence between us. Then I panicked, realizing that Sister Catherine's office overlooked the area in front of the garage. Casting a swift glance up at her window, my heart nearly stopped. There she was, clear as day, looking down at the two of us.

Did she see me smile? I gasped to myself, as the familiar knot of anxiety gripped my stomach.

In that moment, I realized that simply crossing the yard had become dangerous—except, that is, on Monday and Thursday mornings when Sister Catherine hadn't yet returned from her overnight stay with her family. On those occasions, Brother James Aloysius grew bolder in his communication, often whispering, "How's my little princess?" Free of the danger of being seen by Sister Catherine, I too felt emboldened enough to whisper back, "Very well. Thank you."

We were partners in our communication. It was a dance of sorts—silent and outwardly unemotional when we could be viewed from above by Sister Catherine, and cheerfully whispering when the coast was clear.

Sister Elizabeth Ann was assigned to be the dessert cook, which meant that most afternoons she was in the cellar of St. Therese's House making cakes, pies, or, best of all, angel food cake. And because she could sew, she was also put in charge of making all the clothes for the Little Brothers.

I watched her one day as she lined up five or six Little Brothers. "Now hold still so I can measure your arm," she said with a smile as she stretched her tape measure from shoulder to wrist.

I wish she were in charge of making the Little Sisters' clothes. I ached to have that same opportunity for a little time alone with her.

Instead, it was Sister Laura, who had no daughters but was the mother of five of the Little Brothers, who was put in charge of making the Little Sisters' clothes. I wondered about that. *Why did Sister Catherine make sure that the parents couldn't even have a job that let them be with their children?*

* * *

March turned into April, and I began a countdown to the twelfth of the month, the first anniversary of Grandma Walsh's death.

One year before, while we were still in Cambridge, on the morning of Good Friday, we were standing in line in the basement of St. Francis Xavier's House preparing to cross the yard to go to chapel, when Sister Elizabeth Ann hurried down the stairs. Walking straight up to me, she gently took me by the hand and brought me to a quiet corner of the basement. Kneeling down so that she was at my eye level and holding both my hands, she said, "Darling, I have something to tell you." She paused for a moment. "Your Grandma Walsh has died."

I was speechless. My grandma, my adored, gentle, soft-spoken grandma was gone. I'd never see her again. My dreams of our next visit were annihilated.

As tears rolled down my cheeks, Sister Elizabeth Ann pulled out her handkerchief and wiped them away. Through my sobs I whispered, "When did she die?"

"A week ago, sweetheart, on April 12. She's in heaven now and is looking down on you. And she still loves you."

I had been inconsolable for days, crying myself to sleep—out of sight of Sister Matilda, who I was sure would consider my emotion to be a sign of weakness. Now, one year later, I was determined not to let the anniversary pass without finding Brother James Aloysius and letting him know that I remembered. For once, the rule about not speaking to the adults would not stand in my way. I was on a mission.

Kneeling in the chapel that morning during First Breakfast, I prayed to Grandma Walsh to let it be possible for me to see Brother James Aloysius that day. I plotted all the ways I might "bump into him" during the day. He wouldn't be working in the garage, because it was Saturday. But he might be filling in for Brother Pascal on the porter's desk, as he often did on the weekends. If so, I could catch his eye and say a quick word.

But he wasn't in any of the obvious places. I loitered in the porter's room and took circuitous routes to St. Ann's House—but no Brother James Aloysius. For a moment I wondered. *Does he remember what day it is today? Does he know I'm looking for him? Of course he does*, I reassured myself.

It was late afternoon when I spied him heading toward the giant bell that rang the Angelus three times a day. My heart skipped a beat, and I rushed up the stone path by the front of St. Ann's House, heedless of the possible consequences but reassured with the knowledge that Sister Catherine had already left to be home with her family. He saw me, stopped, and his eyes lit up. Without giving him an opportunity to say a word, I spoke as fast as I could, well aware of the danger I was courting.

"This is the day Grandma died," I said. "I remembered her at First Breakfast. I wanted you to know that."

His expression spoke to me before his words, which were soft and tender, and uttered as though he was amazed.

"How wonderful of you to remember, my little princess."

I dared not stay a second longer. I blew him a kiss and then turned and ran back down the walkway in a state of euphoria.

24

Surprises, Good and Bad

1958

It was a snowy afternoon in February, only weeks after we'd moved from Cambridge, when Sister Catherine showed up unexpectedly in the Little Sisters' corridor. She had a surprise for us, she said, and with that she unboxed twenty life-sized baby dolls, selecting one for each of us so that they matched our own hair and eye color. They were dressed identically in a white blouse and blue jumper, the same as our own uniform.

"Now, dears," she said in a serious voice, "you must promise me that you will keep this a secret. You mustn't breathe a word of it to Father. He doesn't understand little girls the way I do."

I got the picture—Father didn't want us to have dolls because they were worldly. But I also pondered Sister Catherine's words—that she understood little girls. I wanted to believe her, and I wanted to think of her in a motherly way. She was now the only person at the Center who could dispense love and I craved it from her. But those moments were fleeting and her love always felt conditional, as though a temporary reward for obedience to her.

Bedtime stories, banished in Cambridge by Sister Matilda, after we were separated from our parents, were re-instituted by Sister Catherine. In addition, she took to reading to us during dinnertime several evenings a week. My favorite book was *Fabiola*, which had the subtitle, *The Church of the Catacombs*. A nineteenth-century novel by the English Catholic cardinal Nicholas Wiseman, it was a tale of conversion and martyrdom, the latter generally depicted in gruesome detail. The heroine was an elegant and brilliant young woman named Fabiola, the much-loved daughter of a wealthy pagan Roman. Her mother had died when she was an infant. Her confidante was Syra, her most valued slave and a Christian in hiding, who eventually converted Fabiola.

While Sister Catherine was endeavoring to inspire us with the honor of martyrdom, what captivated *me* was the vivid depiction of daily life in a wealthy Roman household in the fourth century. I longed for Fabiola's lifestyle, her many-roomed mansion with servants and silver, her elegant clothes and expensive jewelry—in particular, a radiant emerald ring. The vivid imagery provided endless new material for reverie, as I imagined myself as Fabiola. Pagan or Christian, she was my model.

If, instead of engaging in a session of reading, Sister Catherine had business on her mind, it was evident from the force of her stride, from the glint in her eye, the set of her jaw, and the pursed lips, as she took the few steps to her post in the doorway between our two refectories. And she'd come to the point without any small talk.

That's what happened the evening she introduced the Big Punisher. "For those of you who break the rules, there will be a new form of punishment—the Big Punisher—and it will be unlike anything you have ever experienced before. It's for the good of your souls."

She didn't describe it or show it. She deliberately left it a secret, so we had to imagine what kind of device the Big Punisher might be. But the threat was enough to convince me that I would do everything I could to avoid being beaten with it.

The Big Punisher was immediately put into use. At almost any time of the day or evening, one of the Angels could be seen exiting Sister Catherine's spacious cubicle carrying the dreaded black leather bag that held the secret weapon. *What was it?* Only as its use increased did the rumor spread among the children as to what the secret was. Those who were beaten regularly would report back on sightings, when an Angel couldn't thrust it behind her back fast enough to keep from divulging its identity. It was hose—a two- to three-foot section of garden hose, came the word.

It was used at the whim of any Angel or Sister Catherine herself. Some Angels seemed to relish wielding it. Others, like Sister Maria Crucis (my Angel) and Sister Marietta (my brother's Angel), had no use for it.

Frequently, the Big Punisher would be meted out for a full week at a time to a single child, for an infraction as slight as looking out the window instead of at the altar during First Breakfast. A comment that an Angel deemed to be even slightly insubordinate was another reason for a succession of beatings.

There was an aura of secrecy about the Big Punisher—a "code of silence" as it were. Its existence was never revealed outside of the subcommunity of children and Angels inside the Center, not even at community meetings when we met with our parents. Parents they were, but no longer authority figures. I had no reason to believe that they could have done a thing to mitigate the punishments meted out. It would be many years before the truth was revealed to them.

25

First Christmas in Still River

1958

Sister Teresa, the head Angel, hauled a seven-foot balsam fir tree into our corridor on the first Sunday of Advent.

"It's a Christmas tree," she said in her matter-of-fact way as she set it upright in a red metal stand.

The pungent, piney aroma wafted through the corridor as she brought in boxes of ornaments, along with strings of colored lights, tinsel icicles, and long strands of silver garland. At the age of ten, I was decorating a Christmas tree for the first time. When we plugged in the lights, it was like magic, as the corridor sparkled in a multicolored glow of green, red, blue, and white.

When I got into bed that night, I left my curtain open just enough to allow me to gaze at the glowing tree in the corridor. The scent of pine that I'd come to love from hours spent in the woods over the summer was soothing. The kaleidoscopic lights were magnified a hundred times in the reflection they cast on the shimmering streams of silver icicles draped across the branches.

A Christmas tree, a real live Christmas tree. This was different from any other Christmas I'd ever had. I felt joy—deep and peaceful.

As Christmas drew near, the Big Brothers and Sisters decorated the many doors with pine wreaths. Poinsettias dotted the hallways, the chapel, and the great front room. During meals, our single record player provided a constant stream of English, French, and Italian Christmas carols, as well as Gregorian chants by the Benedictine monks of Solesmes Abbey.

Christmas was only days away, when Sister Catherine made an announcement in our refectory.

"Little Sisters and Little Brothers, I have a surprise for you." She paused before proceeding, and I held my breath, hoping the surprise would be a really good one.

"Before you go to bed on Christmas Eve, you will each be given a stocking that you will pin to your curtain. While you're asleep, Baby Jesus will come and bring you some presents."

I'd seen pictures in storybooks of Christmas trees with presents underneath, and I'd read about stockings loaded with gifts, but that all happened "out in the world," not at the Center. And now, Sister Catherine was telling us that we, too, could have presents. *What had we done to be so lucky?*

We chatted among ourselves about what Baby Jesus would be bringing us as presents. One of the younger Little Sisters asked, "How can Baby Jesus carry presents?"

Mariam was quick with her answer. "He's God. He can do anything He wants."

That seemed to satisfy the gathering. I thought otherwise, but decided it was best to keep my ten-year-old's skepticism to myself. I recalled a time before the red fence had been built when I had seen Santa Claus in a big red suit and a white beard in Cambridge. And I remembered, too, how Father had railed against the commercialism associated with Christmas.

"There is no Santa Claus," he'd yell during his sermon at First Breakfast, rubbing his hands together in his rage. "That's a sacrilege. The Jews have turned St. Nicholas into Santa Claus so they can make money. Santa Claus is just a big, fat, ugly man in a red suit. Santa Claus is of the devil!"

I put the picture together—Baby Jesus was *our* Santa Claus.

At eleven o'clock on Christmas Eve, the entire community attended Midnight Mass and when we returned to St. Ann's House, the Angels helped us pin our thick, gray, woolen, knee-high stockings to our curtains, the same stockings we wore inside our boots during winter. Once in bed, as I gazed at the glowing Christmas tree, excitement banished sleep while I tried to imagine what presents I might get in my stocking.

This is going to be the most wonderful Christmas of my whole life, I told myself.

I woke the next morning to the sound of whispers in the corridor and peeked out of my curtain. Mariam was already up. The floor under the Christmas tree was piled high with games of all sorts and large toys—a pogo stick, Chinese checkers, Parcheesi. And the stocking I had pinned to my curtain was stuffed full. Before long Little Sisters spilled into the corridor, trying to keep the rule of silence as they mumbled soft *oohs* and *aahs*.

Suddenly the door opened and in walked Sister Catherine. "Merry Christmas, Little Sisters," she said. "What has Baby Jesus brought you?"

Her entry somehow signaled that it was all right to talk, and the corridor erupted into pandemonium, with Little Sisters in pajamas pulling toys and games out of stockings and sharing their bounty with one another.

Mariam came to my cubicle door. "What did Baby Jesus bring you?" she asked.

I looked at her in astonishment. *She really thinks it was Baby Jesus? She's almost thirteen years old.* But seeing the excitement in her eyes, I could tell she believed it with all her heart.

I had hardly finished opening my stocking when Sister Catherine stood in the doorway of my cubicle. With her was Sister Elizabeth Ann. It was the first time since we had moved nearly a year earlier that my mother was allowed to enter our corridor.

"Anastasia, show Sister Elizabeth Ann what Baby Jesus brought you," Sister Catherine said to me, and together we examined my presents—watercolor paints and a book of pictures to go with them, an origami set, a yo-yo, and a little porcelain bird.

When Sister Elizabeth Ann visited Mary Catherine in her cubicle, she snuggled next to her on the bed and showed her how to make her Mexican beans jump.

The best part of the day was yet to come when, after second breakfast, we had a community meeting in the front room, sharing our presents with our parents for several hours. It was well after lunchtime when the dreaded bell sounded that indicated the end of our family time together.

I grabbed my woolen coat and headed for the door on my way back to St. Ann's House to play with my new games and toys. As I turned to exit the front door of St. Therese's House, I ran into Sister Catherine. She was in a cheerful mood as she leaned down and kissed me.

"Happy feast day, my goddaughter," she said quietly. "Did you have a lovely time at the community meeting?"

"Oh, yes, Sister Catherine," I replied, feeling in that moment that she really did love me. As I paused, reveling in the fact that she had singled me out for special treatment, she reached up to a shelf and took down her hat and pinned it to her hair, the telltale sign she was leaving the property. In an instant, I realized that Sister Catherine was going home to her family in Waltham for Christmas dinner. We left St. Therese's House together, she to get into her car to drive home, and I to walk back to St. Ann's House.

As the afternoon turned to dusk, I watched the sun, a giant orange-red ball of fire, while it slowly drifted toward the horizon in the southwest sky. I was overcome with sadness, the same kind I had felt so many times before when good things came to an end.

I don't want this day to be over. I mused on the wonderfulness of it—a community meeting, new toys, no silence. *If only it could be like this every day.*

26

Our Lady's Army

1959

Sister Catherine had an idea: Our Lady's Army.
"You will be soldiers in Our Lady's Army," she said, "ready to fight against all her enemies."

It was the first stage in Sister Catherine's mission to mold thirty-nine children into a cadre of religious activists.

She wrote the pledge that we memorized and said at the start of each army meeting, a Friday evening event in her office that was closed to the Angels. Standing at attention, with our right hands raised in three-finger salutes to honor the Three Persons in God, we recited:

"As a soldier in the Army of Our Lady, I promise to defend her cause, which is the cause of Jesus, with my life. I promise to be ready to die for her at any moment. I promise to live for her a life so holy that I may win, in the battles against her enemies, many, many souls for her to give to the Sacred Heart of Jesus. I salute her as my Queen and Commander-in-Chief. I give her the complete allegiance of my heart, and I promise her the complete obedience of my will. I promise

Our Lady's Army.

to love Jesus and Mary above all things and to have no other love
before them."

For the next hour or two, Sister Catherine spoke to us about how
we children had been especially chosen by God, as she put it, to save
souls and if necessary to lay down our lives for the cause of the Center,
the doctrine of "No Salvation Outside the Catholic Church." She
warned us that the enemies of the Church were all around us, and the
most dangerous were the Communists.

"The Communists have now infiltrated our country, and they will
soon take over," she said on one occasion. "And when they come it will
be necessary for us to flee to the desert in Arizona."

Her voice took on a transfixed, almost triumphant tone, as though
fleeing was a heavenly journey, the fulfillment of the will of God for
us at the Center.

"We will set up our community in the desert and hide there until
the Communists find us. Then we will be martyred for our faith."

She described martyrdom as a badge of honor that, as soldiers in Our Lady's Army, we must embrace. For my part, I was repulsed by the notion of martyrdom and knew in my heart, never to be admitted in public, that I would never die for my faith.

If we're supposed to embrace martyrdom, then why do we have to flee into the desert? I wondered to myself.

Though I put on a good face, secretly I hated everything about Our Lady's Army—the name, the mission, and the public display. On the first Saturday of each month and continuing for years, we conducted our own army parade out in public. At the head of the parade, one of the Little Brothers carried a giant flag, emblazoned with the words "OUR LADY'S ARMY." We wore parade uniforms—royal-blue jackets with shiny gold buttons and wide white belts. We had boxy helmets, each with a tall pom-pom. Mariam played the bugle, and Leonard played drums.

I thought we looked foolish, dressed up in our uniforms as we marched. The Big Sisters and Brothers, standing along the property that bordered the bypass off Route 110, were our adoring audience, and they clapped enthusiastically when our half-hour march was over. The elderly Mr. Haskel and his ancient sister, Miss Haskell, our friendly neighbors across the road, stood on their porch and watched. Cars driving by on the highway would often slow down and even stop.

Go. Just go, I pleaded silently to the gawking spectators. The flag embarrassed me. What did people think Our Lady's Army was? I felt like a freak and wanted to vanish.

Every few months, the Haskells would present us with a new band instrument, and before long we had a full array—trumpets and trombones, a French horn, a bass drum, a glockenspiel, and, eventually, a tuba. It wasn't long before I was assigned to be a trumpet player, a role I detested. I thought my head would explode when I played the high notes, and in the winter, as we marched in frigid weather, my bony fingers ached and then lost all sense of feeling as I struggled to

Band practice.

push the valves, frozen with frost. When I could no longer take the pain in my head and my fingers, I pretended to play, hoping the Little Sisters on either side of me couldn't tell that no sound was coming from my trumpet.

27

"Birthday" Present

1959

My eleventh birthday came in the middle of August on a hot and humid day. There would be no celebration, but I had become used to that. All I cared about was that I see Brother James Aloysius and hear his whispered, "Happy birthday, my little princess"—a secret tradition we'd established between just the two of us on each of our birthdays. It was Sunday, and this meant the garage where he worked would be closed and we would be playing down in the meadow far from St. Therese's House. This made the prospect of finding each other more challenging, and by midafternoon, I was losing hope.

Where is he? He couldn't have forgotten, could he?

As the other Little Sisters played cowboys and Indians, I paced the field, pretending to look for wildflowers, but all the while keeping an eagle eye on the long, sloping hill that stretched from the barns to our playing fields. Minutes passed like hours.

Please, God, please make him come this way. I'll never do anything bad again in my life.

Scarcely had I finished my prayer for what had to have been the twentieth time that day when I looked up toward the barns. And there he was. I stopped and stared in disbelief. Yes, it was Brother James Aloysius, slowly making his way down the long, rutted road. He looked elegant in his long black cassock, the dress the Big Brothers wore when they weren't working, the neatly folded cincture flapping to the side keeping time with his steps.

He found me. He found me. My prayers had been answered.

Casting a furtive glance at the Angel to make sure she wasn't watching me, I bolted out of her sight. As my father came closer I ran to him, so overjoyed I felt I would cry. We didn't hug or kiss. That was too risky.

"You made it!" I said softly.

"Of course I did," he replied. "Happy Birthday, my little princess," he said, his blue eyes like stars. "Have a wonderful day, sweetheart."

"This is the best day of my life," I replied.

Our meeting was over. I turned and scurried back to where the other Little Sisters were playing, and Brother James Aloysius, in his laid-back Sunday style, turned around and headed up the hill again. The joy inside me overcame the fear that perhaps the Angel had seen me. I didn't care. Whatever the consequences, it was worth every bit of danger.

But in this case, God really did answer my prayer—no one had seen us.

28

And Then It Happened to Me

1960

Father sat at the upright piano in the library, pounding the keys as he belted out his favorite songs, a potpourri of Irish and French-Canadian folk tunes, his black eyes animated by his own performance. I knew all the songs by heart, having heard them dozens of times. For nearly an hour he regaled all thirty-nine of us, and then abruptly he stood up and disappeared into his office. It was March 25, the Feast of the Annunciation, a holy day of obligation. That meant no tutoring. A cold rain, mingled with sleet, pelted the windows. It was the kind of weather that came in March and ruined sledding for the season.

Under the watchful eye of the Angels, we spent the morning popping popcorn over the log fire in the massive brick fireplace, making taffy apples, and playing games.

Suddenly, the towering figure of Sister Catherine appeared in the narrow doorway. She wasn't smiling. Through her clear-framed eyeglasses, her green eyes were glaring—straight at me.

What have I done now? I knew that look well and was panic-stricken. My hands turned clammy, and I averted Sister Catherine's gaze. Stepping into the great front room, she sat down on the low Shaker chair in front of the window, her hands tightly clasped, her back rigid. I pretended to be engaged in the games we were playing, but it was impossible to distract myself from her terrifying presence. Every few minutes, I sneaked quick glances in her direction, only to find her eyes still fixed on me.

Why is she staring at me like that? Then she turned her head. I followed her eyes—she was now staring at Leonard. *Oh, no,* I thought. *It's about Leonard.*

Ever since that day two years earlier when Sister Catherine had forbidden me to speak to Leonard ever again, I had avoided him, not sure if he even knew about the rule. Now sitting amongst my playmates, I was unable to speak—my throat dry with fear.

I grasped a prayer from deep within me, but I sensed that prayers weren't going to do me any good.

When the clock chimed noon and we headed for lunch, I tried to mingle inconspicuously among the other Little Sisters, my insides knotted with terror. But as I approached the doorway, Sister Catherine blocked my way.

"You," she said. Her voice was low, but her rage was inescapable. "Go over to St. Ann's House and wait for me in your cubicle. I'll see you shortly."

I had a premonition of what was to come. As I crossed the yard, my hands were shaking. I was grateful that, because of the holy day, Brother James Aloysius wasn't working on the cars. He seemed to be able to tell when I was in trouble.

Entering my cubicle, I closed the curtain behind me, and sat at the far end of my bed. My face was hot, and my chest hurt. I was too scared to cry. Minutes passed, which seemed like hours, and I started to say my Rosary.

Then the corridor door creaked open, and I recognized the sound of Sister Catherine coming closer and closer by the swishing noise that her stockings made when she walked. She stopped outside my cubicle and pulled back the curtain. I knew it. In her right hand, she carried the ominous black leather bag that contained the Big Punisher.

Her wrath was petrifying. "You know what you did, don't you?" she yelled at me.

"No, Sister Catherine, I don't. I really don't," I replied, hoping that my honest claim of innocence might spare me.

"You were laughing with Leonard during the games," she responded, her voice shrill, her green eyes fearsome. "You'll regret breaking the rule. Get out here now, and go down to the end of the corridor."

Beatings with the Big Punisher were always done in the cubicle farthest from the front hall so that any Big Sisters who might be passing by wouldn't be able to hear the screaming.

I walked to the far end of the corridor and into Mariam's cubicle. Throwing my long blue skirt over my head with one hand, Sister Catherine used the other to retrieve the Big Punisher and began beating me. The first shock of pain practically brought me to the floor.

"This will teach you," she said as she beat away, hitting my back, shoulders, thighs, and backside.

I bit my lip, trying to keep from screaming, hoping that would shorten the number of blows. But after what seemed like endless whacks, I couldn't hold in my cries.

When she finally stopped, Sister Catherine put the giant piece of hose back into the bag before allowing me to stand up.

"Get out," she ordered.

I left the corridor in front of her and headed downstairs to the Little Sisters' bathroom, where I washed away the tears from my face, drank some water, and smoothed my hair with my hands. The welts on my thighs were still rising, but I couldn't see the damage because we had no full-length mirror.

Alone, I crossed the yard to St. Therese's House, arriving late for lunch. For once, the rule of silence saved me from questions from the Little Sisters. What happened would remain my secret. I didn't want anyone to know that I had gotten the Big Punisher. It was too mortifying.

Did she beat Leonard, too? I wondered. From the corner of my eye, I could see he was sitting at his table. There was no way to find out.

It would be nearly fifty years before I asked him that question. "Yes," he said.

"So she told you, too, that you were never to speak to me?" It was a question that I had turned over in my mind for half a century. He nodded his head. It cemented a friendship that had forever been platonic.

The pain subsided and over the next few hours the welts diminished, but not my anxiety. Hard as I tried, I couldn't recall laughing or talking with Leonard.

I barely slept that night, still clueless over how I'd broken the rule that Sister Catherine had devised, fearing that a childhood friendship might blossom into a romance as we grew into our teenage years.

But she's my godmother. I'm supposed to be special to her. Why has she turned on me?

Not long after that hideous day, Sister Catherine entered our refectories and addressed the thirty-nine of us.

"Little Brothers and Sisters," she said. The tone of her voice was pleasant, as though she had a surprise in store for us. "How would you like to be more like your Big Brothers and Sisters? Wouldn't you like that?"

"Yes, Sister Catherine." The reply was instant and unanimous, as it always was when she asked a leading question.

A new rule was coming now. I could just sense it.

"Well," she continued, "the Big Brothers don't speak to the Big Sisters, and the Big Sisters don't speak to the Big Brothers. If you would like to be just like them, then from now on, the Little Sisters will not speak to the Little Brothers, and the Little Brothers won't speak to the Little Sisters."

It was done. One more rule, one more monumental change that we had just "willingly," if unwittingly, agreed to.

I can't even talk to my little brother anymore. I thought. *How will we play baseball and blind man's bluff?* One more sundered family bond.

My instinctive nature was one of optimism. Laughter was my favorite voice, and I couldn't bear to see anyone unhappy. When a Little Sister got into trouble, I'd try to make her feel better with a smile or a whispered word of encouragement. But the beating I received for something I had never done was emotionally paralyzing. In a flash, fear became the new constant in my life, supplanting joy. I tiptoed from day to day with a perpetual prayer in my heart, beseeching an array of saints to keep me safe from the tyranny of Sister Catherine. I hated the person I was becoming—an anxious, insecure, timid girl.

One night, in the darkness of my cubicle, as I pondered my misery, a thought came into my head, one that I would repeat hundreds of times over the next few years.

Someday she'll die, and then I'll be free.

29

Getting Wise

1960

Once again, Mary Catherine had stopped eating. I thought about the secret between her and Sister Catherine that she was forbidden to tell me. It obviously wasn't working.

On a sunny spring Saturday morning, after Mary Catherine had left her breakfast untouched on her plate yet again, Sister Catherine sent for me to come up to her office. There I found Mary Catherine. Her big blue eyes were dull and carried that familiar look, the one that said, "Please help me," and her forlorn expression was intensified by her sagging shoulders, her shaking hands, and the tremble in her lower lip, a telltale sign that she was scared.

Sister Catherine greeted me with warmth.

"Anastasia dear, Mary Catherine and I are going to let you in on a secret, aren't we?" she said, turning toward Mary Catherine and speaking in that gentle, coddling voice I no longer trusted.

Mary Catherine barely nodded her head.

Sister Catherine went on. "Let's go to the Little Sisters' refectory, and I'll explain everything."

I couldn't imagine what was going to happen, but I suspected that the secret that had been so important for Mary Catherine to keep from me was about to be revealed. We entered the dining room and Sister Catherine closed the door behind us. She took Mary Catherine's hand, and I followed as they walked together to one of the windows that looked out to the highway.

Still holding hands, Sister Catherine turned to me and spoke. "Inside Mary Catherine, there's a bad little girl who tells her not to eat. Her name is Suzy. And now we're going to get rid of Suzy. Isn't that right, Mary Catherine?"

Another silent nod.

Sister Catherine unlocked and opened the window. "Okay, all together, on the count of three, let's throw Suzy out the window and get rid of her for good."

Standing next to Mary Catherine, I was stupefied. *What kind of a charade is this? Suzy? That's not even a Catholic name!*

Joining the two of them in this pantomime, I mimicked the swinging motion as Sister Catherine called out, "One, two, three, go!" Then we flung our arms out toward the open window and the highway beyond.

So this was the secret Mary Catherine had to keep from me!

I found the ploy repulsive. It was as though Sister Catherine was saying that my little sister had a devil in her, and we were engaging in an act of exorcism.

If my participation in this ritual was supposed to have helped, it didn't. At lunch, Mary Catherine refused to eat. And the next morning at second breakfast, when Sister Catherine saw that Mary Catherine's eggs lay untouched on her plate, her cajoling ended and the beatings with the Big Punisher resumed.

I felt a sense of hopelessness, knowing that I'd failed. Each day I awoke with dread, fearful that if Mary Catherine didn't eat, pretty soon she would die. *Why is no one able to help her?* I was sure that Sister Elizabeth Ann would be able to get her to eat.

But Mary Catherine's eating problems were kept from my parents. Sister Catherine's determination to shatter the natural bonds of love among family members would not have been served by including parents in any decision-making. The sparse opportunities she did provide for communication, in the form of that increasingly rare but glorious Sunday morning community meeting, were (perhaps deliberately) too short for serious exchanges. And anyway, as I saw it, much as I adored my parents, they had long been relieved of their parental role. They had no authority over me, and I had no recourse to them. Sharing with them the sordid details of punishments and troubles would only lead to their unhappiness. It could serve no purpose.

That didn't mean, however, that my parents were oblivious to the fact that the five of us might get into trouble. Nor did Sister Catherine even try to hide that fact. She set up a system called "Badges." Badges represented an array of virtues, including devotion, obedience, table manners, curiosity (This was actually deemed to be a vice rather than a virtue.), generosity, and more. The Angels determined which badges each of their charges earned or lost each week, and on Friday evening when we attended Benediction, all thirty-nine of us wore a pink satin sash across our chests on which were glued the badges we had earned that week. Missing badges sent a visible message to the entire community that screamed, "I did something wrong! I was bad!" But the rule of silence between children and adults prohibited any opportunity to defend oneself or to explain the painful embarrassment. On more than a few occasions, when my sash was sorely missing prominent badges, Brother James Aloysius would surreptitiously whisper a word of encouragement, for which I was immensely, albeit silently, grateful.

One day, as I was passing Sister Catherine's office, I heard voices from within. My curiosity was piqued, and I slowed my pace. Father's voice suddenly erupted, loud and angry. Moving closer to the door, I could make out a muffled female voice, one that was not Sister Catherine's. A moment later, a forceful man's voice rose and I froze in panic—it was Brother James Aloysius.

"You had no right," he was saying and before he could continue, both Father and Sister Catherine raised their voices in response.

"If you want to keep your faith…" That was Father's voice.

Terrified, I sped out of the library, past the porter's desk, through the refectories, and straight into the chapel. Kneeling down, I shut my eyes, buried my face in my hands, and prayed with all my heart.

Dear God, please protect Brother James Aloysius and Sister Elizabeth Ann. Don't let Father and Sister Catherine kick them out of the Center.

I had never before heard a fight between any of the adults at the Center and couldn't imagine what this might signify.

As the community gathered in the chapel and the organ signaled the start of Benediction, all I could hear in my head were those voices— my parents and Father and Sister Catherine yelling at each other.

That was when the nightmare started. It was the same one over and over. I dreamed I was submerged in a pond of cold water covered with a thick layer of ice. Somehow, I remembered that between the water and the ice there was a tiny sliver of air.

Get all the way up to the top, I told myself. *You can do it. Find the air.*

With my heart pounding, I pushed my head as far back as I could and searched for the thread of lifesaving air. As my nose reached the ceiling of ice, I breathed. I had survived. And then gasping, I woke up.

30

Turning Twelve

1960

My twelfth birthday was nearing and I was excited because, despite the fact that we no longer celebrated the event, it carried significance within the community of children at the Center. Sister Catherine allowed as how becoming twelve signified a migration from child to young adult, the primary evidence of which was I would be allowed to wear silk stockings and a garter belt instead of the blue knee-high socks that were part of our uniform. In addition, I would become the owner of a small wall-mounted mirror in my cubicle, something I had been coveting since Mariam had received one two years earlier. My birthday came and went, unmentioned of course, but not without my ensuring I received the treasured symbols I had been promised.

What I was unprepared for, upon entering my thirteenth year, was finding myself thrust into a world I had no idea how to maneuver— an attraction to boys. The first inkling came through books, as I devoured an array of new arrivals in our library—books on sports figures, mostly famous football players, like Joe Bellino who played for Navy, and Knute Rockne who'd been a star at Notre Dame. Sitting on my bed, I would turn the pages, gazing at the photographs of the handsome athletes in their team uniforms, with their husky builds and their good looks.

This growing interest I shared with no one, least of all Sister Catherine. Her constant exhortation that we share with her, as she put it, "the deepest yearnings of your soul" added to my wariness. Much as I craved to be loved and accepted by her, I had come to the realization that, for reasons beyond my comprehension, I was blighted in her eyes.

Concomitant with my new obsession with books about athletes and boys was my fading appetite for reading the lives of the saints. I read *Tom Playfair* so many times that I had memorized the first few pages.

"Tommy!"

No answer.

"Tommy—do you hear me? Get up this moment, sir. Do you think this house is a hotel? Everyone's at breakfast except yourself."

That's what life was like out in the world, I figured.

But my love affair with these new books was to be short-lived. One day, I was summoned to Sister Catherine's office.

"Anastasia," Sister Catherine said in a tone that meant business. "You are no longer to read any books about football. Those books were meant for the Little Brothers. Do you hear me?"

"Yes, Sister Catherine," I said.

It made no sense. If I wasn't supposed to read books about football, why did Father take us to watch the high school football games in Clinton and Leominster on Saturday mornings?

Sister Catherine went on. "And you've read *Tom Playfair* enough. From now on, all books on boys are out of bounds for you as well. You may leave."

I left her office disheartened and with a feeling of having been trapped. *Who told her I was reading those books? Which Angel?* I was left guessing.

Sister Catherine may have outwitted herself because once she banished the books that were the source of my innocent musings about boys, my fascination turned to the real men around me. Brother Sebastian became my first crush, the Big Brother I had adored as a small child when he told me bedtime stories about the lives of the saints. For reasons I didn't understand, I began to find him irresistible. I'd pass by the chapel where he worked as the sacristan in the hopes of catching a glimpse of him, sure that my preoccupation was my own secret.

So I was more than shocked when, summoned once again to Sister Catherine's office, she came to the point directly.

"Brother Sebastian has complained about you. He says that you're chasing him."

I gulped, not sure how to pretend I didn't know what she was talking about. She went on, her voice not so much accusatory as admonishing. "Now you know the rule about particular friendships, don't you, dear?"

How well I did. It had been another one of those manipulations by Sister Catherine—a "suggestion" from her that she got us children to agree to, thus making it one more ironclad rule. In this case, no longer were we allowed to have a particular friendship or hold each other's hands.

At the time, my best friend was Claudette. We'd spend hours in innocent play together, and I enjoyed holding hands and skipping with her. Now this was forbidden. But I found a way to break the rule without getting caught. As we skipped along the rutted gravel road that led from one meadow to another, I made sure there was plenty of space between us—that is, until we were behind the thicket of elderberry bushes and brambles. Then I'd grasp her hand, and for a few hundred feet out of sight of a spying Angel, we would swing our clasped hands back and forth, throwing our heads back and laughing. When the scrub trees gave way to the open field, I loosened my grip on her hand and we emerged into the view of the Angel, an appropriate distance apart. No one ever caught us.

My parents as Sister Elizabeth Ann and Brother James Aloysius.

Now as I stood before Sister Catherine in her office, I could feel the heat rise in my body as she chastised me for "chasing" Brother Sebastian. As to why I might find him so riveting, there was never a conversation about nature, about my body and why it was changing. Not even with the onset of menstruation a year earlier had Sister Catherine taken the opportunity to discuss human reproduction with me. But then, perhaps from her point of view, since I was in training to be the bride of Christ, in essence having been betrothed to Him from the time I was an infant, what need did I have to know anything about such matters of the flesh?

Not long after this encounter, Brother Sebastian was gone. I searched everywhere for him, but he wasn't at First Breakfast, nor was he in the sacristy or the refectory during dinner. Then I pieced the puzzle together. He'd been kicked out.

Is it because of me?

The ache in my heart took weeks to mend. I pondered over why it was that the people I most loved were taken away—first Betty

Sullivan, and now the man named Charles Forgeron, because he was no longer Brother Sebastian.

Could Brother James Aloysius and Sister Elizabeth Ann face the same fate? Sister Catherine often praised various Big Brothers and Sisters, pointing out their detachment from their children, but it didn't escape me that my parents were never mentioned.

Worrying became part of the daily pattern of my life. I couldn't help it. The premonition that something terrible might happen to my parents consumed me. I wanted them to be safe, I wanted them to be happy, and I wanted them to be loved by Father and Sister Catherine. But I couldn't make that happen. Anxiety lay in the bottom of my stomach like a stone. If they were kicked out, it would be my responsibility to look after my three younger sisters and my brother.

31

Visit from a "Stranger"

1960

The obligatory dinnertime silence was broken by the sound of the front door bell. At first it was a quick chink-like sound. Then it repeated itself, a long incessant buzz. *Who could be there?* I wondered. No one came to our front door during dinner.

Presently Sister Catherine, tall and with an air of command, charged through our refectory and headed toward the front door. She returned shortly.

"It's Betty Sullivan," she announced, clearly not pleased. And then directing her next comment to the Angels, she added, "She wants to come back."

My heart skipped several beats. *Betty Sullivan? The woman I so loved from the time I was a toddler?* While I had long gotten over the heartbreak of her being kicked out, I occasionally wondered what her life was like out in the world. The image was always the same—a gentle woman with a soft voice and melancholy eyes.

Later that evening, a dark and chilly night, I left St. Therese's House alone and headed down the flagstone path toward the driveway, which was dimly lit from above by two floodlights. Suddenly, a figure bounded from the direction of the side porch and sped in front of me. It had an almost ghoulish form, the face contorted, the eyes closed, and the lips grotesquely puffy. Terrified, I leapt to the side and hid behind a tall lilac bush, from which I peered out to witness the gnarled form as it loped across the lawn, one leg seeming to drag behind it, with a large cape billowing out into the darkness.

In an instant, I realized it must be Betty Sullivan. But she resembled nothing like the beautiful woman in my memory. I stood shaking; fear and repulsion was all I felt. How hideous she had become. I raced home as fast as I could. I never wanted to come that close to her again—not in the dark.

That turned out to be only the first of many sightings that materialized like unwanted apparitions. Out of nowhere, mostly in the dark, but sometimes even in broad daylight, Betty Sullivan would scamper across the lawn from the direction of the highway. Her eyes were nearly always shut, and her hair was matted around her head. Her eyebrows were bushy and overgrown, her clothes ragged and disheveled, and she looked as though she never bathed.

Sister Catherine informed us that Betty Sullivan had moved into a makeshift house adjacent to ours, which had expanded with the acquisition of an additional eighty acres. With no running water and no electricity, she lived with several sheep to keep her warm in winter. The dinnertime visits with the incessantly ringing doorbell continued.

As the frequency of Betty's visits increased, Sister Catherine began to ridicule her in front of us. Soon several of the Little Brothers began to taunt her, even going so far as to throw water at her as she stood mute and immobile on the porch with her hand on the doorknob, her deformed and puffy lips parted, her eyes shut. Neither Sister Catherine nor the Angels did anything to stop the abuse. The respect we were required to show to adults, including those in the world outside our community, somehow did not pertain to Betty. It was as though she was now the enemy.

32

Life on the Farm

1961

Within three years of moving to Still River, our farm had become a full-time enterprise. Forty Holstein cows supplied the community with milk (which we drank unpasteurized), and butter. The chicken farm had expanded from a few hens to several dozen, along with two ornery roosters whose favorite pastimes were fighting each other and attacking us children. I loved to collect eggs from the hens, slipping my hand under their warm bodies and feeling around for eggs nestled among the soft down of their breasts. Their half-hearted protective pecks on my hand were like little caresses.

Sister Catherine's vision, as she had described it four years earlier, during that summer before we moved to Still River, was becoming a reality. We had ponies and dogs and cats for pets. And I had my own part in it now, having been given a calf as a Christmas present a few months earlier.

Self-sufficiency was no small endeavor for a group of nearly one hundred people, and it was made all the more challenging by Sister Catherine's decision that we adopt an organic way of life, raising fruits, vegetables and animals devoid of any chemical insecticides. She had become a devotee of Rachel Carson, whose book, *Silent Spring*, convinced her that pesticides, in particular DDT, were a cause of cancer. That mission, too, was influenced by her fervent belief that it was America's archenemy, the malevolent Communists, who were behind the chemical warfare, which extended even to the fluoride in our toothpaste.

Thirty-nine children provided a nearly limitless source of free labor, and for hours each day, from June till September, we could be seen in the fields on our knees weeding and picking strawberries, potatoes, string beans, and corn. As we swatted away the endless reign of terror from deerflies, horseflies, and mosquitoes, one of the Angels would stand at the end of one of the long rows reading aloud to us stories from the lives of the saints. A midday swimming break in the spring-fed watering hole that Sister Catherine had constructed the year after we moved to Still River was a blessed relief.

Each summer also brought with it a challenge—a project hatched by Sister Catherine. One year it might be clearing the brush from acres of land to increase the pastures for our growing herds. Another time we built hermitages, in the image of the early saints who chose to leave society and retire into the desert.

This summer we undertook to build a fieldstone chicken coop under the supervision of the Big Sisters. At twenty by forty feet and ten feet high, its construction required an enormous effort. Gathering the building stones entailed dismantling the generations-old stone walls that ran through our property. Despite the backbreaking nature of the work, lugging boulders and rocks to the site, I reveled in the experience, envisioning myself as a frontier woman, a pioneer of sorts, as I learned how to mix cement and use a plumb bob to ensure that the walls would be straight.

Recreation that summer included our first horseback riding lessons. As Little Sisters, we were required to ride sidesaddle, while the Little Brothers had both English and western saddles. I didn't take naturally to horses, but my interest in riding was augmented by our riding instructor, Brother Dominic Maria. Before joining the Center, he had been Temple Morgan (related to the wealthy Astors and Morgans). He'd gone to Groton School and then Harvard College, where he was a member of the prestigious Porcellian Club. Raised on a stately horse farm in Maryland, he was an excellent rider.

Until that summer, I'd barely noticed Brother Dominic Maria. But when he took my hands to show me how to hold the reins, I suddenly became aware of him in a different way. At six foot two, rugged and wiry, with jet-black hair and deep brown eyes, he was nothing like Brother Sebastian, my first crush of a year earlier, who was short and delicate looking, played the cello, and did indoor kinds of things like arranging flowers and writing poems. I didn't understand my own feelings, but my heart skipped a beat each time I put my left foot into Brother Dominic Maria's cupped hands and hoisted myself up into the sidesaddle.

As I sat poised and ready to ride off with my horse, he spoke in a low tone. "Remember, you're the boss, girl. Don't let the horse get control of you. He can tell if you're nervous."

"Girl"—I loved how he said that. No one said that at the Center. I could scarcely concentrate on the horse, as my insides got all fluttery. And "boss"—another word I never heard spoken. But I knew its meaning and took pride in it.

One day, to impress him, I rode our palomino Regis all the way down to the Nashua River and then cantered back up to the barn through the lower fields and along the rutted road. As the horse panted and dripped with sweat, I sat proudly, waiting to hear what compliment Brother Dominic Maria might have for me.

"Girl, you rode like St. Joan of Arc," he said. My knees began to shake, my heart beat madly, and my mouth became so dry I could barely manage a smile. As he helped me to dismount, I let my body brush up against his.

A few evenings later, Sister Catherine made an announcement in our refectory. "Little Sisters and Brothers," she said, "there are certain words we do not use because they're not very nice. 'Boss' is one of them."

My stomach lurched.

She's talking about Brother Dominic Maria and me, I thought in a panic. I tried to recollect which Angel had been in charge the day he told me I was the boss of the horse. I waited for days, fearing Sister Catherine might call me into her office and tell me that I could no longer take riding lessons. But to my relief, my lessons continued throughout the summer—as did my crush. However, once we were proficient in riding sidesaddle, the lessons tapered off.

By the end of August, the ten-week chicken-coop project was nearing completion. Using ropes, we hoisted long roof beams to the top of the ten-foot-tall structure, nailed plywood to the beams, put on a layer of tar paper, and sealed the roof with shingles. The final touches on the henhouse came with whitewashing the interior walls and installing dozens of nesting boxes.

By Labor Day, a week before tutoring was to begin, we opened the gates to the enclosure and let in over two hundred pullets, the young hens Sister Teresa had been raising all summer. One more step in our self-sufficiency had been achieved.

To celebrate the completion of our project, Sister Catherine treated the oldest of us to a first—a trip to Day's Deli, an unfashionable trailer shack a mile or so down the highway, converted into a roadside takeout spot with picnic tables outside for eating. Nonetheless, this was a reward of monumental proportions, one that seemed to fly in the face of our mission to remove ourselves from any connection with the outside world.

As we arrived and spilled out of the cars, Sister Catherine said, "You may order whatever you'd like, dears."

Whatever we want? The list of possibilities posted on the back wall of the structure was endless, with such oddities as fried clam bellies, onion rings, and a dizzying array of desserts, from frappes of all flavors to hot fudge sundaes, ice cream sodas, and banana splits.

As the other Little Brothers and Sisters murmured among themselves, I gawked at the worldly people inside who were juggling deep-frying baskets and flipping burgers. They were teenagers like me, but so different. The girls wore pretty, colored, sleeveless tops that looked sinfully immodest. And they wore shorts that were very short indeed. I was scandalized but fascinated.

What do they think of all of us with our long skirts and our odd hairstyles? I was embarrassed at being so unconventional. Never before had we been allowed to speak directly to strangers outside of the Center.

While the other children hung back, undecided about what to choose, I walked to the window and spoke clearly. "May I please have a banana split, with a double scoop of vanilla ice cream, hot fudge sauce, marshmallow fluff, and cherries?"

Sister Catherine seemed to enjoy the outing as much as we did, encouraging us to get seconds if we wanted. And to my astonishment, she acted unfazed by the appalling attire of the worldly attendants. This only added to the enigma of the woman who had such power and influence over my every movement, but for a few moments, I relaxed to see her in such good humor as I savored my banana split.

33

A New Glimpse at the Forbidden World

1960

Shortly after tutoring began in mid-September, Sister Catherine assembled the children in the study hall. The room had been set up with folding chairs, and she beckoned us to sit down, Little Sisters on one side and Little Brothers on the other. At the back of the room, Brother Philip sat at a machine with a wheel about two feet in diameter, and in front of us was a large white screen on a tripod. Without an explanation, Sister Catherine pulled down the shades, and the room became dark.

From the machine came a whirring sound. Lights flashed, and then on the screen appeared the words: *The Song of Bernadette*.

It was our introduction to the movies. For a few moments, I was mesmerized. But soon I found myself becoming dizzy. The larger-than-life faces of people and cars moving across the screen so close to my eyes was disorienting. I took a deep breath, and as a wave of nausea came over me, I had to shut my eyes to calm my stomach. For what seemed hours, I sat with my eyes closed, listening to the movie and praying for it to end. At last the whir of the reel subsided, the lights came on, and we clapped. I pretended to enjoy the experience, but inside I wondered why anyone would want to go to the movies.

Things improved when movies became part of the community activity, and we all congregated in the large living room on Friday and Sunday nights. There the distance between the chairs and the screen relieved my nausea, and the subject matter became more interesting for a twelve-year-old girl whose main endeavor was to learn as much as possible about the world beyond the Center.

There were numerous episodes of television serials from the 1940s. *Don Winslow of the Navy*, a twelve-part adventure series about a U.S. Navy commander during World War II, and *Kit Carson and the Mystery Riders* were popular Friday night fare, as was Laurel and Hardy.

But like the books in our library, the movies we watched were prescreened by a trusted Big Brother. Often in the middle of a movie, the screen would go dark, the lens being covered to prevent us from viewing what was considered "inappropriate material." From the context of what we were viewing, I figured out what those "bad" parts were about. It was usually when a girl and a boy came into view together.

Travelogues were among my favorite movies, adding visual stimulus to my years of fantasizing about the many cities and towns I had become familiar with from the lives of the saints. Far-fetched though it might have seemed, I allowed myself to revel in the belief that one day I'd find a way to see the whole world. I'd fly in an airplane. I'd visit all the cathedrals in Europe and eat in fancy restaurants and swim in the Mediterranean Sea. I'd see the cedars of Lebanon and go to the Isle of Lindisfarne.

Someday, I will. I repeated to myself, over and over. *Someday, I will.*

34

The Unthinkable

1962

Where was Brother Martin?

Brother Martin was one of the married Big Brothers, and five of the Little Brothers were his and Sister Laura's children. He hadn't been around for more than a week. I knew he wasn't on a bookselling trip because I kept a mental account of each of the Big Brothers and Sisters who was traveling. I looked for clues to his whereabouts but could come up with nothing. If he were sick, we'd be praying for him. But there were no special prayers, no announcement. He'd just disappeared.

Weeks went by with no mention of Brother Martin. Then one evening, Sister Catherine took her place in the doorway of our refectories and broke the news to us.

"Little Brothers and Sisters, I have something to tell you," she began, her voice serious. "Brother Martin is no longer with us," she said. "He has betrayed the faith and Our Blessed Mother and already has one foot in hell. He is now Richard Cullinane [his name before coming to the Center], not Brother Martin."

I was thunderstruck and terrified. This could only mean one thing: Brother Martin had been kicked out of the Center. *Why?*

I searched the faces of his five sons, trying to see if their expressions were sad. But I could detect nothing. After dinner, I sneaked glances at his wife, Sister Laura, as she did the dishes in the kitchen. She, too, seemed the same as always.

With no further explanation, I became lost in my own nightmare. If Father and Sister Catherine would actually kick out one of the parents, that meant that my parents were no longer safe. For days I was unable to sleep through the night.

I couldn't fathom what a parent might have done to warrant being kicked out by Father and Sister Catherine. I thought back to that terrifying moment a year earlier when I'd overheard my father yelling behind the closed door of Sister Catherine's office.

Will they kick out my parents, too? Jesus, Mary, and Joseph, please, please, please don't let that happen. I will sacrifice anything. Just keep them here. Please.

But I braced myself for the day when it would happen.

35

Challenging Authority

1962

One afternoon in early autumn the year I entered ninth grade, Sister Maria Crucis turned to me as we were crossing the yard for Benediction. "Anastasia," she said, "were you in the study hall this afternoon?"

"No, Sister," I replied

"Are you sure?" she asked. Her nearly black eyes glared at me through her thick glasses. The tone of her voice was accusatory.

I responded in a deferential tone of voice. "Yes, Sister, I'm sure." She didn't let up. "Where exactly *were* you?"

"Down at the barn," I said, irked at this form of inquisition.

What I wanted to say was, "And you should know that I go down to the barn every afternoon to do my chores." But I didn't dare. I could tell she didn't believe me. Powerless, I swallowed hard, trying to bury the anger that was boiling up inside me.

As we arrived at the chapel, I knelt in my place and spent the half hour of Benediction fuming over her horridness. By the time we sat down for dinner, my rage had only increased.

How dare she mistrust me.

When it came time for dessert and we were allowed to speak, I laughed and chatted with the four other Little Sisters at my table but refused to make eye contact with Sister Maria Crucis. When she asked me a question, I answered without looking at her.

"Look at me when you speak," she snapped.

I did so, glaring straight through her thick eyeglasses into her black eyes and enunciated my words slowly to make a point. "Yes, Sister," I said, pausing between each word for emphasis.

Watch out, a little voice in my head said to me. *Ha*, I said back to that little voice.

And I went on chatting with my tablemates, exaggerating my effusiveness with them to make it evident that I wanted nothing to do with Sister Maria Crucis.

Later that evening, the five of us Little Sisters sat on the edge of Sister Maria Crucis's garden as she weeded and watered the small patch of miniature marigolds and pansies that surrounded her favorite statue of the Virgin Mary. While the others lent her a hand, I turned my back, pretending to be bird watching.

"Look," I exclaimed. "There's a rose-breasted grosbeak at the top of the walnut tree." Out of the corner of my eye, I caught a glimpse of Sister Maria Crucis as she dropped her trowel and squinted upward in the fading light. She could always be counted on to engage in bird watching.

"Oh, it's gone," I said. "Too bad you missed it." There had been no bird.

Before heading to bed that night, I lingered in the bathroom so I wouldn't have to say good night to her or accept the kiss she planted on my cheek before turning out the lights. I continued my strike the next morning at second breakfast and was beginning to enjoy the power I felt in being able to shut her out.

She brought this on herself for not trusting me.

Our silent battle raged for days until even I started to tire of the energy it took to stay at war.

How long would we keep up this state of conflict? Forever? One thing I did know: I would not apologize for something I hadn't done.

After nearly a week of standoff, as once again we were crossing the yard to go to Benediction, Sister Maria Crucis turned to me, her eyes filled with tears.

"What can I do?" she asked. "Will you never speak to me again? Is there nothing I can do to make up?"

With all the composure I could muster, I replied, "You didn't trust me, and you didn't believe me when I told you the truth."

"I am so sorry," she replied. "Will you ever forgive me?"

"Yes," I said, doing my best not to let a tear show in my own eye. And with that, the standoff was over. It was an awkward moment, one I'd never experienced before. Children didn't accuse Angels and Angels didn't apologize to the children. I was embarrassed.

On the surface, life seemed to go back to normal. But with that confrontation, I discovered that I, too, could be a force to be reckoned with. The power equation had shifted. It was no longer a one-way street—at least with Sister Maria Crucis.

36

The Attack

1963

On a sunny June morning, only the clicking of metal knives and forks on melamine plates as we ate our fried eggs and toast broke the obligatory silence at second breakfast. Ahead lay another ordinary day of tutoring. Two weeks remained before the start of our summer vacation, and my mind had turned to wondering what Sister Catherine had planned as this year's project.

"Holy Mother of God!" The exclamation shattered my reverie, and I turned to see Sister Marietta leaping up from her Angel's seat in the Little Brothers' refectory.

"Close the blinds. Quick!" she yelled. Instinctively, Angels leapt to their feet, and in a matter of seconds, all seven windows in our refectories were shut tight and the blinds drawn. The brief moment of pandemonium subsided as Sister Catherine entered the darkened refectory, grim-faced. Without stopping to speak, she headed directly out through the kitchen toward the front door. Several of the Big Brothers followed her, unsmiling and resolute. Included in the group was Brother Pascal, our lawyer. His presence meant it was serious.

Breakfast came to a halt as children and Angels sat nearly motion-less. I hardly had time to speculate who might be outside, when Sister Catherine reappeared. She gathered the Angels around her and huddled with them for a few moments. Then they went into action.

"Silence, everyone," came the whispered command. "Come now, quickly. Upstairs, upstairs."

As the Angels herded us out of the refectory, the sound of men yelling came from the side porch. Crouching low, we tiptoed up the stairs and found ourselves in a sitting room I'd never seen before. This was the Big Brothers' living quarters, off-bounds until this moment.

"Sit down," whispered Sister Teresa. "Keep your heads down— don't look out the window, and don't say a word." All thirty-nine of us sat silent and motionless, some on the couch, the rest on the floor, crowded together, knees bent, elbows tight to our bodies, so as to fit in the small space. Fear permeated the room, and I could almost hear thirty-nine hearts pounding in terror. No one dared move an inch or whisper a word.

I wondered where my parents were. And then the most pressing question, the one I always seemed to come back to in any situation.

Are they safe?

The Angels slipped silently in and out of the room but kept a sharp eye on our every move. Minute followed tortuous minute. With no plausible notion of what was going on downstairs, my mind raced with questions.

Whom were we hiding from? Was it the Communists—those demons who were going to bring the world to ruin as Sister Catherine told us day after day? Were we going to be martyred as she prophesied?

An hour went by, and we remained motionless. With my chin resting on my bent knees in the tense silence, I glanced around the room, relaxing my guard a bit. It occurred to me that this was the part of St. Therese's House where Brother James Aloysius had been living for the past five years. The room had an old-fashioned feel to it, with wallpaper and a brass floor lamp next to a homey-looking

The Little Brothers in 1963.

upholstered wing chair. I imagined that was where my father sat when he read his books. He was always in the library searching the shelves for something to read—something spiritual, of course. Those were the only books in our library. It was pleasing to observe the comfort of the room and to imagine him enjoying himself, much the way I remembered those evenings when we were still a family together—the seven of us.

My reverie was interrupted when one of the Angels tiptoed into the room and whispered that we could stand and stretch our legs. She escorted children on quick trips to the bathroom. I made sure to be among them, curious about what my father's bathroom looked like. Then the whispering began.

"Did you see anything?" someone asked.

"There were men outside," came a barely audible reply.

"I think I saw a gun," whispered one Little Brother.

It was close to noon when we were allowed to return to the refectory. There were no vestiges of the mysterious and frightening episode that had erupted a few hours earlier. The blinds were open and, miraculously, the breakfast dishes had been washed, the tables reset, and the sixteen-quart pot of soup was in its usual place on the serving table.

As we ate in silence, the door opened and Sister Catherine appeared. The tension that had been so evident in her body when she marched through during second breakfast was gone. She now wore her motherly look. Glancing around the room, she called out in a gentle voice the names of five Little Brothers.

"Louis, Maurice, Patrick, Magnus, and Brendan," she said. "Would you please come to my office?"

In a flash, I pieced the puzzle together. All five Little Brothers were Richard Cullinane's sons. Whatever happened that morning had to do with him. In the eighteen months since he'd left, we'd heard nothing more about him. And then this crisis. Sister Catherine led the five Little Brothers out of the refectory toward her office without speaking to the rest of us.

It wasn't until she made her usual appearance in our refectory during dinner that she shared with us some details on the morning's events. Richard Cullinane, whom she now referred to as RC, was suing to take the five Little Brothers away from the Center and their beloved mother, Sister Laura, she said. He had come that morning with a sheriff. Sister Catherine's voice became stronger. She rose up on her toes, her steely green eyes blazing, and proclaimed in a fearsome voice, "He is a traitor to Our Lady and her cause, and we will fight him with our prayers and in the court."

What was not shared was that, eighteen months prior, Richard Cullinane had entreated his wife to leave with him so that together they could once again be a family and raise their five boys. She had refused, and he had then taken legal recourse.

The Little Sisters in 1963. I am on the far left in the back row.

In the darkness of my cubicle that night, I replayed Sister Catherine's words in my head. RC was now the enemy.

Could this happen to Brother James Aloysius and Sister Elizabeth Ann?

The thought was terrifying.

37

Preparing for Battle

1963

We were now at war.

"That demon RC is trying to bring down the Center," Sister Catherine said. "We must prepare for battle. If we are to win, you must pray the Rosary and stand ready to die for Our Lady's cause to save souls." Her voice left no doubt in my mind that she was the general in this war.

The battle would be fought in the courtroom that fall. In the meantime, the court had awarded RC visitation privileges with his sons while he pursued his custody battle. Twice a week throughout the summer, the five Little Brothers were taken to meet their father and spend the afternoon with him. At dinnertime, after the five had returned, Sister Catherine would describe to us how RC had exposed his sons to the evils of the world. And in front of us all, she encouraged the five Little Brothers to make life miserable for their father. Her array of suggestions ran the gamut from throwing up in his car to refusing to go to the amusement park with him. Making him miserable, she suggested, might discourage him from wanting to see them.

On one occasion, when RC had tried to take his sons to see the movie *Tarzan,* Sister Catherine praised them for refusing to enter the cinema. "He is intent on destroying their souls," she exclaimed.

I recall wondering, *What is Tarzan about? Why is it so evil?*

Over the course of the summer, Sister Catherine and a small group of handpicked Big Brothers and Sisters spent innumerable hours with a cadre of lawyers to prepare for the court case, which was scheduled for the end of October. It was no surprise to me that Brother James Aloysius and Sister Elizabeth Ann were absent from that inner circle.

It was Sunday morning, a week before tutoring was to start, when Sister Catherine entered our refectories during second breakfast. Her demeanor was relaxed, and I took that as a good sign.

"Little Sisters and Brothers," she began, "we're going to have a community meeting this morning."

My heart skipped a beat. It had been so many months since our last family get-together. She went on. "Today you're going to learn from your parents all about your families out in the world, your grandparents and uncles and aunts and cousins. You may ask them whatever questions you'd like."

I could scarcely believe what I was hearing. *Find out all about my family out in the world?* It took but a moment for me to connect this complete dispensation of the prohibition against PL with the lawsuit. RC had alleged in his custody suit that the children knew virtually nothing about their families and some were even unaware of who their parents were. Sister Catherine needed to prove him wrong.

The questions spilled out as the seven of us Walshes huddled together in the front room. What were the names of our grandparents? Laura and Bill McKinley. I thought of the president by the same name—were we related? No. Where did they live? In Cambridge. Did Sister Elizabeth Ann ever speak to them? Not in a long time. Did she have any brothers and sisters? A much younger sister who had two children.

What was not divulged was that my aunt was twice divorced. Such information was considered scandalous. How many cousins did I have? The meeting came to an end leaving not enough time to have all my questions answered. But at least the Center could now craft a rebuttal to the claim that we children knew nothing about our families.

The court case was drawing near as I entered my sophomore year, at age fifteen. To my surprise, Sister Mary Clare, who normally was one of the cooks for the guests and who also played the organ, was now assigned to be our English tutor.

During the first week of tutoring, she introduced us to Shakespeare—*Julius Caesar, The Merchant of Venice, Macbeth*, and *Hamlet*. As she paced back and forth at the head of the classroom, her vibrant African American black eyes gleamed with energy. Holding the script at arm's length, she impersonated, with gesture and voice, each of the characters in the play, as though she were on stage. Her passion was intoxicating. In a matter of days, English became my favorite subject. I delighted in exploring the world of literature, a world that included Keats and Shelley, Wordsworth and Masefield, George Eliot and Mark Twain.

A few weeks later, when the authorities in the local school district came to observe us in the classroom, Sister Catherine introduced Sister Mary Clare as a "brilliant graduate of Radcliffe with her master's in education." At that moment, I understood the ploy. Sister Catherine had assigned Sister Mary Clare as one of our tutors to prove that our teachers were as good as the teachers out in the world.

That was a savvy move on her part—upgrading the credentials of the tutors—but Sister Catherine chose to keep one step back from truly capitalizing on the intellectual prowess of the adults within the community. Not a single one of the Big Brothers was allowed to be a tutor, despite their array of extraordinary credentials—physicists, mathematicians, writers, geologists, poets. She kept those brilliant men relegated to menial tasks, where they posed less of a threat to her power.

Our history tutoring room now had a newly installed corkboard wall that was crammed with newspaper clippings and articles from *Time* and *Life*, two magazines that Father had long told us were "of the devil." I devoured the information they shed on the Vietnam War, the civil rights movement, and President John Kennedy. And in our meager library, there were now copies of *Redbook*, *Seventeen*, and other periodicals that we were warned not so much as to touch. The wool was being pulled over the eyes of the authorities sent to judge us.

With less than ten days to go before our case went to trial, the atmosphere at the Center grew pensive. Sister Catherine encouraged us to pray day and night, and I did. Despite my fascination with the world beyond the Center, I prayed that we would win our case. The idea that five of the Little Brothers might be taken away was unfathomable.

Then came October 30. Tutoring was canceled as Sister Ann Mary, the principal of our school, and the other tutors were among the numerous members of the Center who had to appear in court in Worcester to testify on behalf of the Center and Sister Laura.

Only a few of the adults stayed behind. Among them were Brother James Aloysius and Sister Elizabeth Ann. He sat at the porter's desk, while she prepared dinner for the community in the kitchen. They spent much of the time talking to each other, an obvious violation of the rule, but they seemed not to care. Out of sight from a spying Angel, I asked Sister Elizabeth Ann if I might help her in the dessert kitchen, and she readily accepted.

Each morning for a week, the adults piled into our black cars and headed to the courthouse, and each evening they returned, somber and silent. The Center itself seemed enveloped in a shroud of anxiety.

And then on November 8, a grim-faced Sister Catherine walked into our refectories and made an announcement. The "evil" Judge Wahlstrom, as she referred to him, had awarded the five Little Brothers to their father, the demon RC. Sister Laura, their mother, was given monthly visitation rights.

We had lost our battle. Immediately, the Center appealed the decision to the Massachusetts Supreme Court on the basis of religious free speech. The fight for our survival, as Sister Catherine referred to it, would go on.

But that fight had consequences. In an attempt to disprove Richard Cullinane's description of life at the Center as abnormal, isolated, and hostile to visits from family members living out in the world, Sister Catherine was compelled to temper the most draconian rules. Almost immediately, families of Center adults, many of whom had been out of contact for fifteen years, were allowed to visit. Each time a new visitor arrived, I got my hopes up that it might be my family. But over and over again, I was disappointed.

38

A New Crisis

1963

It was several days after the shocking news of our loss in court when Sister Mary Dorothy vanished in the middle of the night. That was bad enough—one of the Big Sisters simply disappearing or "running away," but she was the mother of four of the children.

Would there be another lawsuit? I wondered.

But Sister Catherine, leaving no doubt that she was in command, announced that evening in our refectory that the children, together with their father, Brother Theodore, would have to leave the Center. She had no appetite for another custody battle on which a verdict had already been rendered.

Gasps and sobs broke the silence. Even some of the Angels were crying. Sister Catherine herself looked beaten, her normally broad shoulders hunched. But she mustered a smile as she looked lovingly at each of the four children about to depart.

"You will be in our hearts and prayers every day, and we will ask Our Lady to keep you safe from the evils of the world," she said.

Maud, one of the four children, sat at my table. Tears cascaded down her cheeks onto her blue jumper. For the past five years, she'd been my breakfast, lunch, and dinner companion, sitting in the same spot to my right. Despite Sister Catherine's rule against particular friendships, it was impossible not to have a special bond with her and the three other Little Sisters at my table. Being four years her senior, I had played the role of her defender on more than a few occasions when Sister Maria Crucis accused her unfairly of wrongdoing.

The next few days passed in anguish as we hovered around our soon-to-depart Little Sisters and Brothers. The Cullinane case had been awful, but those five Little Brothers were still with us while we appealed the judge's decision. Now suddenly, four members of our family, with whom we'd lived all our lives, would vanish. The questions came fast and furious to Sister Catherine.

How long would they be gone?

"I don't know."

Would they be able to come and visit?

"Of course," Sister Catherine told us, trying to sound reassuring. "Brother Theodore will bring them back for visits." That gave us a glimmer of hope, something to look forward to.

And then the day of their departure arrived. Brother Boniface sat in the driver's seat of the big black car. He was Brother Theodore's brother, and the uncle of the four children. Brother Theodore, his face somber, held the hands of his youngest two children, just eight and nine years old, who sobbed as they walked to the car. It was a scene I hadn't witnessed since we'd moved to Still River: one of the Center parents holding his own child's hand.

"Please don't make us go," they pleaded, one after another. The entire community gathered, silent and tearful, as Brother Theodore helped his children into the car. He walked over to Sister Catherine and kissed her. She dabbed her eyes with her white handkerchief. Then as the vehicle pulled out of the driveway, four little red-eyed faces peered through the back window and waved, and Sister Catherine waved her white handkerchief high above her head as a final farewell gesture.

It was a crushing moment in the life of the Center—as though the four children had been killed in an accident. In one day, thirty-nine children had become thirty-five. The empty chair where Maud had sat at my table was a daily reminder of the loss. We counted down the days to the first visit, then the next and the next. They were joyous occasions, those Saturday mornings when Brother Theodore brought the children up for a few hours. But the happiness was always followed by weeping as the car drove off in the afternoon.

Not more than a few months after the four children had left, Sister Catherine stood in our refectory. Her green eyes were cold, her lips a thin line that displayed anger. She came to the matter with direct force.

"Those four children have been corrupted by the evil ways of the world. After all they were given, after all the prayers that have been said on their behalf, they have betrayed Our Blessed Mother."

What could they have done? I held my breath as she continued. "They were seen window-shopping on the street in Brighton," she said.

As Sister Catherine continued her verbal barrage, I lost track of her words. At the age of fifteen, I hadn't the slightest notion what window-shopping was. *How do you shop a window?* But a new image was forming in my mind. I saw the four of them now dressed in worldly clothes doing worldly things.

I was jealous.

39

A New Crush

1963

I had a new obsession.

My crush on Brother Dominic had subsided after that summer of horseback riding lessons, but by the time I was fifteen, I succumbed to another one: Brother Basil.

Brother Basil ran the dairy farm, and it was he who presented me with my first cow, the ninety-pound, timid little creature on that Christmas morning when I was twelve years old. Despite the fact that we were not allowed to speak to the Big Brothers at any time, Brother Basil had permission to give me instructions on how to feed and care for my new prized possession.

Perhaps it was spawned in those moments of conversation, but my crush erupted seemingly out of nowhere. Brother Basil was good looking for sure—with blue eyes, an easy smile, and handsome, rugged features. Although he was twenty years older than I was, he was a decade younger than my father and so different. My father, gregarious and intellectual, seemed to me to be getting older, most likely because his once full head of black hair had now thinned around his temples and was laced with streaks of gray. Brother Basil, on the other hand, was the picture of youth and vitality. His sturdy build and his strong hands gave him a sense of invincibility. His full head of hair was without a strand of gray.

Brother Basil was married and had five children, a Little Brother and four Little Sisters, two of whom were among my favorite playmates. Long before dawn each morning, he headed to the barn to milk the cows. My cubicle on the south side of St. Ann's House provided a clear view of the barn and milk house.

As I rose and got dressed, I kept an eagle eye on the activities at the barn. The moment Brother Basil left the milk house and stepped into the pickup truck to head back up to the house, I timed my own departure from St. Ann's House so that our paths would cross as he emerged from his vehicle at St. Therese's House. He walked in silence and did nothing to acknowledge my presence, but that didn't dilute my pleasure.

My infatuation was guileless. While my insides would flutter every time I thought of Brother Basil, which was nearly every waking moment, I had not a clue as to the cause of my interest, much less any control over it. When our paths would cross, his unabashed, although silent, acknowledgment with a broad smile made my heart swell. I began to plot ways in which we could bump into each other at least once during the day.

The innocence of my crush was so honest that I had not an inkling of how such emotions might develop into something more. Kissing never crossed my mind, nor did the idea of holding hands. I wanted only to see him and be near him. I was propelled by a bundle of hormones that I could do nothing to stop, and about which I had been taught nothing.

One day, I received a message that Sister Catherine wanted to see me in her office. She came to the point in a hurry.

"Anastasia," she said, sitting upright and arching her back as her eyes narrowed, "you are to stay away from Brother Basil. Do you understand me?" I remained composed as I stood in silence, trying to fathom how she had figured out my interest.

"From now on, when you need to order hay or grain for your cows, you are to ask Sister Teresa. You are not to approach Brother Basil. Have I made myself clear?"

"Yes, Sister Catherine."

I was shattered. My cows had provided a legitimate excuse for contact with Brother Basil, and now Sister Catherine had snatched it away. But even her stern warning couldn't prevent me from doing my best to monitor his movements. I remained mindful of where he was at all times—on the tractor mowing the hayfields or calling the cows to be milked, in the chapel after dinner, or at the movies on Sunday nights.

One afternoon while I was working in the chicken coop, I saw Brother Basil walking slowly across the field with the slight lilt that he had in his step. The flutter in my heart propelled me into action. I calculated how fast I had to walk to cross his path and the precise route I would have to take to ensure that we met. I could almost guarantee that he would smile at me.

I started up from the chicken coop, doing my best to act as though I had nothing in mind, no purpose for my stroll. As I neared the rutted road, he was still a ways off, so I took a detour and came around the other side of the elderberry bushes at just the moment he arrived at the electric gate to the cow pasture. My heartbeat quickened. As he took the plastic handle and opened the single wire gate, he looked up. I smiled at him, and he smiled back at me and we walked on. I was elated.

The next day, I received a summons from Sister Catherine to meet her at the Little Sisters' cubicles at St. Ann's House. When I entered the corridor, standing alongside Sister Catherine was Sister Nancy, one of the Angels. Sister Catherine came to her point without hesitation, and her words were fiery.

"Just where were you going yesterday when you came up from the chicken coop?" she asked, her voice thunderous with accusation.

I could see what was unfolding and knew I had to play dumb.

"I was coming back up to the house," I replied in a quiet, subdued voice.

She shot back. "And why did you go around the bushes rather than come straight up?"

"It was the fastest way," I responded.

"Oh, really?" The sarcasm in her voice was chilling. "Let's go see for ourselves." She strode down the corridor, and I followed her. Flinging open the door, she stood on the balcony and glared at me with fury in her green eyes.

She thrust her arm out toward the field, pointing to the route I had taken, and said, "Tell me, honestly, do you really think it is shorter to go that way," pointing to the route I had taken, "than this way?" pointing to what she indicated to be a more direct route.

There wasn't much difference in the length of the two pathways, and I chose to challenge her.

"Yes, I think the way I went is about the same."

She looked as though she would strike me, and I waited for a blow. Instead, she thrust her hands behind her back and spoke—enraged.

"I know why you walked that way." Her voice was shaking. "You wanted to meet Brother Basil coming in from the field."

I maintained a steely composure on the outside. I wasn't going to back down, despite knowing I'd been caught. But inside, my heart sank, painfully aware that I was unable to escape Sister Catherine's spies. The entire "choir of Angels," all eight of them, was on a mission to watch my every move and report back to Sister Catherine.

I was trapped.

40

Hurtling Toward the Inevitable

1964

Mariam, the oldest child, graduated from high school in the spring, a celebratory moment in the life of the Center. Since the age of twelve, she had expressed her desire to live her life as a nun, the perfect illustration of the success Sister Catherine hoped to achieve among all thirty-nine children.

In so many ways, Mariam was the leader of the children, and she was set as an example of what each of us could achieve. For a year before her graduation from high school, under Sister Catherine's tutelage, she had been encouraged to spend time alone doing spiritual reading in preparation for becoming a nun.

Now this summer, Sister Catherine expanded the spiritual reading to include the next twelve oldest children, seven Little Sisters and five Little Brothers. It was a clear signal that we, too, were being groomed for postulancy, the first of three steps to becoming a professed nun. For one hour each day after lunch, I was expected to find a quiet place to read and to contemplate on my vocation as a bride of Christ.

I chose a secluded spot in the grove of white pines that bordered the hay fields where the alfalfa was high and ready to be cut. The site was ideal for an hour of solitude and reading, but I did neither of those. Instead, I spent the hour peering through the camouflage of pine needles and watching Brother Basil as he sat tall on the tractor and traversed the field, mowing the hay. When my hour of "meditation" had expired, I emerged from the pine grove, precisely as he neared me. We exchanged silent smiles and I basked in the warm feeling that crept through my whole body.

Throughout the summer that I turned sixteen, Sister Catherine spent endless hours exhorting the eight of us Little Sisters to seek joy in a life of prayer and penance, citing examples of the great mystics of the Catholic Church. Her words only heightened my sense of foreboding and the gnawing premonition that I was hurtling toward a day I had hoped would never arrive. I felt powerless to escape the encircling clutches of impending religious life. Dreams of the worldly life I so craved would soon be shattered. Gone, too, would be the childish fantasy I had harbored since I was twelve—that Prince Charles of England, who was exactly three months younger than I was, would somehow find out about me and ask me to marry him. Then I would become a queen one day.

Was I the only one of the children who didn't want to be a religious? I wondered.

Outside of the marathon of spiritual admonition, the summer was much like those of prior years, with farm work absorbing most of our waking hours. We held marathon sessions of canning in August, during which we converted hundreds of bushels of fruits and tomatoes into applesauce, pear sauce, tomato juice, and jams and jellies to carry us through the winter.

Shortly after the start of my junior year in high school, I received a summons to Father and Sister Catherine's office. I was unprepared for what was to take place. Father sat in his usual, nearly supine position in the low red leather armchair, his feet outstretched on the ottoman. He looked feeble, with a tremble in his hands, in sharp contrast to Sister Catherine, who sat ramrod straight on her chair, her head held high.

Father beckoned me to his side and I knelt on the floor, eye level with him. Taking my hands in his, he spoke, his voice tremulous. "Will you offer your entire life to God and be the bride of Christ?" he asked. "There's no greater gift in this world, darling, and you have been chosen by God for this purpose. You won't turn your back on Him, will you?"

Panic struck me. I was trapped. *What am I to say?*

In the silence, Father spoke again, this time raising his voice. "You will regret it all your life if you turn your back on God now. I can promise you that."

The frail man lying before me could still provoke fear. Now was not the time for questions. Now was the time to acquiesce, to accept my fate and say yes—particularly with Sister Catherine looking down on us from her throne.

And that's what I did. "Yes, Father," I answered and felt my heart sink. He responded with jubilation, squeezing my hands with a strength that belied his frailty. Sister Catherine observed the two of us with an air of both approbation and superiority.

"There is much you will need to learn," she said, as though rebuking me.

As I left the office, a pall of dread and anxiety enveloped me. I had just committed myself to God forever and must prepare myself for a life out of sight of the world.

For the next few weeks, Sister Catherine intensified her spiritual instructions to us, the impending postulants. It was during one of our sessions that Father burst into the room. Sister Catherine bristled, as though she resented his intrusion, but he ignored her.

"I want you to hear something," he said, his agitation evident in his quavering voice as he waved a small transistor radio in the air.

Turning first toward me, he put the radio up to my ear and held it there for about ten seconds. It was music for sure, but far from the classical chords to which I was accustomed. The sounds were cacophonous, and the men's voices were harsh.

"What do you think of it?" he asked. And without allowing me to answer, he proclaimed, "This is music of the devil. See what we're saving you from?"

Going to each of the other Little Sisters, he held the radio to their ears and withdrew it after a few seconds. "Have you ever heard anything so awful?" he asked.

"It's terrible," said Mariam. In unison, we agreed.

"They call themselves the Beatles," Father went on. "What a name! What group would name themselves after a bug? That's the diabolical world out there for you. Aren't you lucky to be here dedicating your lives to God for all eternity?"

His piercing black eyes seemed to be directed at me. It was as though he somehow knew that I wanted to be out in that "world of the devil." I averted his gaze and answered with the rest of the Little Sisters.

"Yes, Father." He left, and Sister Catherine resumed her instruction.

Once we became postulants, she explained, we would be segregated from the rest of the children and no longer allowed to mingle or play with them.

By October, the finishing touches were being put on a common room at the end of our corridor. The other prepostulant Little Sisters seemed excited, and I tried to play along, as the days creeped inexorably toward what felt like impending doom. Each evening after dinner, I retreated to the chapel, ostensibly to pray, but as I knelt with folded hands, my contemplation took the form of questions. Why had I been handed this fate? Why could I not get married and have children? Why was the world that I craved to explore about to be closed forever to me?

41

Veni, Sponsa Christi (Come, Spouse of Christ)

1964

The day of our postulancy was November 24. I was sixteen years old. During First Breakfast, the twelve of us—eight Little Sisters and four Little Brothers—knelt on the steps in front of the altar, and Father asked the same question of each of us.

"Do you freely give yourself to God?"

I answered, "I do."

It was a lie.

As the ceremony continued, the Big Sisters sang one of my favorite hymns, but one I had never wanted to have sung for me:

Veni sponsa Christi
(Come, spouse of Christ)
Accipe coronam quam Dominus
(Accept the crown which the Lord)
Tibi praeparavit in aeternum
(Has prepared for you for all eternity)

I would now be known as Sister Anastasia, MICM–a Slave of the Immaculate Heart of Mary. Numb with the burden of what that meant, I rose and returned to my seat. Sister Elizabeth Ann smiled at me, something she seldom did in the chapel. I thought I saw tears glistening in her eyes.

Was she happy for me? I couldn't tell. Or did she know that deep down inside I was miserable and fearful? I knelt down, locking my gaze on Mount Wachusett in the distance. I blinked hard to squelch my own tears.

The atmosphere at the Center that day was one of celebration. To mark the occasion of our postulancy, second breakfast was a feast with fried eggs, bacon, grapefruit, and coffee cake. Sister Catherine announced there would be a community meeting to celebrate the twelve new postulants. This was a much-appreciated surprise, because it had been months since our last one, and I wasn't sure there would ever be another.

As I sat with my family, Big Brothers and Big Sisters came by to congratulate me. I smiled and thanked them, doing my best to seem gracious. Inside I was crying. I wanted everyone to leave so that I could sit with my family. Soon the only family member I would be allowed to talk to would be Mary Catherine, who that morning had become Sister Mary Catherine.

Toward the end of the community meeting, as the crowd was thinning out, Sister Elizabeth Ann tugged on my sleeve, gently pulling me aside. In a quiet voice she said, "Darling, if this is not what you want, if you don't want to become a nun, you just let me know. I will support whatever you want to do in your life."

I was startled. Sister Elizabeth Ann had seemed so pleased for me during the ceremony and at the community meeting. Why this private advice and maternal support? Could it be that she understood the real me? The me who wanted marriage and children? How could she know?

I nodded my head in silence. This was not the time for what seemed to be a dangerous conversation. *What would Sister Catherine do if she found out?*

The bell clanged, signaling the end of the community meeting and the beginning of my new life as a nun.

Unable to sleep that night, I replayed Sister Elizabeth Ann's words in my mind again and again. "If this is not what you want, darling, I will support you in whatever you want to do."

A startling idea came to me. Was it possible that she didn't want to be a nun either? Did she, too, feel trapped? What about Brother James Aloysius?

Are we all in this boat together? I wondered.

I thought back to the days in Cambridge, long before we moved to Still River, when the seven of us Walshes lived as a family on the top floor of St. Francis Xavier's House, and life seemed blissful. How I wished for those days again.

42

A New Life

1964

"Will the postulants please meet me in my office after supper."
Although Sister Catherine spoke as usual from the doorway
between the Little Sisters' and Little Brothers' refectories, the tone of
her voice sent the clear message that she was no longer addressing
children.

Postulants—that word now defined us. It was as though we had
become members of a newly created club—different, better, older and
wiser than the rest of the Little Brothers and Sisters. I felt a fleeting
burst of superiority whenever Sister Catherine referred to us as "the
postulants." But it quickly dissipated.

In reality, the new life of postulancy was both humbling and
confining. Gone were the hours of sports and games on the broad
lawn behind St. Ann's House. Gone the thrill of toboggan rides, of
speeding down the endless expanse of gleaming snow, wind-made
tears turning into tiny icicles on my face.

As postulants, we were forbidden to run or yell or engage in
any spirited activity. No longer considered Little Sisters, we were

prohibited from speaking to the younger ones. But neither were we yet Big Sisters, which meant that they, too, were out of bounds. And as had been the case for years, any contact with the Brothers, both Big and Little, was forbidden. We now sat together at one table for meals, and we reported to a single Angel, Sister Colette, whose role it was to see to our personal needs. Our spiritual needs were in the hands of Sister Catherine.

I hated the isolation from the rest of the community, and I dreaded the next steps in the journey ahead that I was supposed to embrace but could not—becoming a nun for life and taking vows of poverty, chastity (not that I had a clue as to what *that* was), and obedience. I was certain that of the eight of us postulant Sisters, I was the only one who desired a life that seemed unattainable—one of marriage and elegant clothes and parties, a lifestyle that Sister Catherine said was sinful and dangerous to the well-being of our souls.

Day after day, I struggled to be accepted as a model postulant in the hopes of gaining favor with Sister Catherine, but without success. Sister Catherine found fault with nearly everything I did.

I'm different from everyone else at the Center. Sister Catherine knows that. Is that why she's so hard on me? Because she wants to change me? But she can't.

For several hours each week, Sister Catherine met with us in private, instructing us in the ways of a contemplative religious life. Sitting tall on the cane seat of the ladder-back Quaker chair in the front room, she addressed us as we sat on folding chairs in a semicircle around her.

"The love of God must be above all other loves" was one oft-used expression. On other occasions she exhorted us to "fall in love with God."

She exuded a passion that I was unable to resurrect in myself. Love for me meant something different. I loved Brother James Aloysius and Sister Elizabeth Ann with far more intensity than any feeling I could generate for God or Jesus or His Blessed Mother. The spiritual world played a far back seat to my secret adoration of my parents, my intense feeling of protection for my siblings, and my exploding obsession for Brother Basil.

The dream of being trapped under the ice that had disappeared for a year now returned every few nights. First the sense of panic, of drowning. Then the voice inside me that said, *Find the air between the water and the ice. You can do it.* With my head tipped back and my eyes closed, I would rise slowly to the top of the water, searching for the hardness that was the ice so that I could inhale the sliver of air beneath it. And as I gasped in the air, I awoke, drenched in sweat.

43

A Challenge

1964–1965

Thirteen months had elapsed since the Center had appealed Judge Wahlstrom's decision in the Cullinane case, and the Massachusetts Supreme Court was expected to rule within a few weeks. As the time drew near, the atmosphere at the Center became tense, and a pall hung over the usually exuberant Christmas atmosphere.

Finally on New Year's Eve, as we gathered for skits and entertainment in the front room, Sister Catherine and Father, somber faced, broke the news to us. The Supreme Court had reaffirmed the lower court's ruling to give custody of the five Little Brothers to their father, who would take them permanently to his home in Ohio. Sister Laura would have visitation rights.

As a community, we were devastated. Three years of legal battles, along with endless hours of prayer, had come to naught. To add to the Center's dismay, the Cullinane case had attracted national attention, with an article in the January 1, 1965, issue of *Time* magazine that Father shared with the community. The headline was "The Slaves of Leonard Feeney," and it described us as a sect, noting that St. Benedict's "was almost as hard to get into as to get out of." The article included as statements of fact that "Feeney decreed that the Slaves were to take vows of celibacy," "Feeney runs St. Benedict's like a monastery, indoctrinating the Slaves," and "he forbids the Slaves to attend Catholic services in Still River." Those were accurate statements.

The article, which I read many years later, confirmed what I had suspected—that the outside world thought of us as a cult.

* * *

The Cullinane case had thrown a public spotlight on the Center, exposing to the outside world the way of life that Father and Sister Catherine had engineered. No longer could we remain hidden behind a red fence or find protection in secrecy and silence, not even in remote Still River.

Our lifestyle, including the separation of children from their parents, the prohibition against contact with family members out in the world, and even the vows of chastity taken by married couples, became subject to public scrutiny.

The accusations by Richard Cullinane that our education was substandard now forced us to seek accreditation for our school in the State of Massachusetts. This became Sister Catherine's new mission.

When I aced my New York State Regents Exam, Sister Ann Mary congratulated me. In addition to the Regents exams, two of my classmates and I had been practicing for the upcoming SATs, and on a bright Saturday morning in early June, Sister Ann Mary drove the three of us juniors to Groton School, the prestigious boys' prep school in central Massachusetts. As we entered our assigned classroom, I beheld a sea of young men, each more handsome than the next. With long, tousled, dirty-blond hair falling over their eyes and smiles that showed off straight white teeth, they were hard to differentiate—tall, lanky frames with khaki trousers and open-collared shirts. They wore shoes with no socks on feet that shuffled. Slouched in their seats, their long legs stretched out beyond their desks, they had an air about them, as though the place was their domain. My insides went topsy-turvy.

There were girls, too, with lipstick and high heels and handbags and skirts that ended halfway up their thighs. I was shocked—shocked and fascinated.

As I took an aisle seat with my classmates at the back of the giant classroom, I realized that we, too, were being stared at, but for a different reason. Identically dressed in long, pleated navy dresses and white blouses with sleeves down to our wrists, black lace-up shoes, and a hairstyle that seemed more Tyrolean than American, it was evident that we created our own spectacle. I wanted to hide under the desk—to vanish. After a few glances our way, the gorgeous-looking boys ignored us. But I couldn't keep from staring at their broad shoulders from the back of the room.

Concentrate, I told myself. But it was no easy task. It would be a long time before I would forget those young men, milling about, jostling with each other, all-knowing in that foreign, evil world. And I wondered: *Could one of them, one day, be for me?*

44

The Spanish Invasion

1965

Brother Stanislaus served as master of ceremonies at the Center. Originally from Barcelona, or Catalonia as he liked to say, his heavy Spanish accent did nothing to inhibit his perpetual enthusiasm as he spoke his own brand of rapid, staccato English. He was unique among the Big Brothers, by dint of his enormous energy and magnetic personality. It was evident that both Father and Sister Catherine held him in great affection.

Before coming to the Center, Brother Stanislaus had been studying for his Ph.D. in geology at Harvard. Now in the community, it was his role to oversee the altar boys, as well as the rituals and rubrics for our religious services, a job he carried out with meticulous care and great pride.

It was an evening in September, shortly after I began my senior year of high school, when Sister Catherine entered our refectories with Brother Stanislaus at her side.

"Little Sisters and Brothers, Brother Stanislaus has arranged for the choir of the University of Valencia to come for a visit."

She stepped aside and let him provide the details. With his customary mixture of vivacity, gesticulation, heavy accent, and speed, he explained to us that his brother, Jesús, the conductor of the choir, had been invited to the United States with forty of the choir members to participate in the opening of Lincoln Center. But before going to New York, they were coming to stay with us for ten days, arriving in a week's time.

Brother Stanislaus elaborated with exuberance. "They will eat with us, sleep in the guest houses, and be part of the community. We want you to give them a good time, taking them down to the barns, going horseback riding with them, and showing them the animals."

College students from out in the world coming to stay with us? For ten days? It was unfathomable—only the most trusted Center friends were allowed to spend at most a single night in the guest house.

But my incredulity was put to rest when the young men and women, between the ages of eighteen and twenty, alighted from the Greyhound bus. The vision was surreal—an array of gorgeous girls, each a picture of fashion in bright colored blouses and skirts that ended well above their knees. The boys were handsome, every one of them, with khaki trousers and V-neck sweaters or vests. Speaking little English, but overflowing with enthusiasm and high spirits, the troop of Spanish singers turned life as we'd known it in Still River for the past eight years on its head. At all hours of the day, they would come barging through refectories, kitchens, or living rooms, babbling in Spanish or singing and laughing. The rule of silence went flying out the window. While Brother Stanislaus ostensibly organized our activities, in fact it was the Center children and the troop of young Spanish singers who really ran the show.

Sister Catherine seemed a mere bystander, putting no restrictions on any activities, not even for us postulants. For what seemed like an eternity of heaven on earth, she faded into the background, barely a presence in this adventure, and doing nothing to staunch the energetic exchange of high spiritedness among thirty Center teenagers and

The five Walsh children in 1965: (L to R) Peggy, me, David, Cathy, Ronnie.

forty attractive college students. Little Sisters were allowed to talk to the young men and Little Brothers to the young women.

Tutoring took a back seat to entertaining our merry band of singing guests. When we brought them to the chicken coop to demonstrate how to collect the eggs from the nests, the sudden arrival of exuberant strangers caused pandemonium as squawking chickens flew in all directions. Herding the students out of the henhouse, we took them to the barns, where we saddled up our horses and ponies and went on galloping treks through the fields. When they tired of riding, they turned their attention to our giant black Oldsmobiles, careening up and down the driveway from St. Therese's House to the milk barn, burning rubber and raising clouds of dust.

For years, Sister Catherine had warned us about the dangers of "particular friendships," but in this new, unrestrained atmosphere, friendships formed instantly between the young singers and ourselves. Inexplicably, neither Sister Catherine nor any of the Angels appeared to notice, much less reprimand us. When Sister Catherine departed as usual for her home in Waltham, the already relaxed environment became even more comfortable. The rules went into a state of suspension.

Several of the choir members were themselves boyfriend and girlfriend. They openly held hands and kissed, and I feared that the Angels might report such sightings to Sister Catherine. But nothing seemed to be out of bounds during the choir's ten-day stay.

I made one particular friend of my own, a beautiful dark-haired girl named Mercedes. She and I took long walks together through the fields, and I soaked up her every word (in her halting English) of her life in the university and the fiancé she planned to marry. I felt a twang of jealousy, imagining their future together in marital bliss, in contrast to the life I would lead.

And then there was Pacco, a short but ruggedly good-looking young man, who caught my eye the moment he stepped off the bus. His jet-black eyes and his dimpled boyish smile made my heart beat faster and my knees wobble. Each evening after dinner when we gathered in the living room to sing songs and talk in our limited Spanish and English, I tried to position myself next to him. I breathed the scent of his cologne, hoping it would cling to my blouse. Life as a postulant was in abeyance and I wished it could be that way forever.

The ten-day visit came to an end all too soon, and we exchanged addresses with our newfound friends, promising to write. Mercedes gave me a present of a miniature porcelain pitcher, which I still have more than fifty years later. Pacco gave me his address, and I noticed that he put a dash through his seven, a custom I instantly adopted. Then the forty young singers and their conductor boarded the Greyhound bus for the trip to New York and Lincoln Center.

Waving them off and promising to write, we sang a farewell song in Spanish, one they had taught us in four-part harmony. The music was punctuated with sobs. Even Sister Catherine seemed moved, waving her white handkerchief as the bus slowly headed down Route

Center children–1964.

110 on its way to New York City. As it disappeared into the distance, I was gripped with a sense of loss. The last ten days had seemed like a miracle, and now it was over. An ache as hard as a stone sat in my heart. Pacco was gone. So was Mercedes. Would I ever see them again?

* * *

One afternoon, with Mercedes on my mind, I opened the cabinet in our common room and retrieved a bottle of clear nail polish whose sole function was to patch up runs in our stockings. I, however, had a different motive for getting it. No one was around—I was safe. But to ensure privacy, I clasped the tiny bottle in my hand and retreated to my cubicle, closing the curtain behind me. There I applied a thin coat of the clear polish to each fingernail, feeling like a woman of the world. I stared at the sheen on my nails for a few moments and then headed to the sink to rinse off the incriminating evidence of vanity. Rubbing my hands together with a bar of soap under the running water, I saw with horror that the shiny coat remained on each finger. Panicking, I grabbed a scrub brush and an abrasive cleaner, but to no avail. A sickening feeling lurched inside me as I realized that somehow I was going to get caught.

Sure enough, during Latin class the very next morning, Sister Mary Laurence spied my fingers. I anticipated a summons to Sister Catherine's office, but none was forthcoming. When the day went by without any repercussion, I thanked the whole court of heaven.

A few days later, as we postulants gathered for Chapter Meeting, Sister Catherine spoke as I knelt in front of her.

"Dear Sister in the Immaculate Heart of Mary, you show no signs of embracing religious life. You are worldly in your behavior. You are not an exemplary postulant."

The tone in her voice was modulated, but I got the message. The spy network in action had tipped off Sister Catherine about the polish on my fingernails. I felt sick. There wasn't a harsher accusation at the Center than that of being worldly. It was a sentencing—Sister Catherine was announcing that I was a failure, unable to live up to the gold standard she had established for me. That set me apart from the rest of the postulants.

And I knew she was right. I was incapable of measuring up because deep inside me I abhorred the life that I was expected to embrace. No longer could I sublimate my dreams of life in the world. The experience of mingling for ten days with the Spanish choir had thrust me into a new world of desire, a lust for what I had been indoctrinated to believe was evil. I no longer cared. I wanted it—a life in the world and all that went with it.

45

Sentencing

1965

There was a knock on the wall outside my cubicle.

"Sister Catherine would like to see you in her office, dear," Sister Colette said softly. Nothing more.

What could I have done this time?

The usual nervousness grabbed my insides and instinctively I turned to prayer.

As I entered Sister Catherine's office, she greeted me with a pleasant, "Hello, dear, how are you?"

To my surprise, Sister Elizabeth Ann was present. *Why*, I thought. *What's gone wrong?*

Nothing prepared me for what was coming. Sister Catherine's words, cloaked in amiability, unwrapped a package filled with horror—her decision that I was unfit to remain as part of the community in my home and with my family.

For a few moments I was in utter shock, and as reality hit me, I was wracked by a jumble of emotions—the shame of being kicked out, the fear of being abandoned, the sadness at losing my family, and one more—the possibility that I now might be able to achieve the secret dreams of my childhood.

As I sought answers from Sister Catherine that would provide relief, I was brought back to a day not quite a year earlier, that fateful day I had taken the first step to becoming a nun.

The image of my mother came clearly into my mind as she had pulled me aside at the end of the reception that celebrated the first step in my lifelong commitment to Christ. Her words from that day remained indelibly in my mind.

"Darling," she had said in a voice not much above a whisper, "if this is not what you want, if you don't want to become a nun, you must let me know. I will support whatever you want to do in your life."

How had she, who was forbidden to speak to me for the past eight years, uncovered the secret I had buried so deep within me— my ardent wish to be a woman of the world, with a husband, and children, and a beautiful house, and elegant clothes?

Her presence at this meeting with Sister Catherine, though silent, felt comforting. She was with me in my time of need. Despite the fact that she had not raised me for nearly twelve years, my mother knew my heart. I could rely on her to keep her word as I faced this vale of tears, sundering me from my family but launching me into the world I so sought. I left Sister Catherine's office crushed and shamed— and with no idea what would become of me—but armed with the conviction that the person who most loved me in the world would do battle for me.

46

An Application for the Cause

1965

I now carried a painful secret inside me. Each day was one step closer to what amounted to an execution. The carefree public face I displayed as I went about out my daily life belied an all-consuming internal anguish.

Night after night in the privacy of my cubicle, my emotions spilled onto my pillow. A litany of unanswered questions repeated themselves in my mind. What had I done to deserve this punishment? What would the Big Brothers and Sisters think of me when I was "kicked out"? Bound to secrecy, I had no one to turn to. Exhausted by the fruitless search for answers, I eventually fell into a troubled sleep. Hours later when I awoke, the new day brought no respite. I craved distraction from my troubled thoughts.

That distraction presented itself one afternoon, about a week after my sentencing. Sister Ann Mary approached me when I was alone in study hall.

"Sister Anastasia," she said in her exceptionally well-dictioned and modulated voice, befitting her role as the principal of the school.

"We think, dear, that you should make application to some important colleges. It could help us in getting the school accredited."

That she spoke in the first-person plural was normal. There was no "I" in our community; there was no personal claim to anything, not even ideas. I was fully aware of what "we think" meant. Whatever was to follow, Sister Catherine had ordained it.

I interpreted Sister Ann Mary's words as an indication that I had been selected to help save the school. Acceptance at college would validate the Center's claims that our school was worthy of accreditation. The gravity of my assignment was not lost on me—I had to excel for the sake of the community. Despite the apprehension I felt over my own impending expulsion, I held no grudge against the members of my community, whom I considered family. This was a mission of love for them, for my home, and for my school.

I was also aware that this application process would have nothing to do with preparing me for facing life in the world after graduation. Even if I were accepted, Sister Catherine would never allow me to attend college. The words she and Father had used over and over again rang in my ears—colleges in America were "seats of evil, debasing virtue and corrupting the morals of young students." In fact, much of the justification for our isolation from the world was a rebellion against the liberal teachings in colleges across the country.

The colleges selected included one "Little Ivy" (Vassar), my father's alma mater (Bates), and one safety school (Framingham State Teachers College). I was secretly thrilled to read the letter of recommendation that came from Sister Mary Clare, my English tutor. I had never heard compliments like those she used, referring to me as "brilliant…a leader among the students…and endowed with good judgment."

For the reference letters that were required, Sister Catherine asked our neighbor, Lois Watt, who could always be counted on for support. She also conscripted her own daughter, Nancy, to write one for me. I wished I could have seen that letter, which I assumed Sister Catherine had dictated to her. I had last seen Nancy when I was six years old.

Throughout the fall, I heaved every ounce of my intellectual power into this project. My evenings were consumed with studying. Long into the night, after the rule called for lights out, I remained in the common room, studying Virgil's *Aeneid* and doing practice exams for the upcoming achievement tests in Latin and chemistry.

On the night before the exams, I woke with chills and a fever, and the next morning I hid my 103-degree fever from Sister Colette and set off with Sister Ann Mary and two of my senior classmates in a driving blizzard. An hour later, we skidded to a stop in front of Abbot Academy and joined a phalanx of teenage girls bundled up in colorful scarves, ski pants, boots, and bulky down jackets. The three of us, in long black coats, looked more nineteenth than twentieth century. But, unlike that day at Groton, today I didn't care what anyone thought of me. I was on a mission, sick or not.

Too ill to eat, I sat shivering in my coat as I pored over the multiple-choice questions on the chemistry test and fought back waves of nausea. When it came time for the Latin test in the afternoon, I ploughed through the grammar—it was child's play. Then came the long passage for translation. It was by Livy, an author I'd never read before. I'd been hoping that it might be Virgil, whom I could read as though it were English. *At least it wasn't Cicero*, I thought to myself. I despised his paragraph-long sentences. Glancing over the page, I started to relax.

It's all about war, I thought, harking back to Caesar and the Gallic Wars. *There's only so much you can write on this subject.*

I entered my Latin comfort zone, and the passage unfolded.

47

Interview

1966

Sister Ann Mary was beaming as she approached me in the study hall. "Sister Anastasia, dear," she started, her mellifluous voice a balm in the sea of turbulence that was my daily emotion. "The admissions office at Vassar would like to have an interview with you."

Vassar! I conjured up the image I'd imagined many times: a bucolic campus with stately brick mansions covered in ivy, amidst rolling hills. *Now I would get to see one of the Seven Sisters with my own eyes!*

Sister Ann Mary went on. "Sister Catherine has said that traveling to the campus in Poughkeepsie is too long a trip. So we've arranged for you to have your interview in Worcester, at the home of one of the alumnae. It's often done that way when applicants can't get to the college."

Foiled again.

For my interview in Worcester, I was provided with some "worldly" accessories to go with my modest garb. They were hardly fashion statements: cream-colored pumps with sensible heels, a matching beret-style hat, and white cotton gloves. Over my wrist, a pocketbook hung on a small chain; it was empty.

As Sister Ann Mary drove, she shared with me stories of her life before the Center, filling me in on details about her days at Radcliffe and how she'd followed in her father's footsteps by becoming a teacher. This sudden willingness to break the rule about PL (past life) caught me off guard until it dawned on me that this was Sister Ann Mary's way of preparing me to discuss worldly things during my interview. Her words gave me confidence that I was ready.

Arriving at the front door of a brownstone on a tree-lined street in Worcester, I waited as the door swung open to reveal two white-haired ladies, easily in their late seventies or early eighties. They led me into the living room, where we sat and conversed at a small table set out with a tea service.

What was my favorite subject?

"Latin," I responded. *Should I tell them that I had aced the national exam with a 753? No, that would be boasting.*

"Yes, such an important one, isn't it, and not taught nearly enough these days."

"What kind of music do you like?"

That was easy. "Mozart is my favorite. And I love Chopin, too."

It was going well as we sipped tea and ate vanilla cookies.

"And what do you think of the Beatles?"

My heart stopped, and I brought my cup down to the table as I tried to keep my hands from shaking. Grateful for that morning when Father had shared a few seconds of their "music of the devil," as he had called it, I smiled and replied in my most ladylike voice.

"It's not music that I very much enjoy."

"Nor do we," replied one of the ladies.

I exhaled in relief, certain I'd made a good impression.

After more social small talk, our tea was over. Thanking my hostesses, I returned to the car, and Sister Ann Mary and I drove home.

Over the next few weeks, the pressure of waiting to hear from Vassar was tortuous. Hundreds of times each day I thought, *What if I don't get in? I will have let the whole community down.* I dreaded the thought of failing the Center in its time of need.

48

Confrontation

1966

I was summoned to Sister Catherine's office. Before she could speak, Father, who was slouched in his giant red leather chair, yelled at me, "Are you leaving us?"

I panicked. *Sister Catherine has told him*, I thought. "Yes, Father," I replied in a quiet voice.

"You mean to tell me you don't have a vocation?" he asked, his outstretched hand trembling as he looked up at me.

I cringed to see the anger in his black eyes. Or was it anguish? I couldn't tell. I glanced at Sister Catherine in a mute appeal for help. She said nothing.

"No, Father," I said, not sure what else to say.

He paused, and his voice softened, becoming almost cajoling. "Are you sure, dear? Every one of you children was given to God as a tiny baby. You have a vocation. Trust me on that. I promise you. You have a vocation."

Then, his voice rising again, he repeated the words—emphasizing each one. "I tell you, you have a vocation."

I stood in silence, unable to craft a response that would mollify him.

"The world is wicked out there," he said ominously.

My hands were shaking, my throat dry. Still nearly supine in his chair, Father took my hand in his and said softly, "I will pray for your soul."

I looked at Sister Catherine, hoping she would step in and relieve the tension. She tilted her head and gave the half smile that made her look motherly, and then she spoke.

"Sister Anastasia, dear, I have some wonderful news for you. You were accepted into Vassar College. And Bates as well."

Before I could digest this momentous information, Father interrupted, his voice strident. "You're not going to Vassar, are you?"

"Oh, no," Sister Catherine responded before I could. "She applied just so that our wonderful school would receive the accreditation it deserves. And we are so proud of her for doing her part to save our school."

Father paid no attention. "Vassar is the seat of all evil," he said, hissing his words. "You will lose your immortal soul if you go there." He shook a trembling finger at me. "Promise me that you will not go to Vassar! Promise me, my darling." His voice trailed off.

"Yes, Father, I promise you," I said.

He reached out his hand, and I knelt down next to him. Placing his hands on my head, he gently made the sign of the cross on my forehead.

As I left the office, I felt shattered. My hard work for the Center had been successful—I'd been accepted at Vassar and at Bates. But my moment of glory, the triumph of winning the trophy for the Center, had been turned into a scene of anger. As I closed the door behind me, I struggled to hold back my tears.

49

Vassar, No Thank You

1966

"Sit down, dear," Sister Ann Mary spoke as she approached me with a letter in her hand. "I thought you might like to read the letter of acceptance you received from Vassar. I can't tell you how proud we all are of you."

She meant everything she said, and I loved her for it.

Reading the formally worded letter felt surreal. I took in the actual words: "A careful evaluation of your credentials leads us to believe that you…would contribute your own special qualities to the college community." It ended with, "We congratulate you on being a successful candidate at a time when competition for admission to Vassar is keen."

I felt a surge of pride. Only 450 girls in the whole country would be going to Vassar in September as freshmen. But my moment of joy was ephemeral as I remembered Sister Catherine's words to Father a few days earlier: "Oh, no, she is not going to Vassar."

The entire college application process—the testing, the interview, and my essay about why I so wanted to attend—had been part of Sister

Catherine's game plan to attain state accreditation of our school. I had been the ammunition in this battle and had completed my mission with success.

Although the prize lay in the palm of my hand, I was now to relinquish it. Sister Catherine would never allow me to go to Vassar—or any other college. One more duty remained; I must now write the already-crafted letter of refusal to both Vassar and Bates. With a sense of resignation and bitterness, and in my best penmanship, I wrote on the simple white stationery:

April 1966

Miss Jean L. Harry, Director of Admissions

Dear Miss Harry,

Thank you very much for accepting me at Vassar. Unfortunately, it is necessary that I attend school nearer to home this year, so I regret that I will not be attending Vassar College this fall.

Very gratefully yours,

Mary Patricia Walsh

Vassar was now in my past, but it was the Center's crown jewel in their application for accreditation. The school certainly now would be saved. How could it not receive its accreditation when one of its students was accepted at Vassar?

The Center's school had a future. I was the one without a future, without a plan, without the ability to capitalize on my accomplishment. The irony of that juxtaposition did not escape me. Nor, on the other hand, did it evoke a sense of outrage or betrayal. Perhaps that was one of the blessings that came from living within a community that was truly my family.

In due course, the much-coveted accreditation of the Center school was indeed issued by the State of Massachusetts.

50

Family Reunion

1966

Without the distraction of applying to Vassar and Bates, I now reverted to my prior state of anguish. Worry was my constant companion, gnawing at me more each day as graduation approached.

Despite Sister Catherine's promise that she would always love me and pray for me, and although I desperately wanted to believe her, I mistrusted her platitudes. I was sure that once I was gone, she would deride me to the rest of the community for failing to live up to the vocation I'd been called to by God. She'd done that with everyone else who'd left or been kicked out. Why would I be treated any differently?

I conjured up images of my family out in the world, particularly my mother's relatives, about whom I knew so little. It occurred to me to ask Sister Elizabeth Ann if I might visit them, now that I was leaving the Center. But I held back until one afternoon when she and I nearly collided in the small hallway off the kitchen. On impulse, I blurted out the question I'd been pondering for months.

"Sister Elizabeth Ann," I whispered, "do you think it would be possible for me to meet my grandparents?"

Her eyes lit up and her demeanor, normally reserved, switched into a take-charge mode. "Of course, dear," she said, in a low voice. "I'll call them right away."

Without a moment's hesitation, she walked to the porter's desk and picked up the telephone. I watched from the refectory as she began a conversation, which continued for about ten minutes. *She knows the number by heart*, I noted. When she hung up, she motioned for me to join her and spoke in a hushed tone.

"We've been invited to have lunch with your grandparents at their home tomorrow. Don't say a word to anyone about it."

I was elated but, at the same time, apprehensive. In bed that night, a torrent of questions kept me awake for hours.

Has Sister Elizabeth Ann told Sister Catherine what we're doing? What do my grandparents look like? How old are they? I hope they'll be happy to see us.

At eleven o'clock the next morning, Sister Elizabeth Ann (her traveling hat pinned on her head) and I headed out of the driveway for the forty-five-minute ride to Cambridge, the first time I could remember taking a trip alone with her. It was a unique opportunity to talk to her, uninhibited by the presence of any authority figures—to share my anxiety about leaving the Center, and to ask her questions about the outside world. But at seventeen, I didn't know how to confide in her. It had been Sister Maria Crucis, not she, who'd played the role of mother for the last eight years. I was tongue-tied, scarcely knowing how to engage her in casual conversation.

Sister Elizabeth Ann, on the other hand, seemed uncharacteristically excited, which helped to ease my nervousness as she told me about her family, both in Cambridge and in Maryland and Virginia, relatives whom she promised I would meet one day. I reveled in her happiness and managed to slip in a few questions.

"Do you think my grandparents will be happy to see us?" I asked.

"They are dying to see you, dahling," she replied.

"Do they live in the same house you grew up in?"

"The very same one."

That provided a bonus, the opportunity to see where my mother had once lived.

As we wended our way through Cambridge, I was astonished to realize how close my grandparents lived to our original home behind the red fence. My mother made a right turn from Broadway onto Ellery Street and stopped in front of a large three-family house with the number 54 on the door.

"Here we are," she said. "This is my home."

My home—I loved the sound of those words. But as we exited the car, a wave of embarrassment overcame me. My mother was wearing her nun's clothes, with her hair rolled up in a bun that looked like a half-moon and a tiny black hat pinned on her head. I was dressed in my postulant's attire.

What will my grandparents think of our clothes?

But my mother seemed unperturbed as she walked up the front steps, turned the brass knob, and opened the heavy brown door without ringing the doorbell, as though it really were her own place. The hallway had mullioned windows at each floor that let in warm sunlight with a pink tinge. In the air was the scent of cooking, a sign of family life behind the closed doors.

"Our apartment is on the third floor," she said. "Follow me."

Together we climbed the broad wooden stairs, Sister Elizabeth Ann leading the way with a brisk and almost impatient stride, while I followed, holding my breath with anxious anticipation. We reached the second-floor landing, then headed up to the third.

"Hello," Sister Elizabeth Ann called out as we neared the top step.

In an instant, the door flew open, as though my grandparents had been waiting for us with their ears pressed against the door. My spectacled grandfather, tall, broad chested, and bald, was dressed in a blue blazer, white shirt, and tie. He greeted my mother with outstretched arms, unable to speak, as tears streamed down his cheeks. She embraced him, and they hugged, the silence broken only by his sobs. My grandmother stood a bit behind him, dry-eyed but beaming. She was a tiny, white-haired woman, poised and upright, wearing an elegant pink suit and matching pink lipstick.

"Betsy," she said as they kissed. "It's so good to see you." I was taken aback at hearing my mother called Betsy. It seemed out of place, almost a mistake.

After that first emotional moment passed, my mother turned to introduce me. "And this is my oldest daughter."

"Mary Pat," said my grandmother, "you are some lovely young lady." I was flattered, but also caught off-guard. I hadn't been called Mary Pat since Father had changed my name to Anastasia when I was nearly five years old. It was strange to hear myself called by my real name. My grandmother's accent was Southern, and she said my name as though it were one word: "Marepat."

Holding my hand and leading me into the living room, she cooed, "Now dearie, you just call us Grandma and Grandpa."

My anxiety evaporated, and I started to relax. A broad bay window poured bright light into the comfortably furnished living room. "Mary Pat, what would you like to drink? Ginger ale?"

"Yes, please," I replied.

"Grandpa's putting lunch on the table. He's the cook in the family. We'll soon eat."

And what a feast it was. The circular dining room table was set with elegant china, real silver, linen napkins, and crystal glasses. In the center of the table was a platter heaped with seafood delicacies—shrimp, lobster, and oysters—none of which I'd ever had before, all of which were scrumptious. The second course was lobster bisque, served from a soup terrine that matched the china plates and soup bowls. The main course was roast beef with mashed potatoes, home-made gravy, and peas.

As we ate, my mother and grandmother kept up a torrent of conversation about the family—aunts and uncles, nephews, nieces, and cousins in Maryland and Virginia and in nearby towns in

Massachusetts. I found my relatives' names both foreign and fasci-nating—Bernice, Budgie, Charlotte, LaVerne. No one seemed to be named for a saint. Grandma asked about Jim, as she referred to my father, and about my siblings—how old they were and what we were studying in school. My brain was running out of room for all the information about my newfound family, but I didn't want it to stop. Through it all, Grandpa hardly spoke a word as he kept bringing his handkerchief to his eyes to stem the stream of tears.

It was like the parable of the Prodigal Son, I thought. Sister Elizabeth Ann hadn't spoken to them in years, yet they had prepared the most elaborate and elegant meal I'd ever had. She was back now, and the past didn't seem to matter.

After lunch, my mother showed me around the apartment. I was impressed with how big it was. "This was my first bedroom," she said, gesturing into a room with a delicate-flowered wallpaper and a light green bedspread. "I stayed here until my Aunt Bernice got married. Then I moved into her bedroom here," and she walked a few steps down the hallway. A baby doll lay on the bed and my mother explained. "That was my doll Sally, the only doll I ever cared for."

I reveled in this opportunity to uncover a small fragment of my mother's past. Here in her own home, she felt no obligation to abide by the rule forbidding any mention of the life she led before the Center.

As we came back into the kitchen, I started to help Grandpa with the dishes. "No dirty work for my granddaughter," he said.

I laughed. "Grandpa, I do the dishes all the time. Let me help. You wash, and I'll dry." And for the first time since our arrival, he stopped crying, and we chatted quietly in the kitchen.

When it came time to leave, we hugged and kissed, and Grandpa began to weep again. My mother, holding his hands in hers, said, "You must come up to visit in Still River so you can meet the rest of your grandchildren."

"We will come," they promised as we closed the door and headed down the stairs and back to Still River.

I was sworn to secrecy about the meeting that day. But I replayed the day's events over and over in my mind, reveling in all that had happened—my newfound family, my mother's immense joy at the reunion, the unforgettable meal, the image of my weeping grandfather and my beaming grandmother.

And all it took was asking Sister Elizabeth Ann if I could see them. Why couldn't it have happened so many years ago? I knew the answer all too well. This gift of a family reunion was the blessing that came with the curse of being kicked out of my home.

51

The Final Countdown

1966

Graduation was now only a couple of months away. With each passing day, I became more anxious. Keeping the secret inside me was like hiding a terminal illness. I felt cocooned, but without the anticipation of bursting into a brightly colored butterfly like the rest of the postulants as they became brides of Christ.

They knew nothing of my impending fate, as Sister Catherine had sworn me to secrecy. If the Angels knew, they showed no signs of it—not even Sister Colette, who oversaw us postulants. I avoided Father in an attempt to forestall any more unpleasantries. And while Brother James Aloysius and Sister Elizabeth Ann were fully apprised of the plan, I didn't know how to discuss it with them, much less confide in them. It had been a dozen years since they had exercised the parental roles of advisor, guardian, and mentor.

I spent mornings at my desk in tutoring, preparing for final exams in English, math, Latin, French, and Greek. And in the afternoons, I used my free time to work at the barn, always cheered when by chance, or more likely by careful plan on my part, I crossed paths with

Brother Basil. My crush on him had only grown, despite the enduring efforts of the Angels to monitor my every move and to thwart my efforts to be in his presence. What would he think when I was gone? I was sure he cared about me. It was excruciating to imagine a time when I would no longer see him.

Instead of meditating during the required silence at dinner, I counted down the days I had left with my family—the great extended family of the Center that I'd known and loved since my infancy. They were all I had, the only people I'd ever known in my life, the only people I'd ever loved or cared for.

Would the Big Brothers and Sisters hate me when they found out I was gone? I couldn't bear the thought. I couldn't bear to hurt them or let them down. Worst of all was the realization that I would be leaving my four siblings and my parents.

One evening during dinner, overcome by the impact of my impending fate, tears streamed down my cheeks, a silver veil of sorrow. I didn't try to stop them.

Mary Catherine, sitting next to me at the dinner table, looked alarmed. "What's wrong?" she whispered.

I shook my head and whispered back, "Nothing."

When she saw me crying the next day, she nudged me with her elbow, mouthing the words. "What's happened? Please tell me."

I kept silent for a while, but finally replied, "I'm not allowed to tell you anything."

"What do you mean?" she asked.

"Sister Catherine said I can't tell anyone."

But Mary Catherine, now sixteen and no longer the frightened Little Sister she'd been for so many years, took matters into her own hands. The next day, she cornered me down at the barn and said, "I went to Sister Catherine and asked her why you're always crying, and she told me that you'll be leaving when you graduate. She said you don't have a vocation."

She paused and then added, "I don't want you to go." She spoke as my younger sister, not as a postulant. She wanted me to be there for her as I had for so long. It broke my heart to realize I was abandoning her.

"I don't want to go, either," I said, swallowing hard so as not to cry. "But I have to."

"Will you be able to come back and visit?" she asked. I shrugged my shoulders to indicate I didn't know. That was a question I'd never dared ask Sister Catherine, too fearful of the answer.

The notion of abandoning Mary Catherine, my little sister, was unbearable. I thought about the many ways she'd depended on me to help her. We'd shared so many secrets. I knew her fears, her joys, the things she couldn't tell anyone else either because they wouldn't listen or because they couldn't understand. I'd eaten her meals for her when she couldn't. She hated the color yellow, so I had secretly swapped her yellow curtains for my pink ones. I had taped a piece of black construction paper to her window to block out the light of moon, which scared her. I was the one who'd taught her to read music when she wanted to play the trombone. I did her French homework because Sister Maria Crucis, the French tutor, was so strict that Mary Catherine could learn nothing in class. The constant worry about her caused me to lose my appetite, and as my final days approached, I was barely eating at all.

Although Mary Catherine had matured into a vocal and opinionated postulant, she was still frail. For several days each month, she was confined to bed, causing her to miss tutoring. On other mornings, she was allowed to sleep well past second breakfast. When I asked Sister Teresa what was wrong with her, she simply replied, "She needs her sleep."

But fifteen hours a day? I thought. I was afraid for her and felt immense guilt at leaving her. *To whom will she turn when I'm gone? What will she do without me?"*

My father as Brother James Aloysius, around the time of my graduation from high school. He was about forty-eight years old.

* * *

In early June, Sister Catherine called me into her office. To my surprise, Brother James Aloysius was there with her.

As always, he appeared cheerful. "How's my little princess?" he said, approaching me with open arms. We hugged each other, and I was thrilled at this small act of joint defiance in front of Sister Catherine. Pretending to take no notice, she quickly came to the point of the meeting.

"Sister Anastasia, your Aunt Eleanor and Uncle Dan, have agreed to let you stay with them at their house in Quincy for the summer."

I looked up at my father, and his broad smile revealed his own pleasure at the decision. I could hardly contain my excitement, but I didn't want to let on to Sister Catherine.

Sister Catherine as I knew her at the time she forced me to leave the Center.

I'd finally get to see what it was like to live with a family in their own home, to eat meals with them and do the things regular families do, I thought, my heart pounding.

A thought occurred to me. "And will Brother James Aloysius be able to come and visit me while I'm there?" I asked.

"Of course," Sister Catherine replied, "He can come once in a while."

Once in a while, she had said, but that was enough for me. Now he, too, could visit with his family. I was elated and tried to imagine what life at the Learys' home might be like.

Did they play games together? What kinds of meals did they have? What did their rooms look like? Would I be able to go to Mass every day?

Forgetting about what I was leaving behind for just a few moments, I actually looked forward to the summer.

* * *

As my last days of life at the Center loomed before me, the focus of my greatest unhappiness now centered on Brother Basil. The feeling I had had for him for the past several years felt like true love and had not subsided with time. I was wracked with the anguish of never seeing him again. Yet I still had no clue as to whether he knew of my feelings or of my impending disappearance.

My last night alone in my cubicle, I cried uncontrollably for all that I was leaving behind—my adored parents and siblings, my family of Big Brothers and Sisters, and Brother Basil, the love of my life. He might be out of my sight, but I promised myself he would never be out of my heart.

52

Graduation

1966

*D*ear God, please help me to get through this day. Jesus, Mary, and Joseph, St. Patrick, St. Anastasia, St. Monica, St. Helena, St. Elizabeth of Hungary, please pray for me, and help me. I promise to pay you back.

Invoking a litany of saints, on whom I had come to rely for all things spiritual and temporal, I was nearly oblivious to the ongoing Mass. I knelt in my place in the chapel, this room of solemn worship in which I had spent so many hours. It was both rustic and refined. The dark pews seemed one with the roughhewn ceiling beams and window frames, while the four elegantly crafted blond wood statues that stood on either side of the light oak altar were augmented by the embroidered tabernacle cover. I knew every inch of this space. It had been my religious home for eight and a half years.

Tears seeped out from my clenched eyelids, but I dared not wipe them with my sleeve, lest they betray my anguish. Composing myself, I stared at Mount Wachusett on the horizon and let the entire panoply of the last eight years of my life play through my mind. Would I never again enjoy the surroundings that I'd called home for so long?

Dear God, Jesus, Mary, and Joseph, St. Aloysius, St. Monica.... I began the litany again. Prayer and self-control, in a cycle of supplication and exhortation.

Only a few more hours, and then what?

During his First Breakfast sermon, Father made note of the upcoming graduation, specifically naming each of the five of us postulants, four Sisters and one Brother, who would be graduating later that morning. It was a day for celebration, he said.

But not for me.

Sister Catherine sat in her seat in the chapel, her expression composed, her posture erect. I thought I could detect an air of conquest in her demeanor. In just a few hours, she would have me where she wanted me—off the premises, kicked out.

I still couldn't fathom what I'd done to merit this ignominy. I'd tried my best to do what was expected of me. I'd never opened my soul to anyone about my deepest desires for a life that the Center excoriated. That had been my own secret.

I prayed for the strength to get through the graduation ceremonies without breaking down in tears. My head throbbed and my heart pounded as the entire community sang the "Te Deum" at the end of First Breakfast, the hymn of triumph and thanksgiving for special blessings. I mouthed the words, unable to bring up a note.

The Big Sisters had prepared a celebratory second breakfast in honor of the graduates, the kind usually reserved for holy days of obligation, with fried eggs, bacon, crumble coffee cake, and grapefruit. I sat at the table but couldn't eat; a weight lay in my stomach.

Graduation began promptly at eleven in the school auditorium, which the nearly eighty members of the community filled. With my fellow graduates, dressed in black cap and gown, I marched in slow and majestic form down the aisle while Sister Ann Mary played "Pomp and Circumstance."

Graduation from high school. An hour later, I was gone.

As I took my place in the front row next to my graduating classmates, I was astonished to see four of the Big Brothers seated alongside the stage in the place reserved for the graduation speaker. They weren't just any four Big Brothers; they were Brother Francis, Brother David, Brother Athanasius, and Brother James Aloysius, the original Boston College professors whose firing back in 1949 had been a catalyst for the creation of our community. Three of them had a child graduating that day. Brother James Aloysius, who had known for months of my impending departure, caught my eye and winked, which I instantly understood, as clearly as though he'd spoken the words aloud, meant, "How's my little princess?"

The graduation ceremony began, but my mind was elsewhere. I was now a little more than an hour away from being kicked out forever. If only Sister Catherine could have made it possible to say goodbye, to explain to the Big Brothers and Sisters that although I didn't want to be a nun, I would nevertheless always remain a dear friend and I would come and visit often. Then I could have hugged and kissed each and every one of the adults, whom I'd known since infancy. I could have promised them that I would make them proud of me. I could have assured them that I would hold fast to my Catholic faith. There would have been some scolders, but most of them would have been sweet to me—I was sure of it. I never doubted that they loved me the way I loved them. I would continue to love them even when I was gone.

But such a farewell was not part of Sister Catherine's plan. I was to be secreted away within an hour of graduation. No need to tempt the other Little Brothers and Sisters with the idea that life out in the world might be appealing. And what would happen when, over the next few days, it became apparent that I was no longer around? I envisioned the scene as, one by one, members of the community—adults and children alike—would find their way to Sister Catherine's office to ask about me.

What will she tell them?

I hoped she would be kind and simply say I didn't have a vocation. But I couldn't trust that would happen, as she had never answered that question when I asked her. I prayed that, regardless of what she told them, my Big Brothers and Sisters would still love me, as I loved them. I knew they would be disappointed in me. My "going out into the world" would be seen as a rejection of everything they had sacrificed and fought for.

And what would she say to Margaret Mary and Veronica, my little sisters, and my brother too? Would she tell them that they would never see me again? Would they miss me the way I would miss them? Again, questions I had been afraid to ask.

Each of the four professors spoke, but my mind was far away, and their words of wisdom eluded me. I was roused when my name was called, and I stepped up to receive my diploma. Then the entire community rose and sang several verses of "Gaudeamus Igitur" in Latin. I was now graduated.

The five of us slowly made our way out of the auditorium, walking past the applauding members of the community. Swallowing hard, I smiled at as many of the community as I could. For Brother Basil, I gave my biggest smile, which he returned. The weight in my heart felt like a crushing stone. But the memory of that smile would sustain me until I no longer pined for him.

The ceremony was over. Still in my postulant's garb, I rushed over to the chapel and slipped a note under the statue of Our Lady next to the altar. It read, "Dear Blessed Mother, please guide me and help me to remain a good Catholic."

53

What I Carried

1966

A prayer book.
A crucifix.
Rosary beads.
The *New Testament*.
A new, full-length pink silk nightgown.
New, pretty white lingerie.
Silk stockings.
A cardigan sweater.
And a tiny porcelain pitcher, the present from Mercedes in the Spanish choir.

In the solitude of my cubicle, I packed these items—the sum of my possessions—into a tiny suitcase.

I removed my postulant's habit and stepped into the pink dress that had been hidden behind my bathrobe on the wall at the end of my bed. I slipped the white pumps on my feet. My worldly attire felt more like a banishment outfit than an entrée into the world that had held so much appeal from afar. I sat on my bed, the familiar knot of anxiety gripping my throat, my heart, my stomach.

Presently, Sister Colette came by and knocked to let me know that the coast was clear—that meant no one was around, and I could leave without being seen. She stayed behind as I walked alone down the corridor and then exited the front door of St. Ann's House for the last time.

At the top of the walkway stood Brother James Aloysius and Sister Elizabeth Ann. There was no sign of either Sister Catherine or Father. I would leave with no kiss goodbye, no final word of encouragement from her, no blessing from him. It was as though they had already washed their hands of me.

They were leaving it to Brother James Aloysius and Sister Elizabeth Ann, the parents they had stolen from me, to carry out Sister Catherine's plan and to secret me away without the community finding out.

Sister Elizabeth Ann embraced me. "You'll have a lovely summer with your cousins," she said. "And Brother James Aloysius will come down to visit you on Sundays." That was welcome news, but would I see my siblings again? I was afraid to ask.

She turned to Brother James Aloysius. "Give my love to Eleanor and Dan," she said.

As I hugged Sister Elizabeth Ann, I glanced up at Sister Catherine's office window to see whether she was watching us—observing this final embrace, in violation of the rules. If she was there, I couldn't see her.

Brother James Aloysius opened the car door for me, and I got in. As he settled into the driver's seat, he took my hand and said in his reassuring way, "My little princess, everything will be fine. I promise you. The Learys are expecting us for lunch."

We pulled out of the driveway. I turned and waved to Sister Elizabeth Ann. I was now officially kicked out of the Center—my home. There was no invitation to come back.

PART 4

Uncloistered

54

The Summer of '66

1966

The leitmotif of family life was foreign to me. I was the intruder in an alien world, with no grasp of how to fit in. I was jolted into the reality of my new life when my uncle and aunt greeted me as "Mary Pat," a name I hadn't used since I was five years old.

Each morning, while my cousins donned shorts and miniskirts and headed to their summer jobs or to play tennis, I slipped into my painfully unfashionable calf-length, pleated, pink cotton dress, belted at the waist and buttoned to the neck, and made my way to St. John's Church to attend Mass. There, as I knelt in a pew that was neither prominently in the front nor hidden at the rear of the church, I was taken aback to hear the words of the Latin Mass (words I knew by heart) spoken in the vernacular, a result of the Second Vatican Council—an event the Center had decried for its abandonment of the true faith.

But I found it hard to be scandalized by the prayers spoken in English. For sure, I thought, not everyone knew Latin as I did, and the words had to mean so much more when people could understand them. Hardly gone a week from the Center, I found myself challenging their doctrinaire view of the Latin Mass.

Kneeling among the sparsely populated congregation that consisted mostly of ancient-looking ladies with lace doilies on their heads (in lieu of proper veils), I might have appeared to them like a serious young woman spending her last summer in the carefree world before heading into the convent, rather than the failed postulant I was who'd just been kicked out of the convent.

My oldest cousin, Paul, was heading off to college in the fall. He had security in his life. I, on the other hand, was adrift. His road to the future was paved, while I was caught in a jungle without a clue as to how to navigate my way through it. Having been forced by Sister Catherine to turn down my acceptance at Bates College and Vassar, I had no open door to lead me on the path of life.

I found my aunt and uncle's house, while far from fancy, to be a treasure trove of insights into the real world. This world that I was entering felt luxurious in comparison to the paucity of personal amenities at the Center, but no more so than when I retreated into the privacy of my cousin Barb's bathroom, where I encountered a bottle of rose-scented bubble bath that sat at the side of the tub. I opened it and took long draughts of breath, wondering whether it was something very special and expensive.

Then, one evening, I sprinkled a little into the water as the tub was filling up. The small bathroom became suffused in the heavenly scent of roses as the tiny pinkish bubbles plumed like bursting clouds on the top of the deepening water. Stepping in, I lay back and basked in blissful silence, and as the bubbles evaporated on my body, I felt like a lady of leisure, the princess I'd imagined myself to be for so many years, even while a postulant. The fragrance clung to me and became a symbol of my emerging freedom.

Days later, at the drugstore a short distance from the house, armed with the few dollars I'd been given as I left the Center, I would gravitate to the beauty products—Jean Naté cologne, Yardley soap bars, Revlon lipsticks—settling on a small bottle of rose-scented cologne. That purchase, the first I'd ever made in my life, kept me in the presence of something that felt worldly, sophisticated, elegant.

That summer the Beatles were all the rage, and my cousins played their records endlessly. The cacophony of sound was at first beyond what I could appreciate—my understanding of music was deep but narrow. I could parse a piano concerto, solfege a song, and sight-read a sonata, but the breadth of my musical knowledge started with Gregorian chant and ended somewhere around Chopin, with a fragment of Bernstein, whom Father seemed to adore, despite the fact that he was a Jew. Even big band and jazz were verboten at the Center. But as the weeks wore on that summer, I came to enjoy and fully memorize "Eleanor Rigby" and "Yellow Submarine," the summer's hot numbers, despite thinking that the lyrics were inane.

In the evenings, I watched *The Lawrence Welk Show* and *The Red Skelton Hour* with my uncle and aunt, and while I soaked up the world of polka dancers and corny jokes, it wasn't lost on me that my teenage cousins always left the house just as the shows were about to start. Was it the desultory fare they were avoiding, or were they also bolting so they wouldn't have to explain me to their friends?

As to Sister Catherine's dire warnings that television would cause me to lose my soul, I was mystified. I couldn't find the sin, the evil, or the blasphemy in it.

On afternoons when my aunt went out grocery shopping with the two youngest boys, I found books that opened my eyes to the real world. Dr. Benjamin Spock's *Baby and Child Care*, in its paperback version, the pages worn from an abundance of use, was a veritable tutorial on the matter of procreation, a subject so closeted at the Center that biology was proscribed as a course in high school. Alone in the house, I pored over the book, and returned it to its place on the shelf before anyone returned. Within a couple of weeks, I had learned "the facts of life."

At 11:30 at night, the local radio station brought its broadcast to a close with the theme song from the recently released movie, *Doctor Zhivago*. The music was so hauntingly beautiful, so full of romance, it brought tears to my eyes each time it was played, even though I had no notion of the story behind it. A trip to the movies was a venture I was reluctant to take on, lest the word get back to my parents and then to Sister Catherine, who would undoubtedly condemn me to the whole community and ensure that I never saw my siblings again.

My curiosity in the sphere of movies was further piqued when my cousin announced that he and his buddies were going to see the season's newest movie, *Georgy Girl*, deemed by some reviewers to be risqué. Although my uncle claimed to be shocked at their lack of judgment, he did nothing to prevent them from going, and I found myself fantasizing about what might make the movie so scandalous. Before long, I had memorized the popular theme song with its catchy opening line ("Hey there, Georgy Girl…."), but I wasn't yet ready to take that giant step into the forbidden land of wicked movies.

When my father came down for his weekly visit on Sunday, I saw a man more worldly than the cassocked Big Brother of Still River. Clad now in a black suit and crisp white shirt, his required attire when traveling, he'd settle down on the sofa in his sister's living room with a copy of the *Boston Globe*, devouring news on the Red Sox and tennis. He'd chat about things secular—from world affairs to a vast array of cousins. Most particularly, he and Eleanor would reminisce about old times, and I noticed with pleasure how he happily discussed his past life. He was the life of the party at the dinner table, and when he left to return to Still River, I would wonder if he might not prefer the life I was leading to his own.

The weeks passed, and as they did, I found myself a little less lost, a tiny bit more comfortable in putting my foot on the first stepping-stones toward assimilation into the world. Yet I remained haunted by an endless anxiety—what was next for me? What would I do after the summer?

My no-nonsense, commonsense aunt seemed flummoxed—how could I have turned down Bates, my father's alma mater? I had no good response. I wasn't ready to turn on my upbringing, although I could tell that she, a devout Catholic, disapproved of the whole way of life at the Center.

When I suggested that I might go to secretarial school, she guffawed, as though I was too smart for such a career, and I knew deep down she was right. But I was trapped, powerless to make decisions on my own behalf. I had no money, no experience, no knowledge, no mentor, and thus no key to my own future.

* * *

As the summer neared an end, my mother arrived to take me on a vacation, visiting her family in Maryland. Together we headed on the long road trip, first visiting the sights in Washington, D.C., and then on to the countryside of St. Mary's County along the Chesapeake Bay, where we celebrated my eighteenth birthday with my mother's many aunts, uncles, and cousins.

Staying at my great aunt and uncle's house, I felt even more pampered. Uncle Bill and Aunt Laverne had a cook who seemed ever present and a gardener who tended to the orchards that produced the fruits my great uncle turned into wine—peach and cherry, pear and plum—his hobby. During the day, he ran the local bank while she engaged in civic endeavors; together, they were part of the social scene of Leonardtown, a place that seemed fancy and upscale to me.

One morning, when I found myself alone at the house, I put on a pair of white trousers, a piece of clothing I was only starting to get used to wearing. Topping it off with a modest, white cotton eyelet, short-sleeved blouse, I wandered through the orchard and found the gardener, dressed in loose-fitting overalls, the sweat dripping down the side of his cheek and falling onto the deep grass in tiny droplets off his chin as he pruned the fruit trees. The August heat was searing, and he occasionally took a swig of water from a thermos bottle. I sat on a bench and chatted with him. A soft-spoken black man, he told me he had worked on the property for decades, and we discussed issues of farming—insects, harvesting, yield—subjects I knew plenty about but learned more about from him. His manner, though deferential, put me at ease. For those few minutes, I was able to share common experiences in an unpressured environment, a relief from the constant feeling of being hopelessly at a loss for what to say or do next.

I returned to the house, where the cook was eating at the small square breakfast table that sat in a corner of the kitchen.

"Would you like lunch?" she asked me.

"A sandwich would be lovely," I replied, and she set out to make me one.

I took it, thanked her, and sat down across from her at the table, engaging her in conversation as I nibbled away. Like the gardener, she responded, but in a subdued and almost timid way.

When a few minutes later my mother and her aunt walked into the house, I could tell in an instant, from the look on my aunt's face, that something was wrong.

Sheepishly I left the kitchen to discover the source of her ire.

"Don't you know you never eat with the help?" she hissed at me. I looked at my mother for her reaction, but she remained silent.

I was stunned. *What kind of a rule was that?* The "help," as she referred to her cook and butler, were off-limits for conversation? *Why?*

It was increasingly evident to me that the world was far more complex than I had anticipated. I was but a neophyte, struggling to learn the rules—rules that in this case seemed both incomprehensible and vile.

I sensed, too, that my mother wanted nothing to upset her rediscovered bond with her family. They seemed to adore her; she wanted to keep it that way. Whatever they said was fine.

I felt alone, uncertain, anxious.

55

The Gift of Christmas

1966

Christmas was only days away.

A full six months had elapsed since my expulsion from the Center. That banishment had come with an unstated stipulation—I was not to be seen or heard within the community. As far as I knew, that meant forever.

Four months earlier, as August was coming to an end and my mother and I were making our way north from our family visit in Maryland, I had felt increasingly rudderless, having not a clue as to what I would do when we returned. In a moment of panic, I had applied to a secretarial school in Boston, an option Sister Catherine sanctioned.

That long ride back to New England with my mother might have provided the opportunity to seek advice from her, but after a childhood in which she had never played the role of parent or advisor, I was uncomfortable confiding in her. She and my father were still entwined in the life of the Center—it was their home. I was now on the outside, and they could do nothing to change that.

So it came as a shock when my mother broke the news to me at the end of our long ride north.

"Dahling," she said, "Sister Catherine has said that you may stay at St. Joseph's House while you attend secretarial school this fall. And then when you finish the course, you can take up residence at the YWCA in Boston."

St. Joseph's House was a recently purchased guesthouse on the Center's property, but far enough from the hub of activity to be out of sight.

She went on. "Brother James Aloysius will drive you to the bus stop in Ayer in the morning and pick you up at night, and I'll have dinner with you in the evening."

It would be years before I came to appreciate the irony of this new arrangement. Sister Catherine, having failed in her mission to mold me into a bride of Christ, rid herself of me by handing me back to my parents after more than a decade of enforced separation from them.

* * *

In the darkness before dawn each morning, my father drove me to the Greyhound station where I took the hour-long bus ride into Boston to attend secretarial school. Riding in the car with him and engaging in small talk as we made the fifteen-minute journey was a novel experience. "Do you have your gloves?" he would say if the weather was frigid. I adored him, but I wasn't used to his playing the role of father and felt at a loss for how to respond in an intimate way, unfamiliar as I was with the natural role of father to daughter. But I would always give him a kiss as I bolted out of the car.

In the evening when I stepped off the bus, he would bring me back to the seclusion of St. Joseph's House, often accompanying me inside so he could have a brief conversation with my mother, in what seemed like a husband-and-wife kind of way. It pleased me to see them together talking softly. Then he'd depart, and Sister Elizabeth Ann and I would eat in the dining room that she had set up in an elegant fashion. For the first few weeks, our conversation at dinner was reserved, almost formal. I was afraid of scandalizing her with a question or a comment.

After dinner, in the privacy of my locked bedroom, as I did my homework, I turned on the transistor radio I'd bought during the summer, using earphones to keep my secret secure. I'd tune in to WBZ and listen to Bob Kennedy's hour-long show *Contact*, which featured politicians, authors, and celebrities of all kinds, as well as discussions about controversial topics like the death penalty, Vietnam, and abortion.

The show inspired me to read Eldridge Cleaver's *Soul on Ice*, as well as Richard Wright's *Native Son*, books I was well aware would be anathema at the Center. So I kept them hidden under the mattress. My knowledge base was expanding—from the Beatles' "Eleanor Rigby" during the summer to radical politics—and only a stone's throw from Sister Catherine's office. It was empowering, even if I had no one with whom I could exchange ideas or ask questions.

Now Christmas was upon us, and with it came a sense of dread. I could remember something special, something that spoke of joy, about each Christmas for the eight years we'd been in Still River. But this year I would be excluded from the festivities within the community because I was no longer considered a member of the family.

I wanted desperately to be part of the celebrations, but there was only one person who could make that happen, and I had no intention of asking her. Sister Catherine had done nothing to reach out to me since I left—not a letter or even a message through my mother. I was dead to her.

I kept my sadness to myself, not willing to share it even with Sister Elizabeth Ann. There was nothing served by upsetting her, and the last thing I wanted was for her to get into a fight with Sister Catherine as she argued on my behalf. But when my mother arrived at St. Joseph's House one evening carrying a small Christmas tree and an array of ornaments, I was grateful, convinced she sensed my loneliness on this first Christmas as an outcast. Together we decorated the tree, making small talk—she shared her favorite Christmas memories, and after we topped our miniature tree with a porcelain angel, we turned to making Christmas cookies.

"I plan to attend Midnight Mass on Christmas Eve," I said. "I just won't sit in this house alone. I don't care what Sister Catherine thinks."

My mother's response was better than I imagined. "You do that, darling. I'll support you."

There was an inner excitement in my decision—this was my first opportunity to get a peek at the family I'd been missing for the last six months. They'd all be there, crowded into the chapel, no one but Center members because the Mass was not open to the public.

I picked my outfit carefully—a suitably long dark-grey herringbone wool dress and a black square of lace that served as a veil. There was no worldliness in my attire. Over it all, I wore a floor-length black wool coat. I could barely be distinguished from the Big Sisters in their habits. I lingered outside the chapel until the organ blared jubilantly, and Father, preceded by his entourage, solemnly exited the sacristy, walking slowly down the aisle toward the altar.

As the community began to sing the most glorious of Christmas Gregorian chants, "Christe Redemptor Omnium," I slipped furtively into the chapel, selecting my place in the farthest-back seat of the Big Sisters' pew. I was hardly detectable; on the other hand, I had a wide-angle view of everyone.

During the Mass, I scanned the chapel scene from my vantage point, taking note of each of my siblings. Surreptitiously, I checked out Brother Basil, whom I still missed immeasurably. Did he miss me? I wondered.

I stared long and hard at Sister Catherine's profile as she sat regally in her place of prominence in front of the altar, with an air of hauteur, much like a portrait of Marie Antoinette. Her attention was fixed, as though in a trance.

She doesn't even know I'm here.

A surge of adrenaline came over me as I silently gloated on my defiance. This was *my* decision to be here on out-of-bounds territory. I was coming to attend Midnight Mass, and she couldn't stop me. She wouldn't dare.

However, when it came time to join the community in the line to receive Communion, I found myself gripped by that all-too-familiar sense of panic, one I had experienced so many times over the past decade.

Should I slip out and return to St. Joseph's House without taking Communion? The line was forming—I had to decide.

What if Father refuses to serve me Communion? The ignominy of that scene would be unbearable. *What will Sister Catherine do when she sees me?*

I resorted to prayer: *Jesus, Mary, and Joseph, I need your help.*

The line was moving forward, and I was in it. There was no turning back now. A clammy dampness spread across my hands, my neck, and my cheeks, and my knees shook like castanets as I neared the altar. Then I knelt down and waited for my turn to receive Communion.

Don't let Father skip over me, please, I prayed silently as he slowly made his way toward me.

I crossed my hands on my chest, feeling the pounding of my heart inside. Then Father laid the host on my tongue. Before I could stand up, I felt his hand on my head, a soft, silent blessing that seemed to say, "God loves you." My tension evaporated, replaced by an aura of calm. I had come to God, and He had not rejected me.

I rose and walked in procession past Sister Catherine and the long pew of Big Sisters, past the spot where I'd been sitting, out of the chapel and into the wintry December air.

In the midnight darkness, I made my way to St. Joseph's House, feeling triumphant. I had conquered my fear. No one would intimidate me again.

And ten hours later, when Father celebrated the Christmas morning mass, I was there in the chapel again, this time unafraid, uncowed, emboldened.

Returning to St. Joseph's House for Christmas breakfast, I was astounded to see half a dozen beautifully wrapped and ribboned presents under the tree. "They're for you," my mother said as we sat down to a feast she had prepared.

For me? I thought. *Sister Elizabeth Ann got these for me?*

Weeks earlier, I had tried to stop thinking about the fact that I wouldn't get any Christmas presents. Since that first Christmas in Still River when Baby Jesus (whom I never believed in) brought us stockings full of gifts, I had reveled in opening presents—the mere act of untying ribbons and unwrapping paper never ceased to fill me with pleasure.

After breakfast, I opened my gifts with Sister Elizabeth Ann—a pink sweater set, blouses, chocolate turtles with a note of Merry Christmas from my grandparents, and a small box in which there was a gold ring set with three small pearls.

As I slipped it on my finger, my mother said, "That belonged to your great-grandmother, dahling. I thought you'd like it."

"Thank you so much," I replied, in a daze over this unexpected treat.

Sister Elizabeth Ann then headed to the Community meeting and I remained behind, uninvited to share in the Christmas celebrations. I pondered my loneliness, my isolation and then…

Do it, my inner self told me, and I did.

Putting on my long, black, heavy wool coat, with gold buttons in a double-breasted fashion down the front, I opened the front door and made my way briskly down the walkway, across the road to St. Therese's House, through the porter's room, the guest dining room, and the library, and into the noisy front room. Every member of the community was there. Big Brothers and Sisters floated among the families that sat in clusters surrounded by toboggans, coasters, ice skates, and other presents that spilled beyond the branches of a broad, elegantly decorated, balsam fir Christmas tree, topped by an angel ornament that reached to the ceiling. My family was in its usual spot next to the fireplace, and I joined them with a sense of self-assuredness, well aware that my presence would soon be evident to the rest of the community.

From the corner of my eye, I could see the form of Sister Catherine, standing tall near the Christmas tree, her inner circle, her "courtiers," by her side. I was unfazed. She had lost her power over me.

For the next hour, I engaged with my family as though I were once again part of the community, querying my siblings on what they got in their stockings and showing them the new ring on my finger. When the telltale bell rang to signal the end of the community meeting, Sister Catherine stood outside her office door, wishing all a Merry Christmas. I strode past her, ignoring her, while flaunting my presence with my family by laughing and kissing them goodbye in front of her.

That Christmas was to bring me one more present. As I sat down to have dinner with Sister Elizabeth Ann—a meal as elegant as what the rest of the community was having—the front door opened and in walked Brother James Aloysius. My initial instinct was panic.

He's going to get into trouble, I thought. But the confidence with which he gave each of us a kiss and a "Merry Christmas" greeting calmed my nerves. He joined us for dinner, and as we ate and chatted, I reveled in our family togetherness.

But still there was something missing.

Maybe one day all seven of us will be able to have dinner together.

56

Roots and Wings

1967

The secretarial course at the Hickox School seemed like child's play compared to the classes I had taken in high school and I sped through the ten-month routine by February, a record time according to the stout headmistress. But graduation was not until May, and as if to solve the problem of what I would do for the next three months, she asked me if I would stay on and teach. I didn't know how to respond—I had never been offered a job before. Almost without thinking, as though I were responding to an order I was expected to follow, I accepted her offer.

I was now on my own, no longer commuting in secret to the Center, but also no longer allowed to have dinner with my mother or chat with my father each morning and evening. Reality had set in—I was now truly homeless. What I had to call home was a single room in the recently refurbished YWCA on the edge of the unfashionable South End of Boston.

* * *

I sat on the couch in a brightly lit apartment that overlooked Commonwealth Avenue in the Back Bay section of Boston. With me were four girls, all of us in our late teens. I knew only one of them, a coworker who had invited me to join them for wine and cheese. It was the spring of 1967—the season of draft card and bra burning.

I wore my favorite black leather miniskirt, a form-fitting red turtleneck sweater, and platform shoes that made me a full four inches taller than my true five-foot-five height. Fully aware of my status as a neophyte in the world, I tended to be quiet when I was in social circumstances such as this one. I smiled politely and asked and answered impersonal questions, but there was a perpetual queasiness rumbling in my stomach.

As the late afternoon sun spilled warm light across the room, we talked about where we bought our clothes and what stores had the best bargains. Filene's Basement was the unanimous favorite. I feigned interest in the subject but would have preferred to be discussing politics and the growing furor over the war in Vietnam.

During a lull in the conversation, the hostess turned to one of the girls and asked, "So where did you go to high school?"

I nearly dropped my cracker topped with orange cheddar cheese spread, and in a moment of panic, I instinctively bent down as though to retrieve something off the floor, but in truth I wanted to disappear. This was the nightmare scenario I had played over and over in my head. *What will I say if someone asks me where I grew up, or what my father does for a living?* I could come up with no answer. All I could think to do was to run away. My heart was pounding as I made a hasty retreat to the powder room, where I hid until the conversation changed.

As I continued to tiptoe my way into that new world, my roots were deep indeed, but my wings had yet to develop. I was like the fat fledgling robins I had loved to watch in the springtime at the Center. Full of nourishment from weeks of constant feeding, they sat shaking at the edge of their nests, secure in their fat little bodies, but terrified to take to the air, lest they fall. Naïve and uneducated in the ways of the world, I had only my roots, embedded in years of indoctrination, to rely on—that is, until my wings gathered strength and could take me where I needed to go.

Those first few months out on my own found me silent and listening, reserved and observing, reticent to engage in conversation. I stuck to what was familiar while I crammed my brain full of mental notes about what was different, new, and fascinating. I made judgments based on the binary prism through which I had been taught to view the world for nearly eighteen years: good and evil, right and wrong, heaven and hell.

Despite the agony of being evicted from the Center shortly before my eighteenth birthday, I was wed to my faith and determined to keep it. My first encounter with doubt was when a priest plied me with what I felt were inappropriate questions when I was in the confessional. The purity of the sacrament of Penance suddenly seemed tarnished, the priest vile.

That experience led to a period of disenchantment with the Catholic Church, and I put my faith on a back burner of sorts. Admittedly, I was also attempting to discern the true meaning of being Catholic. Was it based on the rigid, dogma-bridled dictates taught to me at the Center? Or was its gift in finding a way to carry out the mission of Christ and the true message of the Gospels? Was it about man-made rules or was it about God's mercy?

In the privacy of my room at the YWCA, I attempted to add strength and length to my wings by devouring books on matters social, philosophical, sexual. I bought magazines—*Seventeen, Ladies Home Journal, Time*—that had been verboten at the Center.

Little by little, as conversation became less perilous, I engaged with greater social ease, but always mindful that I had a secret I couldn't let out. No one must find out where I grew up, or that I had ever been part of the hated Feeneyites.

As my confidence grew, I tiptoed my way into more adventurous situations, sometimes challenging my better judgment. Parties were the right kind of setting to bask in anonymity, as the din of music and the mingling among throngs made serious conversation unlikely. On the other hand, too much alcohol brought with it the risk of overconfidence, of a slip of the tongue that couldn't be retrieved. Then my only solution was to run as fast and as far away as I could.

At a party in Cambridge one night, a loud and raucous affair, I felt the urge to escape and was followed out of the house by a girl a few years older than I was. It was well past midnight and I was hungry, the kind of hunger that goes with having had a bit too much alcohol.

"My house is around the corner," she said, inviting me to come over. I relented—a free meal was a rare treat. As we approached her house, I realized with a start that we were in an old familiar neighborhood. I recognized the houses and was struck with panic when we entered her house—it was next door to Sacred Heart Hall, on Putnam Avenue, the house where Father and the Big Brothers had lived before we moved to Still River.

I wanted to bolt, to disappear, but I was trapped. *Why did I ever let my guard down?* I chastised myself as I followed her into the kitchen that smelled of fried food, that rancid odor that clings to the gritty wallpaper because the ventilation system is broken, or worse, never existed.

Sitting down at the square metal table that filled most of the walking space in the cramped kitchen, I invoked my guardian angel, that heavenly protector I had become less reliant upon as I had gained confidence in the "evil world."

Suddenly the girl seemed vulgar, her voice too loud, her manners coarse.

"Who's there?" came a yell from upstairs.

"It's just my old lady," the girl whispered as I started. "Ignore her."

The creaking stairs told me that the girl's mother was on her way down. As she stomped into the kitchen I found myself repulsed. Bundled in a decrepit housecoat and with rollers in her hair, her sunken eyes and wrinkled face carried the evidence of a life of abuse—too much alcohol and too many cigarettes.

"Whatch youz girls doin' up at this hour?" she barked. "Been drinkin'? Need some eggs and bacon?"

She was already at the refrigerator hauling out items, as though this were her nightly routine. A cast-iron frying pan was sitting on the stove, grease still thick on its black surface. She tossed a package of bacon onto the uncleaned pan, without so much as separating the strips, and as it turned into a ball of curling, fat-spewing, burned-at-the-edges lump of bacon, she flipped it onto a plate and then cracked the eggs into the sizzling inch-deep fat.

This was bacon and eggs? My stomach retched as she passed me a plate laden with the inedible. Only the toast and coffee saved the meal.

It's your own fault, I thought as I contrasted this notion of a meal with the elegance and flavor of meals at the Center. I cringed as the girl shoved food into her mouth, using the back of her hand as a napkin and holding her fork as though it were a weapon. I was failing myself; this was not where I wanted to be.

"You grow up here?" asked the mother, cigarette smoke curling out of her nearly toothless mouth.

Caught off guard by her question I replied, "Yes, near here," realizing with panic that was not the answer I should have given.

"Ya? Where?"

"Right around the corner." Now I was in the quicksand with no way to get out.

"That house next door?"

"Yes."

"With Feeney and them guys?"

I nodded, caught in the truth, but knowing I'd never in a hundred years be stepping foot in that house again.

"Crazy people, all o' them. But I had nuttin' against 'em. They moved. You still with 'em?"

"Oh, no." I let out a half laugh, as though the suggestion were ludicrous, while trying to think of a way I could escape from this conversation, this house, this atmosphere, this netherworld I found repulsive.

With a quick thank you, I rushed back to the solitude and safety of my own space, a sense of shame and failure gnawing at me. But not for long. I learned my lesson, put that experience into its proper place as part of the ups and downs of gaining a foothold in the real world, and moved on. Sometimes my striving wings failed me, and that's when my roots once again took over.

Learning by trial and error was a tortuous affair. After years of indoctrination, my first instinct upon entering the world had been one of distrust. *Don't let your guard down; everyone is out to harm you.*

However, once I had broken through that barrier of self-protection, discernment—how to differentiate the good citizen from the con artist—became the next hurdle. Loans to "friends" that were never paid off brought to life how the asset of a virtue can morph into a liability—generosity can be exploited. But each setback was, in fact, a step forward; each disappointment a lesson learned. I was discovering that good and evil came in myriad shades of gray.

57

Half Nun, Half Mother

1967–1968

was full of confidence the day I signed the one-year lease on an apartment in the Back Bay section of Boston.

Out of the YWCA, on my own, nineteen years old, earning money, and more comfortable about my role in the world, as long as, that is, no one asked me about my past. Which was an impossibility, so I made up answers—my father was a teacher, I'd say, making sure to head the conversation in another direction so I wouldn't have to answer the inevitable follow-up questions: "Where?" and "What does he teach?"

There were four of us in this lease together: three girls whom I barely knew, but who were friends of each other, and me. One of the girls was dating a pitcher for the Red Sox, and we were always at sports parties that went well into the night. Life was carefree, and I reveled in the freedom of being on my own. The scene was much the same night after night—a bash, flowing with alcohol and "Mary Jane" at some guy's pad, dancing under strobe lights, flirting bit by bit more dangerously, and then at some ungodly hour making my

251

way back to the apartment to squeeze in a few hours of sleep before showing up at work on time. Life was pretty much the same for the four of us, so I was stunned when, at the end of the first month, my roommates somehow managed to have spent their rent money and I was left holding the bag. I dutifully paid for everyone, expecting to be repaid shortly.

When a month rolled around and once again none of them had any money for rent, I took the least confrontational approach, politely asking one girl in private, "When do you think you might be able to pay me back?"

"Soon," she said, almost dismissively. I got that sick feeling that used to come over me at the Center when I knew I'd lost control. "I'll have it next week," another roommate promised, while the third, looking chagrined, mumbled, "I just don't get paid enough." I was dumbfounded. Didn't they know a contract was binding? Or did they take me for a fool?

As the third month-end was nearing and I had not been repaid, I suddenly didn't feel quite so self-assured, so worldly, so ready to take on the world. But where could I turn? I was in pressing need of advice—from someone with experience—but I had no parents to turn to on the spur of the moment, no mentor, no friend ready to offer words of wisdom.

I desperately wanted to solve this problem on my own, to prove to myself that I was managing in this new world. To have to cry for help from the Center might give Sister Catherine the upper hand, something I couldn't countenance. My meager financial resources were all but spent when I did the only thing left to me—I called Still River.

As I expected, Brother Pascal, the regular porter, answered the phone.

"St. Benedict Center, good afternoon," he said in his cheerful jaunty way.

I took a deep breath and spoke. "Hi, Brother Pascal, it's Mary Patricia Walsh. Is Sister Elizabeth Ann there?"

His tone turned almost paternal. "Yes, dear, hold on one second, I'll get her for you right away."

When I told my mother my predicament, she snapped into action. "Tomorrow morning at eleven o'clock, I'll arrive with the station wagon. Bring all your things down to the curb, and I'll pick you up."

True to her word, the next morning she was there in the Center's green station wagon, a dilapidated vehicle that likely had a few hundred thousand miles under its belt. I had packed my clothes into two suitcases, and the rest of my possessions consisted mostly of my growing record collection, some secondhand pots and pans, as well as a shoe bag stuffed with more shoes than I realized I had accumulated.

"You can stay in the car," I yelled almost frantically as she pulled alongside the curb. "I can put everything into the back."

The last thing I needed was to have my mother, the nun (not that anyone would have known we were related), be spotted with me. *What if someone recognizes her as a Feeneyite?*

As I slipped into the front seat, embarrassed by my need for help and not having a clue what would come next, she spoke. "I've found a place in Cambridge where we can stay for a while."

I was startled, stunned at her ability to do "worldly" things like that. But I didn't question her—she was my savior at this moment, and I was appreciative, even if I did nothing to express my gratitude.

The place was a glorified studio apartment in a multifamily house, with windows on only one side, a far cry from the open-aired loft-like space of the apartment on Newbury Street in Boston.

What I wasn't prepared for was her staying with me that night. As we unpacked my belongings, my mother brought in a tiny suitcase of her own. From it, she pulled out a black dress and black sweater—clothes of the world, but hardly worldly—and changed into them before heading out to the supermarket to pick up food. I deeply appreciated the gesture, although I found it almost embarrassing to see my mother in anything but the only outfit I could remember her wearing for my whole life. She was a foreigner to me in street clothes.

Although I wouldn't admit it, I was grateful to have company that night. The idea of staying alone in an apartment in a less-than-fancy part of Cambridge was not appealing. When morning came, I dressed for work and she donned her religious habit, slipping unnoticed into the car that was but a few feet from the front door. I made my way to the subway and work.

"I'll see you tonight, dear," she said.

I was not sure I was pleased. *Why couldn't the apartment in Boston have worked out the way I wanted?*

Within a few weeks, my mother had found a light-filled, spacious, full floor of a two-family house in North Cambridge, only blocks from where she and my father had lived when they first were married. It reminded me of my grandparents' house on the other side of Harvard Square—a large dining room, several bedrooms, and an old-fashioned eat-in kitchen with a walk-in pantry. From that day, my mother's life metamorphosed to meet my needs and eventually her own desires as well.

In an interesting juxtaposition, my mother was adopting the role that Sister Catherine had been playing for the past eighteen years—nun during the day and mother at night. From nine to four, she assumed her duties of cook and seamstress as Sister Elizabeth Ann in Still River, returning to Cambridge in time to prepare dinner for the two of us.

"Where do you change your clothes?" I asked her one day, noticing that she drove off in the morning wearing her street clothes and returned in the same attire, but fully aware that she would not show up in Still River in anything but her nun's habit.

"I slip into the Howard Johnson's in Concord and change in the ladies' room," she said, laughing. I knew the place well and asked if she thought anyone noticed her and wondered what she was doing.

"Dahling," she said with a laugh, "I'm sure they do. I'm sure they think I'm up to no good."

Each morning before she left for the Center, she made sticky buns and brewed coffee, generally giving me the once-over as I gobbled them down, noting my outfits with occasional approbation ("The pearls go beautifully with the silk blouse, dear.") or, more frequently, skepticism ("If they made skirts any shorter, you might as well wear nothing.").

I'd harrumph and say goodbye and bolt out the door to the subway and my teaching job, while she'd head back to Still River. By the time I returned from work and levitated my aching feet out of my nearly five-inch heels, I could guess what was for dinner from the aromas that wafted from the kitchen. For the most part, we had a peaceful existence, but I was wary of her intruding into my life. Though grateful for her efforts in my moment of crisis, I wanted no part of her counsel. From my point of view, she was still Sister Elizabeth Ann, while I was now a young woman of the world. "Mother" was what I called her—a practical adjustment to the reality of having to address her in public when we were shopping. Anything more familiar felt uncomfortable after more than a decade of knowing her solely as "Sister Elizabeth Ann."

"Don't tell me how to lead my life," I said harshly on one occasion when she reproached me for refusing to let her know what I was doing for the weekend. "You weren't around for eighteen years, and I don't need you now." I could see the hurt in her eyes, but I was unrepentant.

I offered her 80 percent of my take-home pay, but she graciously told me she only needed 60 percent, and with that, she paid the rent, utilities, and food. It wasn't long before she contributed to the household income herself. Three days a week she no longer showed up in Still River—now she was half Big Sister and half mother.

"What does Sister Catherine say about your coming down here?" I asked her one day.

"She's told me to do what I must," my mother replied. I sensed that, for once, my mother had the upper hand with Sister Catherine.

I observed the ease with which she seemed to adjust to the world beyond the Center. It was as though she had hardly been separated from the real world for all those years. She was particularly at home buying clothes. She knew fabrics and offered advice on matters of quality (which I took) and fashion (which I mostly discarded). She came from an era when handbags were expected to match shoes in both color and texture. I preferred the mix-and-match approach of the late 1960s, perhaps in defiance of anything that seemed rules-based.

She shared with me pictures of herself in the newspaper from her days as a teenage model, and I saw her in a new light. I started reading the society pages of the *Boston Globe*, engrossing myself in a life that seemed almost surreal—cotillions and balls, auctions and fund-raisers, engagements and weddings—and imagining myself as part of that life of privilege.

With little understanding of what was entailed to participate in that lofty world, I blithely asked my mother one day, as we sat reading the newspaper, "Do you think it would be possible for me to make my debut?"

My mother's reaction was spontaneous. With a full-throated laugh, she exclaimed, "Where did you come from? You are the funniest child in the world." I had much to learn.

She went to work as a housekeeper for a young married couple getting their Ph.D.'s at Harvard. Not surprisingly, the three of them became fast friends, and when a year later the couple was expecting a baby, they asked her to be their nanny. My mother accepted the offer with delight. It was almost as though she was seizing the opportunity to re-engage as a mother after having shelved her maternal instincts for so many years.

Until she became a nanny, I had felt sorry for my mother—she was smart and sophisticated, if not particularly intellectual. She had a commanding knowledge of world history and a prodigious vocabulary—both of which she credited to her education at Cambridge High and Latin. I wished she could be doing something that was more stimulating, but in her nun-like fashion, she never complained. Some of our most enjoyable times together were spent watching TV mystery shows—*Hawaii Five-O, Mission Impossible*, and *Columbo*. My mother could pick out the culprit within three minutes of the start of the show, and I had to beseech her to keep it to herself.

"I should have been a detective," she'd say, with an air of supreme confidence.

* * *

A year of teaching shorthand and typing had become tedious. I craved more intellectual stimulation, but quitting never crossed my mind; that seemed to be a dereliction of duty. I found myself more interested in socializing with the students than teaching them, but "fraternizing with the students" was frowned on by the stentorian headmistress, and one day she fired me. I was both terrified and relieved.

Telling my mother that I was unemployed, particularly as I was aware of how much she counted on my weekly paycheck, was not an option. On the other hand, I was exhilarated to burst out of the confines of an intellectually vapid job that was palatable primarily on account of the friendship I had developed with one of the teachers—Mary Cudmore, whose kindness was so genuine that I found myself, on several occasions, on the verge of blurting out my story to her. But I always choked at the last moment.

That evening I scoured my wardrobe for the most respectable outfit and the next morning I walked with confidence into an employment agency on Newberry Street, presenting my credentials. Within a few minutes, the agent offered me two possible options as a receptionist—one with the *Atlantic Monthly*, the other with a broker/dealer, Ladenburg, Thalmann. The *Atlantic Monthly* seemed particularly appealing, as I felt it might open up the literary world to me, and perhaps the opportunity to further my education.

But my first interview was with Ladenburg, Thalmann, and when the partners offered me the job, which included a raise, I accepted on the spot. And thus began my career in finance.

Even as I took on my new position with excitement and energy, I longed to participate in college life, as nearly everyone my age seemed to be doing. So I did it in the only way available to me, enrolling at Harvard University's Phillips Brooks House, where I attended classes three or four evenings each week after a day of work. It was an empowering first step in shaping my own life—studying mathematics, French, political philosophy, and English literature from the very professors who taught those carefree Harvard students whose lives I coveted.

Harvard Square was, in its own way, the center of the universe during the late 1960s. Demonstrations were a daily affair, as professors and students alike voiced loudly and even turbulently their opposition to the Vietnam War. Those demonstrations often turned into riots, as tear gas competed with weed and hashish as the fragrance of the moment in the square.

Hippies, unkempt and unwashed, roamed the square in sandals, tie-dyed T-shirts, and long hair, arm in arm with intellectuals and students and bands of saffron-robed Hare Krishna monks. It was part of the pattern of life in Harvard Square, and I reveled in the spectacle. When the spirit moved me, I could appear as hippie as the best of them. With hair down to my waist, I donned long, flowing, formless cotton dresses and mingled seamlessly among the characters that were the movement of the time. In my apartment, I made candles and macramé baskets, not as a symbol of rebellion, but because I adored craftwork.

Behind the scenes, however, I voted for Richard Nixon in 1968, and I wore a copper bracelet that supported one of the thousands of U.S. soldiers in Vietnam. I was no hippie—what I wore did not define me. Looking the part was a fashion statement, but it bore no resemblance to the person I was, the person I wanted to be, as I carried out my mission to educate myself.

Skeptical of much of what I'd been taught regarding government and politics at the Center, I wasn't sure of the truth, but one thing I did know—our fighting soldiers in Vietnam had no choice in the matter.

The lucky souls who were able to avoid (or at least postpone) the draft seemed to forget their privileged position as they spewed venom on their less-fortunate and less-educated fellow Americans. I found the hypocrisy deplorable.

Over the ensuing months that stretched well into the early 1970s, college campuses across the country were transmogrified into cauldrons of seething anger, instigated by opposition to the war in Vietnam, but soon enflamed by a growing array of perceived—and in some cases, real—social ills.

The rule of law seemed on the verge of annihilation around the country, most notably when students overtook buildings on the campus of Columbia University for five days. The Democratic National Convention in Chicago that summer was the scene of endless riots and confrontations with the police. The fever pitch of hate was foisted directly on those in the military, and as war-weary veterans returned to U. S. soil—those lucky enough to come back alive—they were frequently met with scorn and physical abuse.

But it was the massacre of four unarmed students at Kent State University in May of 1970 that brought the greatest shock to the country, resulting in hundreds of colleges and universities being shuttered for the rest of the school year.

Throughout that era of upheaval, I voiced no opinion on the social issues wracking the country. The discord and enmity felt too close to home. I wanted no more of that way of life, the one I'd been forced to lead for nearly eighteen years at the Center—defying the authorities, challenging the Catholic Church, standing on a soapbox.

Not long after my mother started working, my father began coming down to visit us for Sunday dinner.

My mother was always waiting at the door when he arrived. Their embrace in the front hallway was evidence of their affection. With hands clasped, they snuggled together, almost like young teenagers who were not quite sure it was all right to go further. I made myself scarce, embarrassed by their romance. However, deep inside I was pleased that, away from the prying eyes of the authorities at the Center, they acted like the married couple they were forbidden to be in Still River. Their obvious love for each other was something I had never doubted during my years at the Center, but for which I had little obvious evidence.

Those Sunday dinners were an opportunity for my father to catch up on the news of the world. He read the newspapers that were forbidden at the Center, and when dinner was over, he found reasons to stay on, watching television with my mother as the two of them held hands. It was often long after dark when he bade her a prolonged farewell in the front hall, while I headed off to bed.

I wondered sometimes if the two of them weren't driving Sister Catherine crazy. In my mind's eye, I could visualize the tautness that would grip her face, particularly when my father would openly flout the rules. She couldn't control them, and I relished the distress it must have been causing her.

The true state of my parents' marriage was brought home to me one Sunday evening at our intimate family dinner. It was a homey setting, a freshly pressed white linen tablecloth covering the round dining room table, in sharp contrast to the institutional setup in Still River that was devoid of tablecloths and even place mats.

That evening, when my mother had gone into the kitchen to get dessert, my father turned to me and spoke, his words seeming to be carefully chosen. "My little princess," he began (I relished that he still called me that), "if something should happen to me and I die at the Center, I want you to take my wedding ring from inside my scapular and put it on my finger in the casket. I want to be buried as a married man."

It was a poignant moment—my father making a plea to his now-worldly eldest daughter to ensure that the message was loud and clear that, although he was living a celibate religious life today, in his heart he was a married man who loved his wife.

I was not prepared to probe his heart or his mind on the matter. Instead, I responded with all my heart. "I promise you I will do that, but you're nowhere near dying. You just turned fifty."

His request might have been an opportunity to question him about the Center, about the breakup of the families, about why he and my mother made the sacrifices they did, but I wasn't comfortable going down that path. Instead I buried my burning desire to tell him how much I wanted to see that ring back on his finger, the ring I had played with as a tiny child long before he had been forced to take it off.

In my heart, I felt I knew the reason he was still at the Center—four of his children were still there, and he held firm to his belief that an education at the Center provided the best opportunity for a solid grounding in Catholic doctrine and morals. While Mary Catherine was about to graduate from high school, my youngest sister, Veronica, was not quite fourteen, with several years of school still ahead of her.

Little did any of us anticipate the turn of events that was about to unfold.

58

Cataclysm

1968

My father broke the news to me one Sunday evening at the apartment in Cambridge. We were sitting together on the couch watching news that was consumed with the upcoming funeral arrangements for Martin Luther King, Jr. who'd been assassinated three days earlier.

Out of almost nowhere, he said in a soft and solemn voice, "Sister Catherine is dying."

"Dying" was the word he used—not "sick," not "ill." He was somber, as though devastated by the realization that Sister Catherine was soon to leave this world.

"Is it cancer?" I asked, aware that she'd been rumored to be ill for some time and that she'd been going for treatments that no one discussed.

"Yes," he said, "Hodgkin's lymphoma. She doesn't have long now."

My father's words jolted me—not out of any feeling of empathy toward Sister Catherine, but because it shattered my image of her invincibility. It brought back to my mind the words I had silently said

Sister Catherine, the day after her death on May 8, 1968.

to myself hundreds of times at the Center in my moments of despair. *Some day she will die, and then I'll be free.*

But I was already free—she had seen to that.

Once the news settled in, I saw a certain poetic justice in Sister Catherine's impending demise at the relatively young age of sixty-seven. For twenty years, she had been center of the universe within the community, controlling the lives of nearly one hundred people. But the tide had now turned, and she was about to lose her grip on that control. Mortality was trouncing indomitability. Soon she'd be ashes like all of humanity that preceded her.

During her final weeks, my father would shake his head and say woefully, "What will we do without her?" His words surprised me. Despite the evident pleasure he took in visiting me on Sundays, he was still tethered to the Center—body and soul.

It was early in May, not quite two years from the day I had been forced to leave the Center, when my father called to tell me, in a reverent tone of voice, that Sister Catherine had died. As I sat at the reception desk, an array of emotions reverberated through my mind and my heart, running the gamut from elation to relief and including even a sense of emptiness. I had never known Sister Catherine not to exist. Now she was gone, her power terminated, her authority forever silenced.

I thought of the Community, thrust into mourning, as they made plans for the funeral of their foundress, their once indomitable leader. There was no doubt in my mind that I would attend Sister Catherine's wake, as well as the Requiem mass and burial in the cemetery on the property at Still River. I saw the occasion as an opportunity to visit my family, my whole Center family, whom I missed and still considered dear to me.

Alone, I walked up to the casket, knelt down, and stared at Sister Catherine. I did not kiss her, nor even touch her, as I had the other members of the community who had died. No prayer passed my lips as I knelt with folded hands. My soul was frigid. Suddenly, without knowing why, I spoke to her, under my breath, as if to forestall her coming to life.

"Don't open your eyes," I said. "Don't sit up. You're gone now—gone for good."

And with that I stood up, turned my back on her, and joined the rest of the community. Many were sobbing. All seemed devastated by the loss. I understood their emotion. I did not share it.

59

Together but Separate

1968–1969

I returned to the Center a few weeks later, this time to attend my sister Mary Catherine's graduation from high school.

I came on my own, without an invitation, unconcerned about any negative response to my presence. If the Angels were unhappy to see me, there was no one bold enough to confront me. For the occasion, I jettisoned my conservative attire for a bright-colored pink dress, something that stood out in a sea of black. I boldly posed for pictures as my grandparents clicked away.

Perhaps my visit was less than a cause célèbre because the Center was facing more serious issues than one apostate postulant. The earth was hardly shoveled over Sister Catherine's dead body when an array of internecine battles erupted into what would soon become full-fledged war, primarily focused on a grab for power between the Big Sisters and the Big Brothers. Before long, numerous factions developed, each with its own agenda, much of which was centered on money, power, and control.

My parents took no part in the dissension. For once, being outsiders and nonconformists allowed them to remain above and beyond the fray.

I was blithely removed from the infighting, although my father would bring me news each week of the turbulence embroiling the community. As I pondered the possible implosion of the place I had called home for so long, I found myself scandalized. These were the people who had been held up as paragons of virtue, the only true believers in the doctrines of the Catholic faith, the only people in the world who had a chance of making it to heaven, where, incidentally they fervently believed Sister Catherine now had a place of special importance next to God and the Blessed Mother.

This is holiness? I thought to myself. *Where is the charity that is meant to imbue religious life?*

Much as I was happy to be living out in the world, I still wanted to think of the Center with warmth, as my childhood home with many happy memories, a place where good people lived and prayed and shared the love of God. But with Sister Catherine's demise and the subsequent internal feud, it struck me that she alone had been the glue that kept nearly one hundred highly intelligent human beings together as members of a religious order. Had it been out of their respect, their fear, or their love for her? I could only surmise, but, if their blind obedience to her had been grounded in deep spirituality, why would it fall apart so catastrophically when she was gone? I thought back to the rules Sister Catherine instituted that forced separation between men and women, boys and girls. I remembered how she had told us Little Sisters that we must never trust a man. Now as the place I had called home for so long seemed on the edge of disintegration, I wondered if it wasn't she herself who had planted the seeds of its destruction.

Within days of Sister Catherine's burial, my brother David, who was seventeen and completing his junior year in high school, and my youngest sister, Veronica, who was about to finish middle school,

My father with my Grandmother McKinley, on the day of my brother's graduation from high school, just hours before he left the Center as Brother James Aloysius and became once again Jim Walsh–June 1969.

informed Sister Teresa (Sister Catherine's successor as overseer of the children) that they wished to leave and move to Cambridge with my mother and me. Over the course of the next twelve months, my father decided that if his children wanted to leave, it was his obligation to accompany them into the world.

I myself was becoming increasingly secure in my role as a worldly woman, provided, that is, no mention was made of my past. I had a nice Irish Catholic boyfriend, a couple of years older than I was, whose family lived on Long Island. He was in the Navy and said he was hoping to attend the police academy when he was discharged. Polite and soft spoken, he was courteous to my parents when he joined us for Sunday dinners, and he was blissfully romantic when I could be alone with him. He was my first true love out in the world. We talked of marriage, and he brought me to visit his family, but something inside me kept saying, "No—you need someone who is more intellectual. You will become bored with him." I spoke only of going to college and of all the places in the world I wanted to visit. He'd laugh, not out of disrespect but more in disbelief, as though I was too much for him, not likely to be the kind of wife he needed. When we broke up, I was hurt but not damaged—he was almost too good for me, and I too adventurous for him.

* * *

In June, little more than a year after Sister Catherine was buried, and hours after my brother graduated from high school, my father drove away from the Center with two of his children. The only family members remaining behind at the Center were Sister Mary Catherine, now a professed nun at the age of nineteen, and sixteen-year-old Sister Margaret Mary, a novice. Both appeared happy with their choice.

I had braced myself for a new head of the household—my father, whom I called "Daddy" from the time he started visiting my mother and me in Cambridge. It suited him, the way "Mother" suited my mother. He was casual; she was more formal. He was laid back; she made sure things were in their proper place. I loved her; I adored him.

It had been years since I had to be accountable to either of them, and now I was nearing my twenty-first birthday, accustomed to making my own decisions, leading my own life, traveling where I wanted, building my own coterie of friends. I viewed my father as a neophyte in the world I had come to relish, naïve about social and political issues and hopelessly more religious than I was. Compromise was a virtue I had yet to cultivate.

That first evening as the five of us Walshes sat down to a roast chicken dinner at the now-expanded dining room table, my father, with a certain air of bravado and the full flare of a bishop blessing an entire congregation, made the sign of the cross and announced, "Let us say grace."

I grimaced. Grace at meals was one of those rituals I had discarded shortly after my expulsion. It reeked of being a Catholic, something I needed to hide, lest it invite questions that would wrangle their way into divulging my past.

While the rest of the family spoke the words with respect, I barely moved my lips, fuming inside. After three years on my own, and now a confident and independent "woman of the world," I had a feeling of panic.

Am I about to lose my freedom?

My solution was swift and impulsive. The following day, I traversed the streets of Cambridge and found an apartment on the far side of Harvard Square. At dinner that night, I announced my decision to move out. There was a stunned silence.

"I won't be far," I said, trying to soften the blow, a sudden pang of guilt sweeping over me as I looked at the expressions of shock on the faces of the people I most loved in the world. But I had no appetite for a return to a life that I feared might be regimented and a reminder of the Center.

When my father left the Center, he and my mother requested that they be allowed to take with them the sterling silver dinner service for twelve that had been a wedding present twenty-two years earlier. It came as a surprise to me that the silver I had polished almost weekly as I set Father and Sister Catherine's places at their head table had belonged to my parents. That, together with a check for $9,000, was the sum total that was deemed to be the value of the sweat equity the two of them had contributed over a period of twenty years of living and working and raising money through bookselling, not to mention their donation of the proceeds and contents of their house, which they sold when I was still an infant.

My father was approaching his fifty-second birthday, a middle-aged intellectual with no track record in academia for over two decades. The angst of finding a job and making a living haunted him for the first few weeks, until he was hired by Volvo—"the intellectual's car," as he liked to refer to the company.

He could hardly be described as a salesman, much less a "car salesman." For my father, the business of selling cars was simply one more opportunity to engage with interesting people rather than a challenge to make a sale. This worried me: after all those years at the Center, was he able to face the day-to-day pressure of earning a living, making sure there was enough money to pay the rent and buy food?

He'd regale me with stories about his customers, seldom alluding to whether they'd bought a car. He was particularly pleased one Christmas when he received a personalized letter from Senator John Kerry in appreciation of his services. Years later, when Kerry ran for president, I asked my father if he still had that letter. "You better believe I do," he said with a sense of elation.

Meanwhile, in the freedom of my own apartment, I could retreat into rooms furnished in a combination of Victorian and hippie—orange shag rugs and bookcases crafted from creosoted railroad ties piled on bricks, mingled with my grandmother's mahogany library table that served as both dining room table and desk. Here, I experienced life far removed from the transition my family was making.

For hours on end, I'd sit on the floor, my ear less than two inches from the slowly rotating vinyl, as I memorized the words to the hottest Broadway shows—*Jesus Christ Superstar, Jacques Brel Is Alive and Well and Living in Paris, Hair, The Fantasticks*—and the scores of top ten singles—"(The Lights Went Out in) Massachusetts," "In the Ghetto," "Crimson and Clover"—at the same time delving deep into my studies, writing papers long into the wee hours of the morning, and trekking into the financial district of Boston to open the office well before the partners could shake themselves into cognizance after a martini-laden evening that would soon be followed by a three-martini lunch.

But I was respectful of the two men who ran the office, and while I was a neophyte in the world of finance, it was evident to me that they were not only hardworking but also successful. It was not lost on me that, despite their stature within the office, they were always courteous and made me feel like a member of their team. When I found myself with time on my hands, I'd bounce into their office and ask them if there wasn't something I could do—anything. Before long, I was running errands for them all over town, a welcome diversion from sitting at the front desk and answering the telephone.

I had been employed for eight months, when, at yearend, the partners invited me into their wood-paneled office and presented me with a $1500 bonus check. I was speechless—that was almost half of what I had made since I came to the firm. But equally as rewarding was the realization that these two men, who seemed bigger than life to me, were appreciative of my work.

One day, not long after the bonus surprise, the two partners once again called me into their office.

"We'd like you to do us a favor," they said.

They had been working on a deal, they explained, that was closing at the end of the week, and they needed me to go to New York to collect $5 million in checks from five separate investors.

"Here's a ticket to LaGuardia Airport on the shuttle for tomorrow morning, and a list of the places you need to go. A car and driver will take you to each of the destinations."

Me? Collect $5 million? In New York? On my own? I can do it, and they know I can.

As I took the subway home that evening, I reveled in the realization that I, the receptionist, was selected over the half-dozen secretaries whose responsibilities and income were well above mine.

The chauffeured limousine was awaiting me at LaGuardia, and for the next few hours, I went from office to office. The last appointment of the day was at the country estate of an elderly man, Mr. Rosenberg. He greeted me at the door, his butler supporting his frail frame as he reached his hand out to me.

"Come in," he said, "please join me for tea."

"Thank you," I replied instinctively, "I'd love to."

I was brought back to the days in Still River when I was nine years old and the Thursday afternoon tea parties over which Sister Catherine presided. I noted the difference—on this occasion, I was being served rather than serving. Mr. Rosenberg inquired about my interests, and I felt that stab of panic grip my stomach.

Dear God, please don't let him ask me about where I grew up.

What would a Jewish man say if he knew I was a Feeneyite?

God was on my side, and we found a way to engage in innocuous topics that focused on the cultural scene in Boston, and as I was ready to leave, he handed me a check for $1 million.

"Now don't lose it, honey," he said with a chuckle.

"I promise I won't," I replied as I tucked the precious cargo into the inside pocket of my handbag, along with the rest of the treasure trove I had collected.

Two hours later, I landed at Logan Airport, took a taxi to the office, and handed over the $5 million. The partners celebrated by taking me to dinner at the Ritz Carlton.

As I lay in bed that night, I felt inspired. I saw a life beyond being a receptionist.

I can go far, I thought.

60

Daring Myself

1969

It was a warm, sunny Saturday afternoon in downtown Boston—perfect Indian summer weather two days before Halloween in the fall of 1969. I'd been shopping at Filene's Basement and with nothing to show for it, I was headed to the Park Street station to catch the subway back to my apartment in Cambridge, just four short stops away.

As I walked along Tremont Street, it occurred to me that I might try going home another way. The idea had crossed my mind on occasion in the past, but I'd resisted the temptation.

I'll do it just once, I thought to myself. Hitchhike.

I knew I shouldn't. Sister Catherine's lurid stories about how the Hells Angels would beat up hitchhikers remained vivid in my memory. In addition, she had warned us Little Sisters of the dangers—unspecified, perhaps to frighten us all the more—of being alone with a man. But I had been out in the world for more than three years now, and I had yet to witness the evil to which she alluded.

With an air of confidence, I faced the oncoming traffic and stuck my thumb out. Within a minute, a green car slowed down and pulled over to the curb. The driver was a man who looked to be in his thirties, wearing a red and blue plaid shirt and jeans. His hair was longish, the style of the day. The car looked respectable—not fancy, but not dilapidated either.

"Hop in," he said and I did, after sizing him up and deciding he looked safe.

"I'd like to go to Harvard Square," I said calmly. "It's just over the bridge; I can show you the way."

"I know the way," the man replied as he started off.

And for a few minutes, all was fine. The driver made small talk.

"Do you live in Cambridge?" he asked.

"Yes," I replied, careful not to tell him where.

"How long?"

"All my life," I said, wanting him to know that I knew my way around.

I did my best to sound nonchalant, as though hitching a ride was nothing out of the ordinary for me. But from the corner of my eye, I examined the man closely. The stubble on his face that I hadn't noticed when he first pulled over now gave him the appearance of being unkempt. There was dirt under his fingernails, and the smell of cigarettes hung in the air. Suddenly he looked creepy to me.

Then we missed the turnoff to Harvard Square, and panic hit my stomach. I swallowed hard before saying, "You missed the exit."

"It's okay," he replied. "I'm going around this other way I know."

His answer was plausible, so I let our intermittent conversation continue, attempting to mask my anxiety that was swiftly turning into panic. But within a minute or two, it was evident that the car was not going to Harvard Square. We were now in North Cambridge on the feeder road to Route 2, the highway that headed west from Boston.

My throat became dry, and I was afraid to speak lest my voice betray my fear. Suddenly images of the figures of death leapt into my mind—the names of fiends who had engaged in killing sprees over the last few years: Charles Manson, Richard Speck, and Albert DeSalvo, the Boston Strangler. *Could this be my fate?*

The car was now on Route 2. Soon there would be little traffic around us and no way to escape. My mind was working in frantic overtime.

How do I get out of this car? Should I just throw open the door and fling myself on the road? We're going more than sixty miles an hour. I could be killed.

I knew the road intimately, having traveled it dozens of times. There was only one more set of lights before it opened into a broad four-lane highway. If the light was red, I could jump out.

But what if it's green? I thought. *Then I'm done.*

The gruesomeness of what might happen flashed before my mind. No—no way was I going to die. I wouldn't let myself be murdered by this thug.

The image of my parents, my three younger sisters, and my brother came to my mind, and in that instant I felt a surge of power rise from deep inside me. My fear was transformed into rage. Glaring straight at the man sitting two feet from me, I yelled at the top of my voice, "You turn this car around right now and drive me into Harvard Square."

The driver looked at me but didn't respond. He seemed stunned.

"Do you hear me?" I screamed.

His voice was oddly quiet. "Sure," he said, "if that's what you want."

We were approaching the light, and it was green.

"Make a U-turn here at this light." I said making my voice as steely and cold as I could.

And that's what he did, exactly as I told him. Slowing the car down, he turned around and headed back in the direction we had come. But I wasn't letting my guard down for a moment.

"Now you follow *my* instructions," I said, trying to sound as though I really *was* in charge.

And for the next ten minutes—which felt like an hour—I gave the orders as we drove back to Cambridge. No polite conversation, no small talk.

"Take this exit," I said.

"And now a left here."

"Okay, straight down Mass Ave."

As we neared Harvard Square, I breathed easier, knowing I could jump out of the car and make a scene if necessary. There was no way I was going to let him find out where I lived, so I directed him to the center of Harvard Square and, when we reached the kiosk at the entrance to the subway, I said, "Stop now."

Opening the car door, I stepped onto the sidewalk, slamming it behind me and losing myself in the crowd.

My knees were shaking as I made my way slowly to the muffin shop around the corner, where I sat down and ordered a cup of tea. It remained untouched while I replayed in my mind the experience I'd just been through.

What if I hadn't screamed at him? I thought. *Where would I be now? Deep in the woods somewhere? Being stabbed to death?*

There was no need to berate myself. I'd learned my lesson. I was grateful to be alive.

But I did make a pact with myself, swearing never to hitchhike again in my whole life. I kept that promise. I also decided not to tell my parents what had happened, knowing how distraught they would be. It would be more than ten years before I shared the story with them.

And as I walked home to my apartment, I repeated to myself something I had believed as a child but had forgotten about as a young adult: "I really do have a guardian angel."

I took full responsibility for what happened that day, a brazen and reckless decision that might have ended catastrophically. But a far more heinous incident would occur the following year, when I was not yet twenty-two years old. It would take me many years to forgive myself and decades before I was able to recount the event to others.

My firm was expanding and a number of new brokers had been hired, each with a secretary or two. One new employee was a broker with a rollicking sense of Irish humor, a long client list (generating lots of commissions), and a hail-fellow-well-met attitude. He was given a large office, an obvious indication of his stature as a producer, and his desk was peppered with pictures of his third wife and their three children. Handsome he was not, with his Coke-bottle eyeglasses encased in thick black rims, and a figure that could at best be called portly. His secretary was a charming English girl, a few years older than I was. She and I shared the same sense of humor and were kindred spirits on account of each of us having recently broken up with a boyfriend.

Her boss had a way of inviting us for drinks after work at the 99 Club, a pub frequented by Boston's equivalent of Wall Street traders. It was a pleasant way to end the day before I headed to my evening classes at Boston University, where I was now enrolled.

One afternoon, as he was leaving the office, he asked in an offhand way, "Want to catch a drink at the 99?"

"Sure," I replied, thinking I could have one quick drink before evening school.

I walked into the pub. He was there at the bar, talking to the bartender, and he offered me a seat on the barstool next to him, a broad smile across his face. A drink was awaiting me.

What I next remember is waking up in my own bed in the pitch black, naked, in pain and aware that a man was getting out of my bed. I was jolted out of my sleepiness and stared in shocked silence as the man slipped into his trousers, picked up his shoes, and tiptoed out of my bedroom. His gait, the eyeglasses—they told me who he was, the broker who had offered to buy me a drink.

The apartment door shut behind him, and I lay motionless, racking my brain to try to recreate the events of the prior evening. For hours I lay awake—too stunned to cry, too mortified to call anyone.

How did this happen? How could I have let it happen?

The next morning, I was the first to arrive at the office, taking my place at the receptionist's desk that faced the elevators, and thus allowed me to greet each person who arrived. Long after normal starting hours, the elevator door opened and out stepped the criminal of the prior evening. I grabbed a telephone as though I were engaged in conversation, refusing to look at him as he strode past my desk and on to his elegant office.

Will he apologize to me? I wondered. How naïve I was to think there might be any remorse in that man. Did he think perhaps that I had no idea what had transpired, that I was dead to the world when he sneaked out of my apartment?

I wanted to scream at him, to punch him in the face, but that would entail sharing my nightmare with the whole office.

Would anyone even believe me? I had never heard of such a thing happening to a person—it would be my word against his—he the big producer versus me the pretty receptionist who wore miniskirts. A combination of shame and the fear of retaliation silenced me. I was deliberately ignorant of the array of drugs that were popular among students and young working professionals—Quaaludes, LSD, glue, and a cornucopia of drugs I learned about when I saw the movie of the late 1960s, "Valley of the Dolls." The fear of losing control in a world I was still learning to navigate tempered any curiosity I might have had about experimenting with these drugs.

I confided only in my English girlfriend, who in turn told me he'd tried to rape her on one occasion when he offered her a ride home. It was comforting to share the nightmare with someone who understood—we were now kindred victims of barbarism. But this remained our secret—I did not share it even with my family for over four decades.

61

Martha's Vineyard

1971

The midsummer sun broke from behind the towering plumes of white puffy clouds and flooded us with late-afternoon warmth, its light suffusing the deck in a hazy glow that invited us to bask.

Clad in a pink bikini, I sat with my parents on the deck of the summer cottage on Martha's Vineyard they had been offered for the weekend. Each of us was nursing a refreshing gin and tonic as we gazed out over the rolling dunes to the ocean beyond.

My three sisters had headed out on a bike ride, and my brother was surf casting in an ill-fated attempt to surprise us with dinner. This was summer at its best—a family gathering in an idyllic setting.

A casual observer looking upon this family by the sea might have thought the Walsh clan was on its annual August vacation, a long-married husband and wife bringing together the young adult siblings before a time they, too, would get married and have children of their own, creating the next generation of Walshes.

But this get-together was hardly a yearly tradition. For us, it was the first time in more than seventeen years that we seven Walshes were together as a family under the same roof. It was our first family vacation, and the sheer newness of it was exhilarating.

My father seemed particularly elated, like a king who is proud of what he has wrought in his kingdom. His joy was a family reunited, made complete only a couple of months earlier when the last two of his daughters left the Center and moved into the family home in Cambridge.

"What a beautiful day," my father said. "Beautiful" and "delicious" seemed to be his two favorite words. They expressed his constant state of mind these days—happy. "And how wonderful to have the whole family together."

"Cathy seems so much happier," I responded, referring to my sister Mary Catherine, who had been a particular source of worry to him. Fraught with health problems from the time she was in her teens, she was now twenty-one and, until she left the Center, she had often been confined to bed and frequently in the hospital with ailments that seemed hard to diagnose.

It was a few months before this family vacation that my father and I had driven up to Still River to visit with her. She had seemed dispirited, but Sister Teresa, the superior, had tried to make light of her condition, saying that all she needed was for spring to arrive.

"Once she gets out in the fresh air and working in the garden, she'll be good as gold," she said.

But when my father responded by saying, "I think Mary Catherine could use a little vacation. I'd like to take her home with us for a while," there was no objection.

I stood in silence, not believing what I was hearing. *Allow one of the Big Sisters to take a vacation with her family?* Never had it been done before.

No sooner had Mary Catherine stepped foot into the family apartment than she set herself to work in the kitchen, preparing dinner. As she hovered over the stove in her black nun's habit, I sat at the kitchen table, staring at her from behind, in awe of what I was witnessing. She burst into song as she worked, not a hymn, but a secular melody, exercising a freedom not allowed in the atmosphere of silence that prevailed at the Center. Her gentle soprano voice trilled throughout the apartment.

She's never going back. I thought, smiling. *She's here forever.*

Within days, she had discarded her nun's habit for worldly attire, admittedly more demure than the thigh-hugging miniskirts I wore.

"I want to be a nurse," she declared at dinner one evening. "I've always wanted to be one." She spoke with confidence—the frail, shy child was suddenly bursting out of her cocoon.

"Let's go to Mount Auburn Hospital," I responded. "They have a nursing school, and I'm sure you can get in."

It turned out to be the start of a long career as a nurse.

She admitted to me (years later) that it took her a number of months to get over her guilt about leaving religious life. She feared that God might strike her dead for betraying her vows to Him.

I asked her about her eating problems and how it was that they suddenly seemed to disappear when she was about fifteen years old, not long before I left. She told me that, in a moment of furor over what she felt was an unfair grade on one of her exams, she bolted into Sister Catherine's office and laid out her grievance. Sister Catherine heard her and reassured her that she would take matters into her own hands.

"I found I had a voice," Cathy said, "that I had power, that I could fight back. That discovery gave me back the control I had lost when we were taken away from our parents."

The family was made whole when twenty-year-old Margaret Mary left the Center three months later. Peggy—that's what she became the moment she rejoined the family, a name we had jokingly whispered as her nickname for years at the Center. By far the most easygoing, happy-go-lucky of the five of us, she harbored not a grudge in the world about her years as a nun. Tall and lithesome, she started almost immediately to take dancing lessons—a far cry from her prior routine of selling books and cooking meals for a community of one hundred.

Now a couple of months later, as the seven of us ate steamed lobsters, corn on the cob, and fresh tomatoes, we extended our glasses as our dad poured the wine. It was as though we'd been a family uninterrupted by years of separation. The past was behind us, the future held promise—we were together once again.

62

Back to Normal

1971–1974

That fall, my parents bought a four-bedroom house in the Boston suburb of Watertown—a cottage kind of house with border gardens and a back lawn that was perfect for family picnics. To me, that purchase was evidence that my parents were now part of the American middle class—a giant step from the world of celibacy, communal living, and religious zealotry.

It didn't take long for their home to become the gathering place for many of the Center children, young adults by then, who had been flooding out of Still River for the past six months. Saturday nights at Jim and Betsy's were an open invitation to them, providing an opportunity for conviviality and good food.

My mother would spend the afternoon cooking a meal to rival any at the Center—roast beef with mounds of mashed potatoes or a giant bowl of pasta with salad and garlic bread, always topped off with a glorious chocolate cake or strawberry shortcake or angel food cake. Cooking for throngs of people was second nature to her after her years at the Center. The oval dining room table could comfortably seat ten, but we'd nearly always be cramming fourteen or more.

The longer the evening went, the more boisterous the conversations became—often ending in jovial arguments about the finer points of English or Latin grammar. Jolly was the way to describe the household, and my parents seemed in their element creating the atmosphere of a home away from home for anyone who had been part of the Center.

For me, the world was there for the grabbing, and I became an avid traveler. My English girlfriend had returned to London and I made several trips exploring England. That fall, my best friend Susan and I traveled together, choosing out of the mainstream places behind the Iron Curtain—Budapest and Dubrovnik—and then on to Athens and the Greek islands. A year later, I visited Australia. The daydreams of my childhood were becoming a reality as I explored the world.

The following year, when Susan was offered a job in Philadelphia, she asked me if I'd move there with her and I seized the opportunity like a prize. It didn't matter that there was no job offer for me. I ached to be out of Boston, to be able to spread my wings in a place where I was anonymous, to have the opportunity to climb the next few rungs on the ladder to a career in the business world. With my family now secure and thriving, I no longer felt the need to hover. There was no boyfriend to keep be back. My love life was in the doldrums—maybe Philadelphia would prove to be a springboard for both my career and romance.

I was particularly elated when my advisor at Boston University's Metropolitan College, where I was now enrolled, encouraged me to take courses at Wharton School, promising me that they would count toward my degree.

* * *

The day after I moved into a spacious apartment overlooking Rittenhouse Square in Center City Philadelphia, I had an interview with the research department of The Pennsylvania Group, a broker/dealer located in Bala Cynwyd, a few miles out of the city. The discussion between me and the four research analysts—an all-male cast in a nearly all-male industry—remains vivid. They were looking for a statistician, they said, someone who could put together financial spreadsheets covering an array of industries that included airlines, railroads, hospitality and lodging, as well as insurance.

The position sounded easy—I'd been doing similar work in Boston since being promoted from receptionist to assistant to a research analyst. But challenging, rather than easy, was what I was in search of, yearning for an opportunity to catapult myself forward in the business world, and I was pointed in my request. "I would like to do more than crunch numbers for you. Are you willing to answer the questions I have so that I can understand how each of the companies in these industries work?" They were unanimous in their agreement to work with me and so I took the job.

Helen Reddy had just released her hit song, "I Am Woman," and I felt one with her—I was "strong, not a novice any longer, invincible, with a long, long way to go."

Boston was a six-hour drive from Philadelphia, and that summer I made the trip on several occasions as my siblings and I planned a surprise twenty-fifth wedding anniversary party for our parents. It was exactly a year since all seven of us were out of the Center. My parents were beloved by the Center's expatriate community, and we knew we'd have a houseful. Keeping the party a secret was nearly impossible—the surprise would simply be in the number of friends who showed up.

How distant their days as Brother James Aloysius and Sister Elizabeth Ann now seemed. Urbane and cultivated, my parents spoke of how they wanted to visit the great cathedrals of Europe, a mark of their steadfastness to Catholicism.

The anniversary party was a worldly affair—my mother wore a floor-length blue gown, her hair swept up in an elegant chignon at the back

Mother and Dad's twenty-fifth wedding anniversary with their five children:
(L to R) me, Peggy, David, Cathy, Ronnie.

of her head, while my dad was dapper in his own fashion. The house
was jammed with friends both from the Center and beyond, all there
to celebrate a marriage that had been forced into hiding for so many
years. The seven of us Walshes posed for pictures as a family—there
had been nothing like this before in our lives. It was a far cry from
life only two years earlier. And after the cake and the pictures were
done, the five of us children presented our parents with an all-ex-
pense-paid three-week trip to England, Germany, France, and Italy. It
was the start of a thirty-year adventure that saw them visit and revisit
the great Catholic sites of Europe.

After the guests had left the anniversary party and the cameras had stopped clicking, my parents sat together on the couch. The atmosphere was quiet, and as I plopped myself into an upholstered wing chair next to them, all of us still in our festive attire, it seemed a good moment to talk to them about the Center and to hear from them how it had unfolded, a subject that had been on my mind for the last few years but which I had been reluctant to discuss.

They spoke softly and without rancor of how their faith mattered to them, how they truly believed in the dogma of "No Salvation Outside the Catholic Church." If that meant being scorned by the world and the Church they loved, they were prepared to accept that burden. They may have been excommunicated in the eyes of the world, they said, but in their own eyes they were the true Catholics.

They told me that they had no problem living a communal life, studying together and eating meals as a community, and even going out on the road to sell books.

What they were not prepared for, however, was the rupturing of their family and the loss of their role as parents. My father likened the ever-tightening grip on their lives to a snowball.

"First it was small," he said. "Each new rule seemed insignificant on its own, but before long, it had become monumental, and we felt trapped."

My mother's voice became emotional when she spoke of the separation of the families. "It was the most awful day of my life. Brother Henry, in his cold, haughty manner, told us that all the children three years of age and older would no longer live with their parents but would be under the supervision of Sister Matilda. No rationale was given, no opportunity to ask questions or to discuss, much less object. Brother Henry delivered his edict and left. We were sure he was carrying out Father's orders." She paused before finishing her thought. "There was nothing we could do. We had promised to obey Father when we signed on as religious members in 1949."

I thought she might cry, but she regained her composure and repeated, shaking her head, "It was the most awful day of my life."

That was but the first step in the gradual destruction of family life for them. They had hardly acclimated to that devastating blow when Father summoned them to a private meeting at which he asked them if they would be willing to take vows of chastity; in other words, to forgo their marriage vows in favor of those of a religious nun and brother.

My father told me that he responded with an adamant "No," telling Father that their marital vows were of paramount importance to them.

"I was hoping for twelve children," my mother said, chuckling, "one for each of the twelve apostles. I loved having babies, and I wanted to raise as many good Catholics as I could."

But succumb they did after several more meetings with Father, who let them know that the other eleven couples had agreed to the new arrangement, and they were the only holdouts. It would be decades before I learned that other couples were also coerced into forsaking their marriage vows by Father's duplicity—telling them that they, too, were alone in their decision not to embrace celibacy.

At the time, Brother Augustine (one of the parents who had three boys, the youngest of whom was less than six months old) was seriously ill with cancer. My parents spoke of their soul searching and angst as they gradually convinced themselves that perhaps if they made the sacrifice of renouncing their marriage vows in favor of celibacy, God might cure Brother Augustine. With that rationalization, they acquiesced to the pressure that Father put on them. When Brother Augustine died several weeks later, there was no option to go back to their life as a married couple.

"Did you think you would have been forced out of the Center if you had not agreed to keep that vow?" I asked them.

My father paused. He was generally slow to answer questions that dealt with complex issues, and I could see he was choosing his words carefully.

"That was never openly discussed," he replied, "but your mother and I had the clear sense that if we didn't comply, we would be asked to leave."

I felt a surge of anger—anger at Father and Sister Catherine who, for all those years I was a child, acted as though I had two parents whose sole objective was to dedicate their lives to God as members of a religious order. I was reminded of my childhood reflections: *Why did my mother have to be a nun and my father a brother?* Now that façade was sundered, and I saw Father and Sister Catherine in a new light—as manipulators, driven by zealotry for a cause they decided was higher than the sacrament of marriage. My mother picked up the conversation and went on to recount how a year or two after the families had been separated and they had agreed to forgo the life of a married couple, the two of them confronted Father.

"It was at St. Gabriel's House," she said. "Right in the refectory. We told him that we wanted our family life back, that God did not call us to be religious, but to be parents to our five children."

"What was his reaction?" I asked.

"He got angry and told us we would lose our faith if we left," my mother went on, "and so would the five of you. From the day each of us walked into the Center, long before the trouble started, we had looked up to Father as our spiritual advisor. He was telling us to stay for the good of our souls, and so we felt we had no option but to stay."

My father added, "He told us our vows of celibacy were inviolable."

In the silence that followed, I pondered his words. My father, the intellectual, the man of logic, a student of the writings of Aristotle and Thomas Aquinas, a man of principle—*why didn't he challenge Father about the incongruity of one set of vows superseding another set of vows?* But I swallowed my instinct to ask that question. This was not a moment to interrogate my parents. They had just revealed the backstory that led to the life we lived for so many years. It was evident to me that they themselves had misgivings along the way and had suffered on account of it.

My mother, almost as though to introduce some comic relief, let spill another anecdote. She laughed as she started to speak.

"A couple of days later," she said, referring to their yielding to a celibate life, "we arrived back at our little apartment at St. John's House to find that someone had removed our double bed while we were gone and had replaced it with two twin beds, and anchored between them was a piece of plywood the length of the beds and five feet tall."

"You're not serious?" I said.

"Dead serious."

"As though you couldn't pop into one twin bed together?" I howled with laughter. "Who do you think did it?"

"I'm sure Brother Henry ordered it done," she said.

"Of course," I replied.

"Carrying out orders from on high" was the way my mother phrased it.

It all seemed so counter-Catholic to me, and I asked my parents why they thought Father and Sister Catherine took such a radical step. They admitted that rumors abounded—one being that thirty-nine children were becoming a financial burden.

But my mother said she had an alternate theory, which she based on a conversation she had had with Sister Catherine in Still River, long after the separation had taken place.

"She told me that her wedding night was the worst day of her life. And so she asked Hank [her husband] to agree to a life of chastity between the two of them. I think she abhorred the whole notion of sex and procreation. She was a prude at heart."

I nodded and took this in. The fact that Sister Catherine's two children were adopted suddenly made sense.

It was heading toward midnight, and I changed the subject.

"What did you think when you found out that we were being beaten all those years?" I was referring to a time not long after Sister Catherine died, when turmoil roiled the Center and, in a moment of near revolution, the children told their parents about the beatings with the Big Punisher that were meted out at the whim of an Angel for infractions often created out of whole cloth.

My mother rushed to answer. "We were shocked. Sister Catherine had always told us how wonderful you children were, how good, how obedient and holy. We knew you could get into trouble, but there was never an inkling of physical abuse. I feel terrible to this day and will until I die. To have trusted my children to her and then to discover the treatments they received—for that I can never forgive myself."

"Well, it was all true," I said, not in an attempt to upset them but to reinforce to them the reality of the life that was hidden from them. "But you can't blame yourselves. Why shouldn't you have believed her?"

The room was silent. Everyone was asleep except for the three of us. It was now close to midnight. As my parents rose from the couch and I from my chair, I asked one more question.

"Did you ever think life at the Center would turn out the way it did when you first joined?"

"Never, darling, not in a million years" was my mother's reply.

She spoke without bitterness but with a sense of disbelief and regret. What had she done, unwittingly? How had she and my father, wanting only the best for their five children, managed to cause so much suffering?

But lugubriousness was not a state of mind for either of my parents, and I was blessed to inherit from each of them the "life will be all right" gene. As Daddy would say on many an occasion, "Don't waste time regretting the past. There's nothing you can do about it. Look to the future and find happiness there." He didn't say it as an excuse for his own decisions and actions. To the contrary, he had expressed profound regret for having unintentionally subjected his children to a regime he had never fathomed. Rather he spoke as befit a philosopher.

I took his admonition to heart and was blessed in discovering the benefits of optimism and hope embedded in his words. I held no grudge against either of my parents. While I could not imagine having made the sacrifices they agreed (albeit reluctantly) to make, I did not judge their motives nor resent their actions. There was only one person I found to blame, and she was now dead. Father Feeney, who should have been the strong leader, had been outmaneuvered by her. As I saw it, he was more pathetic than blameworthy, although there were others, my parents included, who laid the blame solely at his feet—he had been the spiritual leader of the Center.

* * *

It was the spring of 1974, and the economy was in a deep recession, the result of the quadrupling of the price of oil by OPEC a year earlier. The decline in the stock market was wreaking havoc with brokerage houses, and I found myself, at the age of twenty-five, among the ranks of the unemployed.

So I journeyed from Philadelphia back to Boston and my parents' home. Philadelphia had been an interesting and rewarding two-year experience, providing a giant step forward in my career, as I migrated from a statistician to a research analyst while simultaneously continuing my studies in economics at the Wharton School of Business. But my social life could best have been described as a dud. Center City Philadelphia in the 1970s was but a shadow of the vibrant, cosmopolitan, youthful metropolis of today. I'd had my fair share of romances, but each was fraught with unsustainability. Leaving Philadelphia was easy to do, but returning to my parents' home had never been in my plan. I was on a journey and had no intention of letting my career get mired in my hometown. This was just a stop-off on my sojourn.

I had hardly entered my parents' house when my father, in a rather jovial manner, popped a question at me. "My little princess, how would you like a challenge?"

I could see from the whimsical look on his face that what he had up his sleeve was well beyond the realm of my ability to guess. He explained that he had recently sold a Volvo to a woman whose name I had never heard, but which he knew well from his days as a young bachelor. Brenda Diana Duff Frazier Kelly Chatfield-Taylor (the last two surnames having been acquired through two unsuccessful marriages) had been debutante of the year in 1938, her picture on the cover of *Life* magazine. She was now living in Boston, my father explained, and needed someone to drive her to and from her daily sessions with a psychiatrist in Newton.

"What?" I exclaimed. "I'm here to find a job in the investment business, not drive some old lady to her shrink."

"It's just while you're looking for a new job, princess," he cajoled. He paused and then went on: "I told her you would call her this evening."

More to please my dad than to earn the five dollars an hour that Mrs. Taylor grudgingly agreed to pay me, and convincing myself that this position would be for a few weeks at most, I tiptoed my way into scenes of a life of both privilege and horror. The position of chauffeur lasted for less than a week, by which time it had morphed into a mélange of roles including gal Friday, confidante, friend, lunch companion, *and* chauffeur. Mrs. Taylor (as I addressed her) needed help to bathe and dress in the morning because her breakfast consisted of a handful of pills (her "vitamins" as she called them) washed down with several large gulps of "water," as she described clear liquid, which was quite obviously vodka.

The routine was the same each day. After extricating Mrs. Taylor from her bathtub, terrified that I might break her rail-thin bones either by holding on to her too hard or by letting her slip and fall, I helped her through what generally ended up as a two-hour dressing ritual. Stumbling her spindly legs into a pair of white linen trousers was the first step in the process. Once seated at her makeup table, she embarked on a ceremony of sorts—namely, re-creating Brenda Diana Duff Frazier, debutante of the year 1938. Between sips of what she kept referring to as water, but I knew better, she drew with a deep black makeup pencil the shape of her eyebrows, which were nonexistent, as well as her once famed widow's peak, which was now simply part of her nearly bald head that she adorned with a jet-black wig, another replica of days gone by. By the time she powdered her face and painted on her ruby-red lipstick, she looked more Kabuki than debutante, more a caricature than a re-creation of her once exotic beauty.

Despite her intense reliance on pills and alcohol, Mrs. Taylor had a bright eye, a sharp tongue, and a wickedly good sense of humor. And deep inside there was also a kind, but badly broken, heart. Snippets of stories from her past that spilled out of her as we drove each day depicted a woman who craved love because it had been denied her. For a reason I couldn't explain to myself, likely because I was well aware that this was a temporary employment situation for me, I found her fascinating rather than revolting.

After visiting her psychiatrist, who seemed oblivious to her state of addiction, she and I would lunch at the Ritz Carlton, the same meal every day—beef tongue on rye bread with mustard for each of us, accompanied by a double martini (for her alone). By then she was inebriated as well as exhausted, and I took her home and helped her into bed, leaving her to the staff, which took over with understandable trepidation—I'd hardly be out of the bedroom when she'd start screaming at her maids.

In the few hours that were left in the day, I scrambled to set up interviews and secure a job that would take me where I was determined to go—up that ladder in the financial world.

So I was unprepared when the psychiatrist called me in to his office one day. "You realize, don't you," he said, "that you're the only person in the world whom she loves. Would you consider moving in with her? It would help her immensely."

Poor Mrs. Taylor was all I could think. *She loves me because I'm the only person in her sphere who's not afraid of her—not her tantrums, nor her wailing, not even her histrionics when the police come to the apartment because I've inadvertently set off the alarm on her jewel-stuffed safe, evidence of the many lovers in her past life.*

Before replying, I asked him if he had any idea that Mrs. Taylor was blind drunk by the time she arrived for her daily visit. He was nonplussed, and I realized at that moment she was just a paycheck to him.

No, I wouldn't live with her, I told the doctor, but I promised to stay with her until I found a job. I didn't share with the psychiatrist that, despite Mrs. Taylor's eccentricities and her own self-loathing, there was a way in which I did love her.

She and I flew to her house on the Cape, another home stocked with staff. There I discovered her insomnia. Come the time I was ready to retire for the night, she bade me sit at the foot of her bed and for the next six hours she regaled me, between gulps of vodka, with tales of a life lived long in the past and lived hard. The eastern sky was spreading the light of dawn by the time her increasingly garbled storytelling came to an end and she fell back on the pillows exhausted.

When my birthday came around in August, I was touched by the presents she gave me—a painting of a hummingbird that she had done while we were on the Cape together and a leather briefcase with my initials engraved on it. She wished me good luck in my search for a job.

Perhaps that present was my good-luck charm, because by September I had found a job that became a stepping-stone into the world of finance in New York City, where I was hired three months later.

63

Woman Strong

1975 and Onward

was twenty-six years old when I arrived in New York in January 1975. The city was teetering on a metaphorical cliff, ready to hurtle into bankruptcy. The daily headlines were replete with reports of the dire straits that faced the most powerful city in the world. But for my part, I could see only the upside. Gotham was my key to the world, a giant open door beckoning me to reach for the highest rung on the ladder of success. The Big Apple was my "ticket to ride." I was but one college paper away from receiving my degree in economics from Boston University, a milestone that had taken nearly nine years to achieve. Nothing could stop me now.

Long days and even longer nights, with travel to places like Peoria, Illinois, and Des Moines, Iowa, Pocatello, Idaho, and Morgan City, Louisiana—I reveled in the freedom to explore the world of finance and I marveled at the luxury of working in an industry that paid me to learn. It wasn't long before I was building my own reputation as a go-getter analyst and had expanded my industry coverage to include the energy sector, a hot area in the market because of the rising price of oil.

But growing success failed to relinquish me from the bonds of my still deeply held secret past. My comfort with the world at large was unable to unleash my inhibition to reveal anything about my childhood. The words wouldn't form when I tried to imagine how I might tell my story. I feared being considered weird. I feared my parents would be derided. I feared the unknown.

It was two years after moving to New York when I found the courage to step through that door. I had been dating a man for about a year, a respected oil analyst on Wall Street, whom I'd met at a business lunch. This man whom I adored was twenty years my senior, and in the short time we'd been together, he had unearthed a world that was far beyond the reveries of my once childish imagination. Together we traveled to exotic places—Egypt and Tobago. On the moonlit balcony of our room at the Oloffson Hotel in Port-au-Prince, Haiti, he read to me—poems by Stephen Spender and passages from E. M. Forster. For Christmas, he gave me a copy of Skeat's *An Etymological Dictionary of the English Language* before presenting me with a pair of gold earrings from Cartier.

I sensed he relished the role he played in my life—the older man opening up the world of culture and literature to a receptive and energetic young woman. Perhaps a bit like Professor Higgins, although I hoped he didn't consider me quite Eliza Doolittle. "Gamine" was what he sometimes called me. At first I wasn't sure if that was a compliment or a put-down, but I came to understand it as a term of endearment—I was the raring-to-go, not-quite-settled girl and he was the already accomplished man of Wall Street.

On a warm summer evening, I was sitting with him in his apartment on New York's Upper West Side, coddling a glass of white wine, the light of day still pouring into the living room through the skylight above. I had my feet tucked underneath me as I excitedly explained my upcoming business trip to Paris. He mentioned that his mother lived in the town of Orgeval, a few kilometers outside of Paris. She had recently broken her hip, he said, and was struggling with her recovery.

"I'd love to visit her," I told him. That's when he got silent, and I sensed something was wrong. "Tell me," I said. A tear came to his eye, and he reached out his hand, with its slight tremble, to take my own in his.

The words formed slowly. "My mother's a lesbian," he said, and the tear rolled down his cheek. His pain touched me—he'd spoken of his mother before, but only in reference to his parents' divorce when he was barely old enough to walk and how he would go for months at a time pining for her. I knew deeply what that separation felt like, yet I had not braved sharing with him the story of my own parental loss. But in that moment, something sprang free in me. That his mother was a lesbian seemed to me hardly a matter of shame. Compared to the tale I was hiding, I thought it trivial.

His emotion acted as a catalyst, and I burst out, "Well, I have a secret, too." And for the next hour, I let spill out of me for the first time ever the tale of my life. Punctuated with sobs and even laughter, I unveiled my story while he listened intently, without interrupting, his soft blue eyes moist with emotion. And when I was spent talking, he expressed his fascination with my childhood and his interest in meeting my extended family. I was immensely grateful for his interest and particularly for his lack of prejudice toward my parents. I found it surprising that he knew nothing of the Center because he was a Harvard man—class of '51—which put him in Harvard Square at the very time of the disruption that shaped my life. But his sybaritic life as a member of the elite Fly Club at Harvard during that tumultuous time kept him far removed from the revolution at the Center.

He told me he loved my story—the unusualness of it, the fact that I still cherished the place I knew as home for so many years. We shared our childhood sorrow over losing the daily love and affection of our parents—he because his mother ran away from marriage, I because my parents were convinced that sacrificing their marriage would help to save my soul.

I brought him to Still River on numerous occasions, and he came to know by name the grand array of my "uncles and aunts," so many of whom had attended Harvard or Radcliffe. I found myself wondering what my Center family thought of me and this relationship. Although I was fully relaxed and at home among the Big Brothers and Sisters, I had been careful to keep my social life separate from my Center life. Only now, nearly ten years after I'd been spirited out of the Center, did I bring a lover with me and it wasn't without trepidation. But there was not a word of disapproval; to the contrary, my partner was embraced.

Was I now above reproach because I was a sophisticated woman of the world, a successful businesswoman and a benefactor of the Center? Was my role as lover of an older man less shocking because he was gracious and respectful to them? Or because he hailed from Harvard as they did?

The Center was now a far cry from the place I had exited a decade before. The outside world was no longer the enemy it had once been. It felt like home again, but better than before.

My partner became an integral part of my large family, and he was particularly fond of my father. The three of us traveled together to places that included Haiti, Bermuda, and Mexico. While the two of them read and played chess together, I did things they thought insane—parasailing in Mexico (long before it was safe), trekking alone into the congested iron market of Port-au-Prince. The sybaritic atmosphere brought out the best in my father, and I reveled in the pleasure he took in acting like a man of leisure.

I developed a deep friendship with my lover's children, attending the weddings of three of his four children. But my closest relationship was with his mother, whom I came to adore, from that first visit in France and for years after when she moved back to New York and took up residency at the Gramercy Park Hotel. Tall and handsome, her daily attire was a pair of tan Chanel trousers topped with a white silk blouse and a hacking jacket. Her closely cropped white hair was complimented by elegant gold earrings and a bold shade of lipstick.

Me at the Oloffson Hotel in Port-au-Prince, Haiti–1978.

She was profoundly urbane, and we bonded despite our more than forty years' difference in age. Sadly, I lacked the courage to share my childhood story with her. Given her own life, lived daringly and openly as a lesbian in the literary and cultural mecca of post–World War II Paris, she would most likely have lent a tolerant ear and provided words of support and wisdom.

* * *

Within a year of leaving the Center, I had shed much of the yoke of puritanism that had been engrained in me for nearly eighteen years. I saw the folly in Sister Catherine's prudish dictates and in her sequestering of any emotion bordering on romance. There was no tug of conscience when I chose to see the movie *A Man and a Woman*, the

Claude Lelouch production that scandalized many who weren't even Catholic. I thought it beautiful, artistic, and erotic.

However, there was one holdover from my indoctrination at the Center. For eighteen years, I had absorbed the hateful rhetoric espoused by both Father and Sister Catherine that the Jews were a cursed race for having killed Jesus. Somehow (although they never explained why) that sin transmogrified the entire Jewish race into an amoral, money-grubbing, not-to-be trusted people. While still at the Center, I questioned (to myself only) how it was that two thousand years after Jesus was put to death the Jews could still be tainted with His death. No rationale was offered, and it was one of those issues that was easier to accept than to challenge. It was not surprising then that I left the Center wary of anyone who was Jewish.

But a year later, I came to know several Jewish brokers at Ladenburg Thalmann. One was a pleasant man in his early thirties, the proud father of three young daughters, whose framed pictures covered his desk. When I asked him about the one with Santa Claus, he laughed and said, "My girls love Santa Claus. We have a menorah and a Christmas tree. Anything for my girls." I took his words to heart. This was a good man, I thought, not an evil Jew.

Still I harbored an instinctual bias, until some years later when, now in my late twenties, I was playing hostess one weekend at my boyfriend's house in East Hampton to a couple of young creative geniuses from the London office of Ogilvy & Mather. One was the epitome of proper English breeding. His associate was a tall, gangly, bespectacled fellow whose perpetual attire was black on black (long before it was all the rage in Hollywood). He had an easy laugh, a brilliant sense of humor, a kindly manner, and an extraordinary mind. With his beguilingly charming and self-deprecating humor, he made endless fun of his orthodox Jewish upbringing. His gentle humanity left me with a raw sense of guilt over my bigotry. I was miraculously cured; my prejudice was gone, and with it any instinct to distrust Jews simply because they were Jews.

After six years of what seemed like married life, my lover abruptly left me for someone younger than I. It would take nearly a year before I was able to re-engage with him and carry on as friends. This we did for the next twenty years, as he became increasingly frail, afflicted by the ravages of Parkinson's disease. He had been the only person outside my immediate family with whom I had shared my life's story. The next time I would do so was with the man who would become my husband.

Not long after our breakup, and following a few interim dalliances, I found love again, this time with a man with whom I had been working for nearly two years, without the remotest interest in him. Over a simple lunch, we ended up discovering that each of us was in essence single—I recently ditched and he in the midst of a divorce after eighteen years of marriage and three children.

We dated for some months before I felt comfortable telling my story for only the second time in my life. John had grown up in Washington, D.C., in the 1950s, in an era of debutante balls and society dances, and his instinctual reaction to my tale was one of disbelief at the life I had missed, one he had taken for granted. As I shared my story with him, I found myself laughing and using one of my favorite expressions, from the then famously popular song in the Broadway musical, *Evita*, "Don't cry for me, Argentina."

Three years later, almost to the day, we became husband and wife in an intimate ceremony that included only our closest family. The fact that he was divorced made it impossible for us to be married in the Catholic Church, which disappointed me but not him. He, an Episcopalian, liked to call me kiddingly a "mackerel snapper." For my part, I told him (in good humor) that his religion was based on the selfish whim of the Catholic King Henry VIII. If he hadn't demanded a divorce from his wife because she couldn't produce a son, there'd be no Episcopal Church. My parents voiced no objection to our mixed marriage, for which I was enormously grateful. In truth, they thought the world of my husband and were more than happy to remain silent on the matter of religion.

However, the depth of my own concern about what my Center family might think of my getting married outside of the Catholic Church was revealed to me through a dream I had several nights before our wedding. In my dream, I was visiting the Center and excitedly telling the Big Brothers and Sisters about my upcoming nuptials. I was careful to omit the word "Episcopal" from the name of the Church—St. Paul's—hoping they would think the wedding was to take place at the beautiful church of the same name that was directly across from the original Center in Cambridge. A sense of relief came over me when I realized that I hadn't slipped up on the "Episcopal" part. After describing the music and telling them that my brother David and my sister Cathy would be singing the Ave Maria—sure signals, I trusted, that this was a Catholic wedding—I offered to show them my wedding dress. As I pulled it carefully out of its garment bag, I choked back a gasp of horror—instead of the crisp white beaded designer dress I had picked out in London, my wedding dress was a lifeless stone gray. My heart sank. This was a dead giveaway, I was sure, that I was not getting married in the Catholic Church. I awoke from my nightmare and realized how strongly I was still tied to my childhood home, how much I wanted to ensure that I did nothing to lose the love of my "uncles and aunts" at the Center.

* * *

From the time I was a child, I had imagined myself in the role of mother. But real life was unfolding differently. I was thirty-six years old on the day of my wedding and as I neared my fortieth birthday, my career was barreling forward.

Not that the trajectory was a straight line up. The journey had been arduous at times—in no small measure on account of the unique circumstances of my childhood. At the age of nineteen, with not a clue as to how to finesse my way in business, much less with any notion of a career path, I had the good fortune to find myself on the bottom rung of a ladder in the world of finance and investing. I've sometimes

My parents, siblings, and my daughter, Caroline—1998.

My wedding—1985.

wondered how the course of my career might have been altered had I instead become the receptionist at a car dealership, or a travel agency.

The Center had, in a way, been a proving ground, particularly during the years of the court case when I had been perspicacious enough to realize that the very existence of the Center's school rested on my shoulders. Rather than find the challenge frightening, I thrived on the pressure that acted like adrenaline. Once out in the world, what I lacked in knowledge and sophistication, I attempted to make up for with will power. The status of ingénue did not inhibit my drive.

I entered the jungle of Wall Street at a time when professional women were almost an anomaly in the industry, and was fortunate to have had an array of mentors (all of them men) throughout my advancing career. Their guidance was sometimes direct but more often subtle, and perhaps their greatest value was inspiring me to play a similar role to young women (and men) in their own careers as mine was maturing.

The glass ceiling was real, and I was aware that my drive and energy were at times a detriment to my advancement—the same work ethic in male counterparts was treated as leadership and rewarded. But resentment was a waste of energy and could only detract from the exhilaration I experienced in the charged world of investing. So, I gave myself the same advice on more than a few occasions when I knew I had been denied a promotion I deserved: *You have two options. You can quit and go somewhere else, or you can prove them wrong.* In all cases, I chose the latter, and never with regret.

Around my fortieth birthday, my husband and I were having dinner in Manhattan and I let the words spill out without premeditation. It was almost as though I were being led by my guardian angel.

"I don't want to have a successful career at the risk of not having any children." He was silent. It was an odd moment, because in our five years of marriage we had managed to elude a serious discussion about having children of our own. His three children, by now attending college or having graduated, were the focus of his energy, and I played my part as a supportive stepmother. He seemed content; I was not.

But it was only a matter of days before he jumped on board and for the next four years we moved heaven and earth, engaging the most renowned specialists to bring to fruition what had been my, and now became our, dream. It wasn't without its moments of grief with unsuccessful attempts at pregnancy. But there were also moments of hilarity. After one particular whirlwind business trip, I regaled my husband with the tale of how I'd headed off to the airplane lavatory to drive a two-inch needle into my backside as the airplane was going through a particularly rough patch of weather because the hour had struck for my next hormone injection. After three years of emotional ups and downs, science and religion, in the form of doctors and prayers, collaborated in producing a successful pregnancy.

I worked until two days before my delivery when, at the age of forty-five, I gave birth to our healthy twins, Caroline and Jim.

You can stop climbing the corporate ladder, I told myself during my three months' maternity leave, and I really tried. Now ten-day trips were crammed into four so that I could be home before (I hoped) the children had time to realize I was gone. I found a way to work from home a day or two each week and for a while it worked. But the corporate world is ruthless, and opportunities passed up can prove fatal to one's career.

The tireless work was rewarding. But I was fully aware of the downside—I was not seeing enough of my children.

My husband brought the reality home to me when we were on a late summer vacation. "This isn't a vacation for you," he said. "I'm at the beach with the children [now five years old] and you're on conference calls." He was right.

I lay awake for much of the night thinking of his words and when I awoke to the sun pouring into our bedroom, it was with a new energy.

(Left) Me with my children, Caroline and Jim, at age one, on the beach—1995.

(Bottom) Caroline and Jim, in the gardens their father cultivated.

"Darling," I said, "on Tuesday morning when I get back into the office, I'm going to quit. I promise you I will be retired by the end of the year."

It was 1999. I had just celebrated my fifty-first birthday. I kept my promise.

* * *

And so I started the new millennium as a full-time mother, taking my children to school each morning, driving them to their skating lessons (peering over the top of my Wall Street Journal to catch their eyes as they twirled past me), their gymnastics classes, their playdates. These were novel activities for me, having never enjoyed them myself as a child.

The experiences of childhood form the base of one's own approach to parenting, and one either revisits those experiences with the next generation or eschews them. In my case, there were three elements of my upbringing that guided me immensely in raising my children, and they came with varying degrees of complexity. It took no soul-searching to be convinced that hitting a child served no purpose other than expressing one's own frustration. More complex was a deep instinct within my mothering wellspring that related to food, and I was well aware that it reflected the agony I experienced during my childhood, as I watched and mostly was helpless to solve the eating problems of my sister Cathy (that started when she was only four years old). As an adult and a mother, I was emotionally incapable of forcing our children to eat anything if it didn't appeal to them. So I let them pick their meals—breakfast, lunch, and dinner—each day. It was gratifying to observe that such a philosophy had a more salubrious outcome than might be expected—the child who liked white toast with the crusts cut off also loved raw green vegetables. The one who found it difficult to chew beef adored chicken. On occasion, dinner consisted of as many different meals as there were people at the table.

It might be criticized as being overindulgent, but I was determined that mealtime would be stress-free.

Growing up in the milieu of monasticism, I became accustomed to every facet of daily life being regulated and rule bound, strictures that chafed at my innate free spirit, and I fantasized about exploring the world unimpeded. Once out of the Center, both as a professional and as a parent, I made it my endeavor to say "Yes" rather than "No." And when I had to say "No" to my children, I tried to find a way to keep a door open for the future. Was it simply in my DNA to engage in making things work out, or was it a sub-conscious response to years of disappointment?

For the intellectual stimulation I craved, I maintained my crack-of-dawn appearances on CNBC to opine on the markets, and I'd rush into the city in the afternoon for *Your World with Neil Cavuto*, and I continued to sit on the board of an insurance company as I had for the past eight years. I joined the church choir and a choral group, satisfying my long-held desire to sing, something that a Wall Street career was unable to accommodate.

Pro bono work crept into the vast empty spaces of time I now had, those hours in the day when the children were at school. It was a new and rewarding world for me—committing serious time, talent, and treasure for the benefit of others, sharing learned skills for the common good. It resonated with many of the values of my childhood—living a communal life inevitably meant sharing, relinquishing claim to personal achievement, rejoicing in the success of others.

The more I became involved, the more doors opened—and it wasn't solely in the eleemosynary world. I became an expert witness for a number of cases that dealt with the financial crisis of the moment—the collapse of Enron in 2001 and the fraud that was perpetrated by that and other companies on unwitting investors.

It wasn't long before search firms were knocking on my door—would I consider going on corporate boards? Slowly a second career

With my husband, John, and children, Caroline and Jim.

was unfolding in front of me, one that allowed me to keep my promise to my children that I would be home to make them breakfast and drive them to school, at least most of the time. In fact, they were more than agreeable to my accepting one new board position when they discovered they could come with me each spring to Bermuda for the annual meeting.

When my husband retired while the children were still in grade school, we'd laugh together and ask ourselves, *Do our children think that this is the way all families are—both parents home all day?* Being "older" parents certainly had its benefits as well as its eccentricities.

One day, after my husband and I attended a school play, our daughter said, in a tone of voice that had an edge of disdain, "You know, Mom and Dad, you're the oldest parents in the whole school!"

I was quick with my comeback, "That may be true," I said, "but we surely don't act like the oldest—right?"

With my siblings and their families, celebrating my 70th birthday, in the summer of 2018.

She agreed without hesitation and was pleased to point out some of the benefits of having "old" parents, most particularly the array of world traveling we did together as a family.

The children were entering high school when I began to write my memoir. They had been visiting the Center since their infancy and came to know my "uncles" and "aunts" as extended family. However, they knew nothing of the history of my family's life there, until it started spilling out as they asked questions.

They were astonished, then curious, and soon became skeptical, most particularly my daughter, as she matured, graduated from high school, and attended college. She found my childhood deeply disturbing, and on one trip home from college, she demanded that I "drop everything," as she put it, until I finished my book.

Now I have finished it.

Epilogue

The Center of my childhood was much changed by the mid-1970s. Leonard Feeney, under the auspices of Cardinal Madeiros of Boston and Cardinal Wright of Worcester, had become reconciled with Rome in the early 1970s and died in 1978 a few days shy of his eighty-first birthday.

After more than a decade, the infighting among factions at the Center in Still River simmered down, and the two communities found a way to split up and yet remain on speaking terms with each other. I had taken no sides in their conflicts, and each of the separate entities reached out to me in a warm and welcoming way. In a turnabout, they sought me out for advice, most particularly on matters that had to do with finance, and I was happy to help them in whatever way I could.

St. Therese's House became a Benedictine abbey, changing its name to St. Benedict Abbey. It remains a vibrant community today. The Big Sisters at St. Ann's House became a pious union of nuns under the Catholic Diocese of Worcester, teaching catechism and preparing children for First Communion, for which they are beloved by Catholic families in the local community. A number of the original Center

Leonard Feeney
towards the end of
his life.

members moved to Petersham, Massachusetts, and established their
own Brother/Sister Benedictine monasteries, St. Mary's Monastery
and St. Scholastica Priory, under the auspices of Pluscarden Abbey
in Scotland. Three other splinter groups settled in Ohio, New Hamp-
shire, and California.

During the late 1970s, on one of my visits to Still River, I was
astonished, as I entered the library, to find Betty Sullivan sitting in
the red leather wing chair next to the piano. She caught my eye as I
approached and her face lit up—as much as her doleful eyes would
allow. She no longer looked decrepit. It was evident that whatever
mental illness she had suffered years earlier was at least under control.

For the next couple of hours, we shared reminiscences and caught
up on our lives. She knew, to my amazement, that I had a career in the
financial world. That pleased me—that she had made an effort to keep
me in her sights. For her part, she said she had taken up oil painting
and followed it with, "And I'd love to paint your portrait, and Davey's,
too," referring to my brother's name as a baby.

"That would be wonderful," I replied, intrigued by what she might produce. Sadly, time ran out before her dream became reality. She was ill with breast cancer at the time and succumbed before she had a session with either of us.

In an act of Catholic kindness, the prioress of one of the splinter groups of Big Sisters admitted Betty into their convent on her deathbed, fulfilling a request she had been making for years—that she be allowed to rejoin the Center. She was buried in the Center's cemetery, and the stone on her grave is inscribed: Sister Mary Elizabeth.

After I had been living for several years in New York City, I reconnected with Charles Forgeron (formerly Brother Sebastian). He was single and often in need of an escort in his active social life and for several years in a row, we attended an annual ball at the Pierre Hotel. Sadly, he, too, died young, of a heart attack at the age of sixty-three.

Over the next couple of decades, the bond with the "uncles" and "aunts" of my youth remained as warm as when I was a child. They rejoiced in my marriage and shared in the joy of the two children that followed.

A year before my children were born, my husband's ex-wife died. I pondered the fact that my husband was now a widower, and in the eyes of the Catholic Church I was free to be married as a Catholic. But I let the idea percolate without acting upon it until I was closing in on my fiftieth birthday. My sister Peggy had organized the annual "Center Children" reunion. It was to be held on August 15, the day before my birthday.

I told my husband that I would like to have our marriage receive a Catholic blessing by Abbot Gabriel, and he was all in favor of that. The abbot had been one of the Big Brothers who became ordained as a priest after the Center reconciled with the Catholic Church and subsequently was elected abbot when the community joined the Benedictine order. To me he remained one of my favorite "uncles."

When I reached out to the abbot and let him know of my wish, his response, not surprisingly, was one of elation. He promised a very

With Charles Forgeron (my first crush at the age of twelve when he was Brother Sebastian) at a ball at the Pierre Hotel in 1981.

quiet affair, as I requested—nothing that would get the attention of the rest of the large crowd that would be arriving for the picnic, and he reassured me that we would go off premises to the small Catholic church in the center of town. My dearest friend, Alexandra Trower, agreed to be my witness, and the only other attendants were my parents.

What I had not anticipated was the abbot's decision to turn a requested "Catholic blessing" into a full Catholic wedding, concelebrated by one of the other priests from the abbey. I was on the verge of giggles when, during the ceremony, the abbot asked the question that is part of the Catholic wedding ceremony, "Are you prepared to accept children lovingly from God?" I was about to be fifty and my husband was fifty-nine. I answered in the affirmative; I'm not sure my husband did.

My Catholic wedding was indeed the best fiftieth birthday present.

* * *

As I entered my fifties, I reminisced on the uniqueness of my childhood experience and felt an urge to record my personal recollections as a legacy for my children and theirs. The Center of my childhood was now extinct, and within a generation or two, there would be no one left who had a firsthand memory of the life we had lived.

In one small way, my story was the same as that of thirty-eight other children. But in reality, there were thirty-nine stories that could be told, and I could tell only mine. I was struck by how differently the thirty-nine of us approached life, religion, and relationships after the similarity of our upbringing, defined by the deprivation of parental affection and a regime of rules and punishments.

Only two of the thirty-nine remain in religious life. Several others made a commitment to that life but eventually left in their twenties, thirties, and even sixties. Some of the thirty-nine remained resolutely Catholic, while others took a more laissez-faire attitude toward religion and more than a few abandoned religion entirely. There were marriages and divorces, as well as couples who chose to live together unwed. There were Ivy League graduates and those who did not attend college at all; straight and gay; financially successful professionals, with careers in medicine, psychiatry, engineering, and finance; and a few who struggled to face life's daily challenges.

Despite a staunchly conservative upbringing, there was a large contingent of Democrats, as well as some Republicans, Libertarians, and Independents. Some enjoyed gathering at an annual summer reunion in Still River, while others refused to speak to anyone at the Center again. In a way, we represented a microcosm of society in this country, notwithstanding the unusual circumstances of our early life.

Thirty-nine children were raised in an experiment—part of the vision of a woman who believed she could supersede the "evil" forces of nature and mold human beings into a cadre of religious zealots who would follow her, in cult-like fashion, embracing a celibate way of life for God.

Where was Leonard Feeney's input in all this? He was the spiritual leader of the Center. Sadly, once we moved to Still River, his role as leader was titular at best. A romantic at heart, he needed to be admired and praised, and he sought the approbation of those who would give it. That weakness gave Catherine Clarke the upper hand, and despite the fact that she could not hold a candle to Feeney on matters of theology, she usurped his role. He was not strong enough to counter her.

Was Catherine Clarke's vision conceived in the moment of crisis that forced the Center into hiding in 1949? It seems more likely it was honed piecemeal as she became increasingly enamored of her own power. Did she ever concern herself with the thought that she might get pushback from some sixty highly intelligent, educated, and sophisticated men and women as she manipulated them emotionally? How could she be assured that they would forever sacrifice their personal ambitions and dreams and adopt her vision?

If she ever doubted her prowess, there was no evidence of it. Her actions, over the course of nearly twenty years, influencing the lives and emotions not only of the children but of their parents as well, implied that in her mind, any means were valid to justify the end.

Whatever deep-seated pathological conditions in her past may have influenced Catherine Clarke's decisions concerning the lives of parents and children will never be known. One can only conjecture how a mother who chose to keep her own family intact, spending nights at her private home away from the Center, could, with blithe indifference, have sundered the family bonds of twelve other families.

The evidence was monumental that to her dying breath she had no remorse over her actions. My youngest sister relayed to me that as recently as three days before Catherine Clarke succumbed, she called for the Little Sisters to assemble in her bedroom as she lay on her deathbed. She then excoriated my sister for her "particular friendship" with one of the other Little Sisters. A day or two later, she slipped into a coma from which she never recovered.

While she lived, Catherine Clarke's experiment seemed to meet with success. She simply rid herself of those, like me, who stood to thwart her plan. For that treatment I eventually became immensely grateful. Upon her death, however, no one could take on her mantle. In the end, her experiment failed. Her motives may have been honorable in her own mind, but her tactics were abhorrent and destructive.

It is interesting to note that since her death, there has been no body of work regarding her life, her role at the Center, her impact on humanity. On the other hand, one can find numerous articles, books, and references to Leonard Feeney, who will likely live on for centuries as a force in the American Catholic Church from the 1940s through the 1970s.

* * *

On my fifty-fifth birthday, in 2003, I was sitting with my parents at the beach house my husband and I had bought several years earlier. We were nursing our summer gin and tonics as we rocked in the white wicker chairs and took in the magnificent vista of whitecaps on the Atlantic Ocean off the coast of Rhode Island, much as we had done thirty-two years earlier on our first family vacation on Martha's Vineyard. My father was now eighty-five, my mother seventy-four.

Without any preparatory thought, I said to them, "I've been thinking about writing a memoir. I look back on my childhood with great pleasure. I know that may seem strange, but I did not grow up as an unhappy child, and I want to tell that story for my children and my grandchildren. In fifty years, long after I'm dead and buried, there won't be anyone alive who was part of the Center."

I was aware that I could offer only my own account, which might differ from other eyewitness versions, but growing up in St. Benedict Center was part of the history of the Catholic Church in America during the mid-twentieth century, and firsthand versions are better than second and third, or speculation and hearsay.

Their response was unsurprising: "Tell it exactly as you remember it. It's a part of history. Yes, there are things that we wish we could do over, but you should tell the story."

After thinking about the project for a full five years, I finally put pen to paper (or fingers to keyboard) a little more than ten years ago. In truth, my initial instinct was to hide behind a pseudonym. I was still anxious about what the world might think of me. But as I started to share the unfolding chapters with the women in my memoir writing group, I was encouraged by their reactions. They found the story fascinating. They expressed empathy for my parents. It was Sister Catherine whom each of them despised. Through their encouragement and support, I was able to overcome my anxiety about publishing my book.

The first rendition was more diary than memoir—a blithe recollection of anecdotes, events, and memories. But the more I wrote, the more I became involved in the depth of the full story. I engaged in the dual roles that are the prerogative of the memoirist—to be both protagonist and narrator, both insider and observer. The passage of so many decades from my childhood to the recording of it was beneficial because it allowed me to have a better sense of perspective and a deeper sense of perception.

At the heart of my story is a tale of love—the story of a family that may have been separated but could not be broken. A family that found a way to spin an endless and unbreakable web of devotion so strong that when the day came and they were reunited, there was no rancor, no need to rebuild trust. The family was whole, and so it remained.

For nearly forty years after life at the Center, we were once again a complete family, until my father died peacefully during a nap, four months shy of his ninetieth birthday. My mother, for the next eleven years attended daily Mass and was abundantly cheerful—enjoying her five children, ten grandchildren and eleven great-grandchildren. She passed away as this memoir was going to print. She read it in its entirety and it had her blessing.

Afterword

Friends have asked me why I'm not angry, why I don't hate my parents, and why I seem so "normal." To be honest, I have spent little time analyzing why I'm happy.

That is not to imply that I have been free of any anger; rather that the anger I *have* felt has been directed, not at my parents, but at Catherine Clarke.

From an early age, I had a subliminal conviction that my parents were somehow victims of the powerful Leonard Feeney and Catherine Clarke. It appeared to me that my parents, my siblings and I were thrust together in a world that was foreign to our kinship. With the benefit of adulthood and maturity, I came to realize that my parents were free to have left the Center and thus to have prevented our family from being sundered. They allowed their religious zealotry to supersede their parental obligations and the joys associated with them.

When I try to understand why my parents did what they did, I cannot. I could never have made such a sacrifice. Nor do I pretend that I didn't wish my childhood had been different. Those endless hours consumed craving family life, wondering if we were the only thirty-nine children in the whole world who were being raised in a religious order, forbidden to call our parents "mummy" and "daddy." This incomprehension is real, as is the pain.

What anger I have experienced is aimed fully at Catherine Clarke, the power behind the throne of Leonard Feeney. Tall and powerful, she exuded an Amazonian force. As a mere child, I was her challenge—unmalleable, a free spirit in the claustrophobic world of the Center. She and I engaged in a battle of the wills, and try as she might, she was unable to forge me into a submissive member of the community. And so she banished me. At the time, I felt like a failure, but in truth it was she who had failed. I was David to her Goliath.

Despite the pain and the anger, I am most conscious of the many ways in which I have been blessed, not the least of which is that I'm hardwired to tackle challenges, disappointments, humiliations, and other hurdles in life. I'm an optimist through and through—no matter how bad the news, or how daunting the situation, my instinct is to create a solution and see it through to make the situation right again.

I left the Center at the tender age of seventeen, brokenhearted and feeling deserted. But that door through which I was kicked out was the same door that opened onto a world I had so passionately wanted to explore since I was a small child. The optimist in me seized the opportunity to learn (silently and timidly at first) and to vault forward on the expedition of my life. Some ventures were formidable, but the journey has been extraordinarily fulfilling. There simply has been no time for self-pity.

If I let myself dwell on the emotional pain I experienced, I would unfairly ignore all the good that God's grace has showered on me, not the least of which is the blessing associated with raising my own children in a warm and loving family environment.

Happiness is finding peace, joy, and inspiration in the array of things one does in life. It is also moving on from what cannot be undone.

I am thankful for the grace that allowed me to find a way forward uninhibited by remorse and anger.

Acknowledgments

When it takes ten years to write a book, a memoir in particular, there are likely to be many, many people who have provided invaluable support, guidance, criticism (most appreciated), and hand-holding. I thank them all, with particular gratitude to:

My parents, who from the moment I told them about my idea, were supportive. Although my father did not live to read this memoir, my mother went through it line by line and never wavered in her support.

My siblings, Cathy, David, Peggy, and Ronnie, without whose encouragement I would never have been able to find the strength to take on this challenge.

My husband, John, and my children Caroline and Jim, my intimate fan club. Particular appreciation goes to my daughter, who read and reread my manuscript, putting my feet to the fire when writer's ennui inevitably set in.

Mother Mary Clare Vincent, OSB (in memoriam), my English tutor at the Center, for her unswerving support, love, and encouragement throughout my writing.

Jessica Bram, the founder of Westport Writers' Workshop, to whom my appreciation knows no bounds for her tutelage, and Dr. Suzanne

Hoover, as well as my "sisters in crime," the group of memoirists with whom I met sometimes twice weekly for six years as together we learned the art of writing, and whose moral and emotional support was invaluable—Kathy van der Aue, Diana Bowes, Karen Como, Betsy English, Jody Foote, Nancy Galasso, Jacque Masumian, and Sheila Traub.

Ursula Streit—friend, confidante, and publisher par excellence in Switzerland, who read my manuscript twice and challenged me to tell the stories I wanted to keep hidden, and selected the title. "It's obvious," she said. "It has to be *Little Sister.*"

My friends who agreed to read my story and offer advice on how to improve it, most particularly my cherished friend Alexandra Trower, who loved it and gave me the courage to share it with other dear friends, including Deborah and Chuck Royce who also provided invaluable advice and insight, and Nina Lesavoy, Alexander Craig Morrison, Bryanna and Jonathan Kallman, Addy Bachrach, Linda Munger, Tanya Zlateva, Katherine Moran, Michael Shapiro, Hilary Hatfield, Rudina Seseri, Robert Ainsley, Tricia Boyer, Kamie Lightburn and Phoebe Lightburn, Tania Clark, Joel Fletcher, John Copenhaver, Lil McCarry, Phillip Watson, Gary Dell'Abate, Mary and Sherif Nada, Susan Martin, Paul Mendelson, Olga Goff, Richard Greene, Barbara and Russ Jones, Lucy Hedrick and others as well.

My Catholic friends who were able to see the story through special eyes and thus offer invaluable advice—Mary Gordon, Mary Ellen Markowitz, Sister Susanne Ashton, Jolyne Caruso FitzGerald, Kerry Walsh (no relation), Liz Wooster, Mary and John Redvers, Howard Cannon (in memoriam) Michael Colopy, Betsy and Ed O'Reilly, Aundrea Amine, Ted Murphy, Cee Greene Verbinnen, Mother Mary Elizabeth Kloss, OSB, Sister Gemma Meade, OSB, Heidi and Bert Garvin, Rosemary and Michael Jeans, Edward DeGraan, Dan Fitzgerald, Michelle Coppola, Deb Canales, and Judi Klappa and others who found it, in their words, "fascinating."

Fellow Little Sisters and Brothers who, while they may not have read my manuscript, shared stories and stimulated my memory in ways that added to the texture of the memoir.

Gail Harris, my copy editor, who put the first tangled mess of pages into respectable shape so that I could send it to Trena Keating, who read my first rendition and had the decency to refrain from throwing it in the wastebasket but instead directed me to my first editor, Peternelle van Arsdale, who forced me to turn, as she described it, "a diary into a memoir." And Kelly Notaras and Nikki Van De Car, who directed me to my second editor, Carolyn Flynn, who saw in my memoir a love story, not a mommy dearest tale, and guided me with such brilliance and sensitivity. And Jon Ford for his skill in chopping 105,000 words down to 84,000 and improving the story in the process.

The string of begats that took a raw manuscript and made it what it is today: Alexandra Trower, who introduced me to my lawyer Ellis Levine, who read my manuscript and then sent it out to agents, including Michael Carlisle at InkWell Management, who called within three days of receiving it, saying he wanted to represent me because the book spoke to him.

My doctor, Erika Schwartz, who introduced me to her publisher, Anthony Ziccardi, who said "yes." A partnership was formed that day, one that has turned into a genuine friendship. I will forever be indebted to Anthony and to his talented team at Post Hill Press—Michael Wilson, Madeline Sturgeon, Devon Brown, and Cody Corcoran. It has been an immense pleasure to work with you. And to my publicists, Emi Battaglia and Jenn Hansen-dePaula, and my audiobook producer, May Wuthrich.

For the vast array of friends who have accompanied me on this journey, I am full of gratitude.

About the Author

Photo by Joanne Bouknight

Patricia Walsh Chadwick was born in Cambridge, Massachusetts in 1948. She received her BA in Economics from Boston University and had a thirty-year career in the investment business, culminating as a Global Partner at Invesco. Today she sits on a number of corporate boards, and she blogs on issues social, economic, and political. She also mentors middle school girls at Our Lady Queen of Angels School in Harlem. In 2016, she founded and is the CEO of Anchor Health Initiative, a health care company that serves the needs of the LGBTQ community in Connecticut. She is married and lives in Connecticut with her husband. They have a daughter and a son.

Readers' Guide

Resilience is a strong theme running throughout *Little Sister*. Is there something in Patricia's upbringing that leads to her resilience or does it just come to her naturally? Are there times when she seems to lose her resilience? Have you experienced situations in which you were able to overcome adversity and felt empowered because of it?

Patricia's parents and the other members of the Center were highly educated and intellectual. Why do you think they didn't resist the draconian rules imposed on them? This story takes place in the aftermath of World War II and many of the men at the Center saw the horrors of war firsthand. Is it possible that PTSD played some role in their actions? How does the Center compare with similar situations in the recent past?

Catherine Clarke was a powerful and controlling figure in Patricia's life. Is there a point when those roles were reversed? What was the catalyst? How did it shape Patricia's life after that? Have you experienced a situation where you were able to change the power structure in an important personal relationship—at home, in the workplace, among friends?

Despite the fact that Patricia is immensely curious about the world outside the Center and wants to experience living in the 'real' world, she is wracked with grief when Catherine Clarke tells her, at the age of seventeen, that she will have to leave the Center. Why is she conflicted? Discuss your own experience of wanting something but realizing it will require giving up something else you love equally.

Patricia does not use the word "cult" in her book. She says that she never thought of the Center as a cult, although today she readily accepts the fact that it was just that. Why might that be? Have you experienced or read stories of other cults? Are there similarities to Patricia's story?

Almost immediately after Catherine Clarke died, the Center fell prey to infighting. Why might this have happened? What does it say about a regime built on blind obedience to a leader? Are there other examples in contemporary times when the demise of a charismatic figure led to the disintegration of a community/cult/group?

Forgiveness plays a strong role in *Little Sister*. Is there something about Patricia's life at the Center and her upbringing that allows her to be so forgiving? Why do you think she feels no anger toward her parents? Could you put yourself in her shoes? Have you been able to forgive and move on in an important relationship?

What role do you think Patricia's position as the eldest of her siblings played in her strength of character and care over her sisters and brother? Does it bring to mind any other stories of survival?

Some people who had undergone such an experience as Patricia's might have emerged very damaged. Patricia, however, has gone on to create a fulfilling life. How do

you think that this is possible? What might have contributed to her ability to achieve this?

Patricia's Catholic faith does not appear to have been
destroyed, despite her upbringing. Why do you think that
might be? Can you empathize with her reasoning, giv-
en all the harm that has been inflicted on people by the
Catholic Church?